<u>Exhibiting</u> <u>Architecture</u>

<u>A Paradox?</u>

Edited by Eeva-Liisa Pelkonen
with Carson Chan and David Andrew Tasman

Yale School of Architecture

Exhibiting Architecture is published by
Yale School of Architecture
P.O. Box 208242
New Haven, Connecticut 06511
www.architecture.yale.edu

Copyright 2015
Yale School of Architecture
Yale University
All rights reserved
Printed and bound in the USA

Distributed by
Actar D
355 Lexington Avenue
New York, New York
www.actar-d.com

Dean, Yale School of Architecture
Robert A. M. Stern

Publications Director
Managing Editor
Nina Rappaport

Editor
Eeva-Liisa Pelkonen

Assistant Editors
Carson Chan
David Andrew Tasman

Copy Editor
Ann Holcomb

Graphic Design Concept
MGMT. design, Brooklyn, New York

Designer and Layout Editor
Amy Kessler

ISBN 978-1940291-59-8
Library of Congress Control Number: 2015934199

Contents

Preface

Robert A. M. Stern

Exhibitions large and small held in major museums, architecture schools, veritable hole-in-the-wall galleries, and as part of multinational biennales and more regional art festivals have played, and continue to play, a major role in architecture culture. Not only have they introduced new architectural ideas and resurrected forgotten architects but they have embodied the inherent paradox of such an undertaking: how, indeed, can architecture be exhibited? The book at hand discusses some of them: full-scale plaster cast replicas, models, drawings, and urban happenings.

The "Exhibiting Architecture: A Paradox" symposium was held at the Yale School of Architecture's Paul Rudolph Hall, which is home to one of the major architecture galleries in the country. While the discussion was going on in Hastings Hall auditorium, the gallery played its part: on view was *Everything Loose Will Land,* curated by Sylvia Lavin, an exhibition featuring the intersection of art and architecture in 1970s Los Angeles that showed vividly how exhibitions have been instrumental in fostering the convergence of art and architecture in a particular locale. Over its fifty-year history, the gallery in Rudolph Hall has played an important role in bringing art and architecture together, never more dramatically than in April 1968, when it was the setting for *Project Argus,* a mylar-covered structure designed by Charles Moore, Kent Bloomer, and Yale students that served as a temporary stage for the light-sound event of the Pulsa group.

During the symposium, essays and historical case studies of exhibitions that made architectural history were discussed and contemporary practices were reviewed by architects who themselves curate and design exhibitions as part of their individual practices. By the symposium's conclusion, we were left convinced, all in all, that not only do exhibitions play a major role in how architecture is represented, produced, and experienced, but exhibitions can also affect architecture's social role.

"Exhibiting Architecture: A Paradox" was the fifth J. Irwin Miller Symposium. Miller (B.A. 1931, L.H.D. 1979), long-time head of the Cummins Engine Company based in Columbus, Indiana, was one of this country's great patrons of modern architecture. We are grateful to William I. Miller (B.A. 1978), Catherine G. Miller, Elizabeth B. Miller, and Margaret I. Miller (M.A. 1968) for their generous endowment supporting symposia that honor their late father's memory. We also gratefully acknowledge an anonymous donor who made this publication possible.

Introduction

Mining the Paradox

Eeva-Liisa Pelkonen

This book, *Exhibiting Architecture: A Paradox?,* brings together, in print form, the lectures, paper presentations, and panel discussions that took place at the eponymous symposium at the Yale School of Architecture from October 3 to 5, 2013. The symposium was convened by associate professor Eeva-Liisa Pelkonen with David Andrew Tasman and Carson Chan.

The inquiry into the topic began with a seminar, Exhibit Architecture, at Yale in spring 2012, that focused on how architects use exhibitions as laboratories for architectural ideas. This framework led us to focus on smaller experimental exhibitions organized by architects themselves, often far from a cultural metropolis, and often held in alternative places. Students in that seminar—Anya Bokov, Edward Hsu, Surry Schlabs, Katharine Storr, Violette de la Salle, David Andrew Tasman, and Juana Salcedo, the teaching assistant for the class—deserve credit for their thorough research which informed the content of a class website. With Kevin Repp, the Beinecke Library's curator of European books and manuscripts, we were able to explore the Library's rich collections of exhibition catalogs and exhibition posters as primary source materials.

One of the class favorites was a little-known 1969 exhibition, titled *Space Electronic,* that took place in a nightclub and was organized by the Florentine collective Gruppo 9999. To complete the experience, the catalog—a copy of which can be found at the Beinecke—came with a fur and tin cover. We also learned that many group formations and projects originated from the exhibitions: Archigram came together for the first time when curating *The Living City* in 1963 at the Institute of Contemporary Art in London, and Superstudio mounted the *Continuous Monument* in Trigon '69, in Graz, Austria.

We also learned that, unlike real commissions, exhibitions throughout the twentieth century and beyond have allowed architects to take extremely speculative positions. Hans Hollein's "architecture pill," presented at Trigon in 1969 stood out as an end point: architecture reduced to a medically induced condition. Some exhibitions we discussed charted a completely new terrain for architecture. For example, Finnish Team X member Reima Pietilä's 1972 exhibition, *The Zone,* investigated the relationship between form and language, opening architecture to yet another type of experience.

Additional examples were explored by the presenters in the Yale symposium. Exhibitions—particularly those from the 1960s and '70s—also remind us that architecture should not ignore its historical and social context. Group shows, such as the 1968 Milan Triennale's *The Greater Number* and the Trigon '69's *Architecture and Freedom* captured, for example, the political ethos of the late 1960s. At the other end of the spectrum, the topic of the 1980 Venice Architecture Biennale, *The Presence of the Past,* placed architecture within a longer historical *durée* (duration). All in all, the case studies cited by the presenters demonstrate that architecture exhibitions have not only played a role in canonizing architects and buildings, but remind us about the spectrum of possibilities for what architecture can and should be.

Yet, as the title of this book suggests, the ambition to exhibit architecture always entails a paradox: how to exhibit something as large and complex as a building or a city, and how to communicate something as elusive as an architectural experience that unfolds in space and time? To be sure, architecture poses a challenge to exhibition as a medium—indeed, what do we exactly exhibit when we exhibit architecture? Should we be satisfied to exhibit photographs of buildings and sites, or should we aim to display whole buildings, or, if that is not possible, fragments and models of them? These were among the questions the organizers posed to a group of architectural and art historians, practicing architects, and curators, who were invited to participate in the symposium. Their discussions ended up addressing not only the exhibition as a medium, but challenged the stability of our preconceived idea that architecture is an object, easily transported and displaced from its site, which opens up a whole range of possibilities for how architecture is made, experienced, and discussed.

The book opens with Barry Bergdoll's essay "Out of Site/In Plain View: On the Origins and Actuality of the Architecture Exhibition." Four thematic sections that explore historical precedents follow. The first section "Exhibition as a Medium," looks at various exhibition formats and techniques developed from the nineteenth century onward, from displaying plaster cast copies of historical masterpiece architecture (Mari Lending) to models of modernist buildings (Wallis Miller) and urban happenings (Romy Golan), all of which share the key question facing curators of architecture exhibitions: is it a matter of replicating and reproducing likeness and simulating experiences?

The second section, "Immersive Environments," focuses on new material techniques that challenged how architecture is experienced, such as Trigon '67 which was entitled, suggestively, *Ambiente/ Environment,* and which took place in Graz, Austria (Pamela Burleigh); *Structures Gonflables,* a 1968 exhibition in Paris, that explored the potentials of inflatable structures (Craig Buckley); and the E.A.T. (Experiments in Art and Technology) installation at the Pepsi Pavilion at the 1970 Osaka World Exposition (Mark Wasiuta)—a technological, media-saturated environment.

The third section, called "Public Encounters," looks at how exhibitions have provoked and promoted public engagement: Simon Sandler writes on Theo Crosby's seminal *How to Play the Environment Game* from 1973, which sought to convey the myriad forces that shape the built environment; Federica Vannucchi writes about the 1968 Milan Triennale, which addressed architecture at the age of population growth; and Andres Kurg considers the alternative paper architecture exhibitions during the Soviet era, which poked fun at the official state building projects.

The final section, "Curatorial Acts," focuses on significant curatorial "acts" by various curatorial impresarios in different settings: Helena Mattson discusses the architectural exhibitions at Stockholm's Moderna Museet initiated by the legendary Pontus Hultén; Liane Lefaivre's piece covers Hans Hollein's various curatorial activities; and Irene Sunwoo Alvin Boyarsky's ideas about exhibiting architecture during his tenure at the Architectural Association; while Léa-Catherine Szacka considers the planning and format—a full-scale architectural environment—of the first Venice Architecture Biennale, *The Presence of the Past.* It is worth noting that the authors represent twelve nationalities, thus mimicking the lively international exhibition scene they chart in their essays.

The thematic sections are followed by the two panel discussions. The first one, "Contemporary Exhibition in Dialogue," moderated by David Andrew Tasman, involves Yale School of Architecture faculty members Brennan Buck, Ariane Lourie Harrison, Nina Rappaport, Joel Sanders, and co-editor Carson Chan. The panelists discuss their own exhibition projects, which ranged from material installations to the use of exhibitions as a platform for activism and social engagement. The closing panel, "Exhibitions Matter," moderated by Carson Chan, involves leading contemporary curators discussing the significance of architectural exhibitions today.

The paradox mined by the various contributors to this volume is a productive one: at best, architecture pushes exhibition as a medium and, in turn, exhibitions force architects and curators to redefine the discipline, over and over again.

Out of Site/In Plain View: On the Origins and Actuality of the Architecture Exhibition

Barry Bergdoll

What does it mean to exhibit architecture? Isn't architecture, once it is built, always already on display, even without going to the extremes of putting it in a display case, as in the case of the building-scale glass box over the house of Domingo Faustino Sarmiento, the great Argentine hero and seventh president of the country (1868–1875) located in the El Tigre delta outside Buenos Aires? This 1855 house, which is visited by some fifty-thousand people a weekend in summer, has been a protected building since 1966, and an object in a vitrine since 1996. If we felt that buildings needed a curatorial voice, and not simply an authorial voice, perhaps we could take to issuing buildings with wall texts and labels, as for instance has been done in a recently completed cultural center, the last work—commissioned in 2005 and completed after his death in 2007—by the great Colombian architect Rogelio Salmona: the Casa de la Cultura de Moravia. The center is located in a poor neighborhood of Medellín, where the building, which has a clear relationship to local tradition, is not allowed to speak for itself, but is aided by wall texts. These explain the historical sources of each component of the building—ramps, patios, etc.—and provide explanations of Salmona's design. To an extent, this project is not new; in the eighteenth century, Horace Walpole had prepared a guidebook to Strawberry Hill, one of the earliest of many antiquarian houses in which dwelling and display were merged. Plaques and texts have long ago begun to convert our cities into open-air museums, but perhaps with less didactic insistence than the Colombian case.

As is well known, it is notoriously difficult to bring architecture into the space of the gallery where, for centuries, works of painting, sculpture, and other two-dimensional arts have found a home. Nearly every lecture on the architectural museum or the architectural exhibition begins by rehearsing the truism that architecture can only be exhibited through simulacra, substitute objects, or representations—originally drawings, models, mock-ups, prints, illustrated books, or other images—created after the building's completion or original design projection. Later, photographs, films, and computer simulations joined the arsenal of means of representing the art of architecture in a place other than where it stood. The architectural exhibition then is, with few exceptions, almost always a radical deracination of architecture—simulacra and deracination, a substitute representation or a displaced original. But what, we might ask, would it mean to craft a history not of the poor substitute that is an exhibition condemned to work with placebos, but rather a history of the potentialities of the architectural exhibition?

We might begin by asking why the habit of exhibiting architecture in the gallery first became common practice during the Enlightenment? This began in London in the 1760s, followed soon after in Paris, and then by the end of the century in Berlin, St. Petersburg, and nearly every other major or second-tier European city in which there was an academy, even if we can find isolated and quite specific cases a half-century earlier, notably in papal Rome. To ask the question: To what extent did the phenomenon of displaying architecture change the very nature and possibilities of architecture? With the title, "Out of Site/In Plain View," I propose that part of the very essence of a self-consciously modern architecture is wrapped up in the ability to put architecture on display, to take it out of its original site, and to return it to plain view. It is my contention that exhibitions, in the most diverse formats, have been vital instruments for advancing some of the greatest features of modern architecture since the Enlightenment, facilitating the emergence of a critical discourse on the public character and responsibilities of architecture; the invention of a history of architecture with its consequences for the exploration of architectural meaning and its capacities to build national, regional, and local identities; and the capacity of architecture to project entirely new programs and environments that we associate with the very condition of the avant-garde.

Of course, there had always been a way of putting architecture in a frame of sorts via rhetorical methods of calling attention to architecture through representations. One thinks of the role of the architectural model as it developed in the Renaissance as a way of seeking approval for a work, while at the same time refining its design and qualities. In this regard, think of Michelangelo's great dome of St. Peter's as depicted in a well-known painting by Domenico Cresti, or the role that miniatures of buildings played in portraits of saints or in underscoring the role of patronage, seen notably in the donors' portraits of buildings often held by those who financed all or part of buildings from the Middle Ages on. Not to mention the role of buildings in painted and sculpted iconography, in general. But I am not interested in sketching a history of architecture as iconography, but rather of architecture as itself on display. In short, I think we can ask: Is architecture's status as an art, in the first instance, and later, as an autonomous discipline, not, in some large measure, assured by the mechanisms of display and of the exhibition? But even this calling-attention-to is not necessarily what I have in mind, for what I am interested in is the larger rhetorical and narrative structures of the exhibition, not the fragment of display, even if the two are intimately related.

The possibility of exhibiting architecture out of site but in plain view is essential to creating a modern discourse on architecture, not only in terms of public discernment but also about the values of projects for urbanism, for the public good, and the like. Here, the key decade is the 1760s it seems to me, in which for the first time architects began to exhibit for a public outside the profession. It is true that exhibitions of architectural drawings were part of the academic tradition in training architects almost from the earliest Italian academies. And, with the rise of the academic competition—first with the Concorso Clementini at the Accademia di San Luca in Rome from the very late seventeenth century—the practice arose of pinning up drawings for the jury to compare, as in an oft-cited example by Juvarra. The student projects, though unsigned, were numbered, and only the secretary had a corresponding list of names, a practice that may have already been in use in the occasional competition from the Renaissance on to decide building commissions of great import. We know, from the research of Helmut Hager, the great historian of the Accademia di San Luca, that, beginning in 1695, the winning projects were exhibited to the public for a week, along with the names of the designers, and then kept in a great cabinet in the Sala di Studi of the Academy as study materials for the students. Although, as early as 1708, a Parisian student project for a purpose-built building for the Academy included a gallery for exhibiting the results of the competition, this does not seem to have been the practice in France before the mid-nineteenth century when more and more sophisticated pin-ups of the drawings were created for the exclusive use of the judges—even though, as early as 1758, the great teacher Jacques François Blondel, teacher of a whole generation in his own school, called for a gallery for exhibiting architectural drawings within the academy. But it is not this, per se, which interests me, for no doubt in architecture studios, for centuries, drawings had been pinned to the wall and discussed among equals.

Something changes in the mid-eighteenth century, and this is not simply the admission, of the public in Rome. It seems also, in Madrid, to view firsthand that the academic competition's role in establishing the artistic credentials of the architect—the ability to project a complex building design independent of a building site, or even a real commission—evolved. Too, the public reception and debate of architectural projects, not only as works of art but as issues of public concern and of the public good, took on a new aspect. Before the mid-eighteenth century, there are isolated examples of displays related to competitions, notably for the Baptistery doors in Florence. Evonne Levy, in her *Propaganda and the Jesuit Baroque,* has discussed the case of how the Jesuits, almost unwittingly, were forced into allowing their choice of an architect and design for the chapel of St. Ignatius in the left transept of the church of the Gesu in Rome in 1709, to become a matter of public scrutiny. They had recourse to a public display of designs, a display that has left no visual record of the display technique, but is documented in a careful recording of all comments overheard in the display. At the time it was noted that, once word spread, the display was under way: " . . . it is unbelievable how many ran from every part of the city to see it, stimulated by curiosity which had been aroused by the shrill tones of earlier that had already spread word around the city. Innumerable cardinals, bishops, prelates, princes, gentlemen, architects, painters, priests, monks, and laymen of every sort came. There was, in sum, a continuous flow of people, almost a fleet at sea." But, as Levy demonstrates, the Jesuits' concern was to manage gossip and to use the display as a mechanism of propaganda, not to seek discordant opinions or to foster public debate. It is that interest in soliciting rather than controlling public opinion, I would argue—following, of course, in the classic analysis of the interaction between press and coffeehouse by Jürgen Habermas in his influential (and controversial) 1962 *The Structural Change of the Public Sphere*—that marks the gradual entry of architecture into the public exhibition in London and Paris in the mid-eighteenth century, just as both cities began a significant period of urban change. In 1760, in the free market of London, was created the Society of Artists (incorporated by Royal Charter in 1765), the first of a series of venues where within a few years architects would freely exhibit their works without being enrolled pupils or admitted members of an Academy. At first, these were largely prints that would be sold as individual images or bound books. The illustrated book, we might say, was the first traveling exhibition. But, soon, other types of projects began to find their way into display and thus into the columns of the new public handbills and magazines, and the exhibition quickly changed from being an advertisement for a multiple that could be purchased, to making claims for architecture as an art form and for its stake in public debate. Much research remains to be done on the development of architectural exhibitions in Britain where a free market reigned and where it would seem, at a cursory look at the hard-to-come-by catalogs of these exhibitions, that lesser known architects were primarily attracted to this possibility to make a name. Leading exhibitors include the otherwise little-known Matthias Darly who exhibited architectural designs regularly at the Society of Artists from 1765 to 1771, although he is primarily known as an engraver of architectural ornament. Indeed, the earliest use therefore seems to have been to promote sales, first of the prints themselves, later of architectural services. Charles Cameron, however, who was to make his name with designs for Catherine the Great in Russia, exhibited examples of his work in 1767 at the Free Society and then again in 1772 at the Society of Artists, something that could be interpreted either as a way of sending newscasts home and maintaining his reputation far away from his adopted country, or as an appeal for other clients. And, by the end of the century, John Soane, a brick builder's son, had risen to fame partly through regular exhibition at the Royal Academy, and would give throughout the 1790s, through powerful renderings, almost annual updates on the progress of building at the Bank of England, a worksite off-limits to most. Many of these drawings were by Joseph Gandy, who, along with Piranesi, was one of those eighteenth-century architects who chiefly made their living and reputation through dramatic architectural representation, representations that could circulate not only in the explosion of the architectural publishing and printmaking industry which has been so well studied, but also in the space of the exhibition, which has not been adequately documented.

The French Academy created a very different situation. In the same years in Paris, the artist who pioneered the exhibition as a form of self-promotion, Charles de Wailly, opened with his first act. Michel Gallet reminds us that when De Wailly in 1771 exhibited his project for the Château de Montmusard, near Dijon, it was an unprecedented act made possible by the fact that the Marquis de Marigny, the director of the King's buildings, had promoted De Wailly directly to the first class of the Académie de Peinture, a rare case of an architect who was a member of both the architecture and painting academies. Only members of the Académie Royale de Peinture et de Sculpture had the right to exhibit. Charles Louis Clérrisseau—the first architect ever admitted, in 1769, to the Académie de Peinture— took advantage sometimes with views of antiquity or caprices; and from the first they were noticed and discussed, notably in the *Mercure de France.* And, once Clérrisseau moved to London in the 1770s, he exhibited regularly at the Society of Artists and the Royal Academy, to mixed reactions. *The London Chronicle* found his drawings "remarkable for taste, correctness and variety of tints—a circumstance seldom met with in compositions of architecture," while Horace Walpole noted, in his 1772 catalog of the Royal Academy show: "too much like a scene in an Opera." But De Wailly was the first to exhibit his own architectural design, and, more importantly, is the only one to have exhibited his own work—either buildings under way or already finished—so that it was both his skills as an architectural designer and as a painter depicting architecture that were on display. Most important here then is the promotion of a building not yet designed, peopled with future or imaginary users, who could take on many of the same rhetorical gestures and functions of figures in history painting. This became then a valuable instrument in the emerging public discourse on contemporary issues of architecture and urbanism, on the crafting of the public realm, something more famously associated with the first works of architectural criticism by Voltaire and by Étienne La Font de Saint-Yenne in the 1750s, when both published pamphlets urging Louis XV to take up essential tasks, such as the completion of the Louvre palace as a monument worthy of Paris, and the selection of an appropriate site for the permanent exhibition of Bouchardon's equestrian portrait of the King, a frame for sculpture that would also become a stage for a new public life. While the competition entries of the Place Louis XV in the 1750s had been exhibited only to decision makers, De Wailly now used his opening wedge into the annual exhibition that was the Salon to imagine the public realm that could be created by his current commission, along with the architect Marie Joseph Peyre, to design a new home for the Comédie Française. De Wailly's *morceau de reception* at the Académie de Peinture, which he in turn exhibited in the Salon of 1771, was in fact a depiction of the future vestibule and staircase of the projected theater, inviting the public to partake of the Comédie Française as a place of public assembly and a forum for modernity that was in some way a recreation of the forum of the ancients, replete with a cast of theatergoers straight from the world of history painting.

De Wailly was not alone in exhibiting architectural images at the Salon. Though painters of ruins such as Hubert Robert and Pierre de Machy created a critical discussion of the genre of *vedute,* or view painting, De Wailly was the first to take De Machy's radical gesture of exposing a representation of a future project into the space of the gallery and the Salon, where a lively critical discourse emerged. I am referring, of course, to one of the most spectacular architectural exhibitions of the eighteenth century: De Machy's enormous scaffold-supported painting at 1:1 scale of the future portico of J.G. Soufflot's royal church of Ste. Geneviève erected for the cornerstone ceremony in 1764. The occasion of the exhibition made it possible even for the builders who were given the day off to attend, and the general public—and not only those who could afford the engravings that were circulating—to appreciate the royal munificence (the real point of the event) as well as the proposal to erect the first-ever, colossal, antique-style portico in Paris. For the King it meant the possibility of obtaining instant political capital from his great investment, something with precedents back to the triumphal arches of the ancients and so in vogue again in the mid-eighteenth century. But what was new was that, for De Machy, it meant the possibility of public discourse; the combined mechanisms of an emerging press and a free print market, along with the Salon, meant that the image could circulate in a different space. The event was engraved, discussed in print, and even reexhibited in a modestly scaled painting at the Salon, which is generally on view today in the Musée Carnavalet in Paris. De Machy, moreover, extended beyond a mere representation in two dimensions a future sculptural space, and also projected the layout of a new hemicircular space, evidence of the extent to which spectatorship and the theatrical were entering into not only the exhibition of architecture, but the curation of the existing city fabric. This, but a few years after Voltaire wrote in his seminal essay on the "Embellishments of Paris" that, in order to ornament Paris as a city that could rival the beauties of ancient Rome, it was necessary to *dégager*—that is to "make way by clearing," or "to free up," or "disencumber"—more than to build.

De Wailly especially liked to use the Salon to unveil his great projects of urbanism. In the 1789 Salon he had an impressive ensemble of drawings of a comprehensive plan for the urban renewal of Paris. This presaged the rapid expansion of the architectural exhibition as a forum of public debate under the Revolution. In 1793, an architecture section was created at the Salon, mirroring now the free-market conditions that had long prevailed in English cities. At first, De Wailly and his pupils, who shared the same style of rendering, which often depicted figures themselves as stand-ins for viewers, dominated the exhibits. This approach gained a huge legacy in the nineteenth century when the profession of the architectural renderer became fully established.

The year 1794 to 1795 was a key moment in Paris, for in those years two new functions of the exhibition worked in tandem with the unfolding project of the Revolution to remake both the spaces of public life and the consciousness of the *citoyen:* the Competitions of the Year II and the founding of the Musée des Monuments Français past and future, both to be taken into public arena and debate. In the same year, a vast plan for restructuring the city, the so-called Plan des Artistes, was put on display, having taken up and reworked De Wailly's plan first exhibited at the Salon in 1789. The Competitions of the Year II played an important role in the emergence of a public debate over the form and functions of architecture. (These competitions were much studied twenty years ago in the context of the bicentennial of the French Revolution, in 1989, right at the moment when President François Mitterand was again rebuilding the French capital and international competitions gave rise to international exhibitions of French architecture.)

In 1794, the competitions were an open call to architects and artists to submit works in support of the newly emerging societal order. In painting and sculpture a whole new dimension of public iconography was called for, but in architecture—though there was little money or even political stability for much building—a veritable encyclopedia of new building types was created, from practical markets and tribunals of justice to monuments for new rituals meant to create the emotional and psychic infrastructure of the first Republic on the European continent since antiquity. The results were not published, but rather displayed in a great exhibition, accompanied by a catalog, arguably one of the first catalogs of an architectural exhibition. One hundred and twenty-seven paintings were received, 110 proposals for sculpture, and 195 proposals for buildings; for the first time ever, architecture would dominate a public display of the arts.

The exhibition, moreover, was not one of either existing buildings or buildings under construction, but rather the projection of a future architecture for a future state, the exhibition then becoming an integral part of the Revolutionary project itself—something to be reborn in nearly every major political realignment, notably in the decade following the Russian Revolution of 1917 or the reunification of Germany in 1989. As James Leith explains, in *Space and Revolution* (1991), a book built on the discovery of the registry in which the projects were entered as they arrived over the course of May to August 1794, the artists of France, suffering from the collapse of royal patronage on which the arts were based:

> Responded with a series of projects . . . that were eventually grouped together and
> later judged by a single jury in what has come to be known as the Concours de l'an II.

The government called on painters to portray subjects of their own choice related to the Revolution. It appealed to sculptors to submit versions of three of the temporary monuments erected for the Festival of Unity and Indivisibility the previous year: a figure of Nature Generated rising from the ruins of the old prison on the site of the Bastille; a huge figure of Liberty for the Place de la Révolution; and a figure of the French People trampling down Feudalism for the esplanade of the Invalides. Sculptors were asked to submit models of a monument first proposed by David the previous November for one of the most conspicuous sites in Paris, the promontory of the west end of the Ile de la Cité, near where the statue of Henry IV had once stood.

But it was the architects who were asked to depart the most significantly, not simply inventing new iconography but inventing whole new building types and functions. They were to design a permanent version of the monument that had marked the second station in the Festival of Unity and Indivisibility; a triumphal arch commemorating the march of Parisians to Versailles that had forced the royal family to take up residence in Paris on 6 October 1789; a monument for the Place de la Victoire, honoring those citizens who had died on 10 August 1792; a column for the Pantheon commemorating those who had died in defense of the Fatherland; a Temple to Equality for the Beaujon Garden on the Champs Elyssées; and covered arenas to be built on the site of the old Opéra between the Boulevard St. Martin and the Rue Bondi where the citizenry could celebrate republican victories and national festivals. To these symbolic and ritual tasks—themselves the concrete elements for reconstituting urban space as well as turning Revolutionary events immediately into a new historical symbolic order—were added a roster of projects associated with plans to modernize Paris and to give it a suitable symbolic center. In the spring and early summer of 1793 the Convention had passed a series of decrees asking artists to submit plans addressing the problem of how nationalized property could be exploited in order to produce revenue, while at the same time widening streets, enlarging squares, and beautifying urban space. At first, the Convention called for proposals for developing the area around the Tuileries Palace, so as to give the legislature a proper setting and to improve lines of communication with the rest of the city. Several artists prepared plans, some of which were later submitted to the Competitions of the Year II. The commission comprised eleven members: four inspector-generals of thoroughfares and seven architects. Their planning, based on the detailed map of Paris made recently by Edme Verniquet, gradually spread to take in the whole city.

But, while the Commission of Artists was busy with its plans to improve the urban infrastructure, and the Committee for Embellishment was working to create a symbolic city center, artists submitted designs in response to government appeals in separate decrees and announcements in the press. Here, then, was a project that began to extend the paper museum of an ideal monumental public architecture that Etienne-Louis Boullée had been at work on since the mid-1780s, although there is little evidence that he ever publically exhibited many of the watercolors, such as his famous project for a museum as a place of elevated sentiments of citizenry in a public setting.

By the end of 1794, a veritable museum of modern architectural types had been put on display, judged and awarded prizes, and submitted to public scrutiny and extensive discussion in the burgeoning press and broadsides. Projects ranged from the most elevated tasks—a new kind of national assembly, a temple of laws, a veritable prototype for so many nineteenth-century courthouses, a project for an Odeum National, or a national music hall by one Bernard, and the astounding projects of the young Percier and Fontaine partnership for a National Theater. Numerous architectural innovations took place here as well. First among them was the quest for an architecture that could speak through a more abstract language of form, rather than a deployment of the literal classical orders of architecture—most famously in Durand and Thibault's Temple of Equality, or through writing and inscription, either of memory in the case of Percier and Fontaine's Monument to the Defenders of the Fatherland, or literally to the celebration of the newly codified laws of the Republic and the idea of a constitution proposed by Durand and Thibault in a prototype design for a small primary assembly that could be built throughout the reorganized territories of the French Departments. The country was to be untied now by a legal system of public consensus, along with a new educational system that was intended not only to make citizens equipt to read the monumental forms essayed in the competition entries, but also a standardized French proposed by the Abbé Grégoire in important papers on a linguistic reform, which included the wonderful proposal to collect regional dialects into a museum of the French language. This temporary display of a veritable new Republican typology of public architecture, which included also a full range of buildings of a more quotidian use such as markets and schools, was to be made an instrument for reference and architectural training a few years later when the same J.N.L. Durand published his great elephant folio *Receuil et parallèle des edifices de tous genres,* perhaps the first time that a book derived from an exhibition, rather than the other way around. The exhibition was not firmly established within the economy of the circulation of architectural images and types nor within the politics of public debate about buildings, their forms, their placements, and their language. Here it seems too that the idea penned by Boullée in his unpublished *Essai sur l'Art* was realized:

> If one were to raise the objection and say that the government cannot give out monuments to build the way it commissions painting and sculptures, I would reply, 'Yes of course.' But we can turn to architects for model solutions . . . And with time we would thus comprise a museum of architecture (one of the first mentions of this topic to which we must turn next week), a museum which would include everything one has a right to expect of this art form from those who have cultivated its practice.

Indeed, the Jury that judged the competition concluded in its session of 9 June 1795: "These models will be carefully conserved in order to constitute, along with others that will be added annually, a collection of architectural models . . . using of course the word 'models' in both senses of sculptural representations of buildings and of standards for emulation."

The competitions of 1794, moreover, did not go unnoticed. After that date, there was a spike of the presentation of projects that were possibly speculative in other academies. A high point was reached with the so-called competition of 1796 for a monument to Frederick the Great. This was, as we know from the most recent research by Michael Bollé, not an open competition at all but rather an event staged by Carl Gotthard Langhans, Berlin's most prominent architect and the author most recently of the Brandenburg Gate, to try to force royal action. All the leading figures of the Berlin School presented themselves, perhaps one of the earliest examples of a school of thought being constituted in part by the event of an exhibition: Heinrich Gentz, Friedrich Gilly, Langhans himself, Johann Gottfried Schadow, and Aloys Hirt. One year later, they all submitted their projects to the annual Berliner Akademieausstellung. While it did not lead to immediate execution of the project—it would take some forty more years—it did cause a young student to abandon his plans to study music in favor of a career in architecture. This student was Karl Friedrich Schinkel whose first biographer, Gustav Waagen, claimed in the booklet prepared for the Schinkel Museum that it was the apotheosis of the quest for an architecture capable of embodying the highest values of a society that convinced the sixteen-year-old Schinkel to enroll in the young Bauakademie.

Schinkel would complete his studies at the Bauakademie before the studios and collections found a first home in the upper floors of Heinrich Gentz's new multipurpose building for the Prussian Royal Mint on the Werderscher Markt in the center of Berlin. This was commissioned in 1796 to provide not only a factory for minting coins but also a headquarters for the state administration of mountains and mines—the Berg-Departement—with, on the upper floors of the building, its mineral cabinet, eventually to be organized as Prussia's first public gallery of mineralogy, and its plan room with topographic and technical documents on all mines in use. In 1798 Gentz exhibited a wooden model and nine sheets of plans of the project at the annual exhibition of the Academy, but in the following year the project changed when the Bauakademie and the Ober-Bau-Departement were added to the program. In addition, Gentz accompanied his display with a text defending the style of the building, first published in the catalog of the display and then reprinted in David Gilly's newly founded *Sammlung nützlicher Aufsätze die Baukunst betreffend, Für angehende Baumeister und Freunde der Architektur,* the first sustained German architectural periodical. That text, in which he defended his mixture of references from different styles in his search for the most appropriate functional and civic character of the new building, was a landmark in the critique of neoclassicism and the emergence of a modern synthetic historicism, but also in the emergence of the idea that the communicative power of style and the intellectual engagement with its meaning were themselves constituent acts of the public. If some find the building Greek, others Egyptian, and others even Gothic—as it was described in the popular "Berlin, eine *Zeitschrift für Freunde der schönen Künste, des Geschmacks und der Moden*"—this is their right. He was delighted that, by 1801 in the *Zeitung für die elegante Welt,* "the unusual feature of columns without an entablature at entrance" led to a critical article and debate. The exhibition and the press then had formed an alliance to create a public space for architecture paralleling the period's fascination with the creation of worthy physical spaces. The model entered a new discourse when it became part of the display of models inside the building, a historical lesson now for the students. With the emergence of a critical debate about the appearance of public buildings and their legibility, architecture had—in Berlin now as in Paris and London earlier—begun to find its public, and the public found architecture in a set of overlapping dialogues which connected the evolving metropolis, the burgeoning press, and conversations in places as diverse as the coffee shop, the public reading room, and exhibition spaces—from the august Salon to commercial displays.

It is a possibility for architecture that would take us through a number of key incidents, one being the insistence that the competition entries for rebuilding the Houses of Parliament, after a devastating fire swept the Palace of Westminster in October 1834, should be put on public display. The Houses of Parliament competition has long been seen as a threshold in an emerging battle of styles—with the association of medieval and Elizabethan styling as expressive of both Englishness and of the great Parliamentary tradition of government in opposition to the then dominant neoclassicism of expression in public building—as well as in the history of the use of the architectural competition as a democratic way of soliciting building designs for public architecture. The competition is equally important in the extension of the democratic claims of public exhibition of architectural designs, and their role in engendering needed public debate. Writing under the pseudonym "Candidus," John Claudius Loudon, in the lively *Architectural Magazine,* penned the first of many columns that followed the Houses of Parliament affair, under the title, "A Word on the rebuilding of the Houses of Parliament . . . ." While Parliamentary officials had given in to the demand for a display of the leading contenders, Loudon wanted all entries to be given a public viewing:

> We cannot see the wisdom of limiting to the leading men of the profession; because if this principle were adopted and acted on generally, it would exclude all the rising talent, and all extra-professional talent. If there is to be an exhibition of the designs, what have the leading men of the profession to fear from the designs of those who are not leading men? . . . For our own part we advocate not only free competition, but public exhibition, and public discussion of the plans; the deviser of each design having permission to come forward and explain and defend it if he thinks fit. Why should not the subject of a proposed public building be discussed in public and reported to the world in the newspapers, as well as a proposed public law?

A month later, he returned to the subject and proposed that the public exhibition be an integral part of the decision making. "There will, I trust, not only be a public exhibition of all the designs for the Houses of Parliament, but the exhibition will be allowed to take place before a definitive choice of any one design be made; so that those with whom that choice ultimately rests shall be able to ascertain, in some measure, what is the general public opinion." Letters poured in, responding to Loudon's advocacy of exhibition, with Mr. John Weale, an architectural publisher proposing an exhibition portfolio of the unsuccessful designs, one that could extend the exhibition throughout the country. Loudon picked up on this and concluded:

The British Public is just beginning to exercise an opinion on matters of taste in arts and manufactures, and such a publication as proposed would give a wonderful stimulus to architecture. All the public libraries throughout Europe and North America would be eager to possess a copy of the work; and we have no doubt that, in consequence of the recommendations of the Committee on the Fine Arts of the House of Commons, government would purchase a number of copies, and present them to Mechanics' Institutions, and other institutions to be formed in large towns, for the purpose of encouraging art.

And thus, soon, by popular demand, the projects were put on display in the newly completed first wing of William Wilkin's National Gallery on Trafalgar Square, the first architectural exhibition ever held there. This would become common practice in nineteenth-century Britain, the heyday of the use of the competition as a type of referendum on design. We see this impulse just one decade ago, when the citizens of New York demanded, after 9/11, that a competition be held for the redevelopment of Ground Zero: when the projects were put on display and a referendum was taken within the exhibition itself. Like so much else about the tragic event, and the hope for civic engagement that briefly followed, it is at once something that seems entirely of this young century but belonging to a longer history.

Exhibition as Medium

Out of Place: Circulating Monuments

Mari Lending

Architecture curators and exhibition historians often claim that the display of architecture is more cumbersome than the presentation of other art forms. While sculpture and painting, once produced for site-specific admiration, quite peacefully found their way into collections and museums and over the centuries became naturalized in their new habitats, architecture has remained something of a problem in the modern world of collecting and display. This problem is as old as the architecture museum itself. "[B]uildings are made to remain fixed on the spot where they are originally erected, and are of such a scale that they cannot be collected together in any gallery, however large," stated James Fergusson, at the time manager of the Crystal Palace at Sydenham, on the occasion of the incorporation of the Architectural Museum into the new South Kensington Museum in 1857.[1] Fergusson compares displays of capitals and cornices, fragments and details to "a collection of fingers or toes of sculpture, or eyes or ears out of paintings." Certainly, while most art works can be presented as "the real thing," architecture on display normally involves matters of representation, or, alternatively, severe fragmentation. Exhibited and collected, architecture is always somehow out of place, and concerns the *oeuvre* rather than the *ouvrage,* to borrow a distinction drawn by Jean-Louis Cohen, namely that such curated spaces present designs, models, drawings, photos, and intellectual work, as opposed to the built work.[2]

Despite his skepticism, James Fergusson did not dismiss the possibility of an architecture museum catering both to a generalist and a specialist audience. Several attempts had of course already been made. He mentions Sir John Soane's Museum, as well as Hôtel de Cluny and Palais des Beaux Arts in Paris. He could have stirred Alexandre Lenoir's short-lived Musée de Monuments Français into the mix as well. However, none of these experiments captured exactly what he had in mind, which is perhaps why he was so palpably discontent with the two contemporary museums he was involved in himself. The plaster casts in the Architectural Courts at Sydenham were criticized for being populist, and accused of polychromic excesses. The manager was among its critics: "There are some minds which can only be approached by having their wholesome food so clogged with sweetness or so savored with spices as almost to destroy its nutritious qualities." The only sound exceptions were the Pompeian House and Owen Jones' Alhambra Court.[3] The Architectural Museum, on the other hand, appeared to Fergusson myopic in its Gothic profile, and "too exclusively mediæval to perform."[4] He did, however, have the recipe at hand for an architecture museum that would give England "a more complete illustration of architectural art than any nation of Europe," a museum laid out "on a proper scale" and "established on a sufficiently broad basis and carried out with a proper cosmopolitan liberality of feeling."[5] The one solution for a modern architecture museum was a scientifically arranged collection of plaster casts ("I need hardly add that they must be arranged chronologically"); casts with surfaces treated to look exactly as the monument in situ, not restored back to an imagined former glory.

For all his self-doubt, Fergusson basically launched the program for the grand collections of full-scale monuments that, over the next decades, would furnish museums from Moscow to Chicago. Before falling out of vogue in the first decades of the twentieth century, the plaster cast was a major architectural mass medium, developing in parallel to and closely interwoven with photography. A key document in this trajectory was the "Convention for Promoting Universally Reproductions of Works of Art for the Benefit of Museums of All Countries" that Henry Cole had fifteen European princes sign during the 1867 World Exhibition in Paris [Figure 1]. The convention laid out an apparatus for the exchange of national monuments, implicitly theorizing a new mass medium and outlining a boundless museum based exclusively on reproductions whose merits and characteristics could be assessed across time and space.

Fergusson's plaster vision and Cole's Convention were remarkably successful. Soon, this was the prevailing mode in which architecture was presented for a broad audience: full size, in three dimensions, and to varying degrees imitating the surfaces of the original monuments. Plaster reproductions were promoted, both in the U.S. and in Europe, as a compensation for those who could not themselves go to see the monuments in situ: "It is difficult to determine for what purposes such strange and mixed assemblage of ancient works or rather copies of [cast from] them, for many are not of stone or marble, have been brought together—some have suggested that it might have been to the advancement of Architectural knowledge by making the young Students in that noble & useful Art who had no means of visiting Greece and Italy some better ideas of ancient Works than would be conveyed thro: the medium of drawings or prints," John Soane muses in a hallucinatory 1812 note, fantasizing about what posterity would make of his plaster heaven home at Lincoln's Inn Field in London.[6] At the time, Soane used his private collection of architectural fragments for teaching purposes. The public cast collections obviously served didactic ends, however their main purpose was to show architecture, as close as possible to the real thing, for a broad audience. From a number of vantage points, it was argued that reproductions were better suited than originals to display architecture. The benefits of casts resonated with a variety of nineteenth-century scientific taxonomies played out in the displays, among them chronology, evolution, style, and comparison, unachievable in even the best-equipped museums of originals.

The cast collections confirmed the emerging opinion that architecture was actually best experienced out of place, in well tempered, light-controlled curatorial environments. In fact, in 1818, the prominent museophobe Quatremère de Quincy—who in the 1790s had risked both his career and life criticizing the French looting of European masterpieces and claiming that museums killed art—gave one of the most illustrious reasons ever presented for the superiority of experiencing architecture in the museum. Traveling to London to inspect the Elgin Marbles, Quatremère was mesmerized not only by finally seeing pieces from the Parthenon first hand, but of the effect of the fragments as curated collectibles. In a captivating suite of seven letters to his friend Antonio Canova in Rome, Quatremère states that disintegrated building elements offer a more genuine understanding than an original building could ever provide, whether intact or in ruin. Not only out of place but relocated in time as well, the temple fragments induced, according to Quatremère, a veritable time travel, propelling the observer back to their moment of creation. From a provisory gallery adjacent to the British Museum then under construction in Bloomsbury, he reported to Canova that you find yourself "on the construction site or in the atelier, with your hands on the objects, which appear in their real dimensions, you walk around them, counting the pieces, combining the relations between them and their dimensions."[7] [Figure 2] Your imagination, he goes on, describing in depth the heavily dismembered fragments of a ruined structure, "is compelled to contemplate the entire ensemble of works, makes you speechless at the thought of all the labour and expedience invested to fulfil this enterprise, in such a short period and with such a degree of perfection." Quatremère is of course talking about originals. Exposed to the Elgin Marbles, however, he outlined the tropological basis for the display of architecture as full-scaled reproductions that took on speed and popularity a few decades later, namely, the synecdoche, the *pars pro toto,* in which the displaced fragment lets the eye and the mind envision lost or otherwise inaccessible totalities. It is worth noting that while Quatremère was studying fragments from the Parthenon in the Temporary Elgin Room in 1818, orders for casts of the marbles were already being placed at the British Museum, soon to catapult bits and

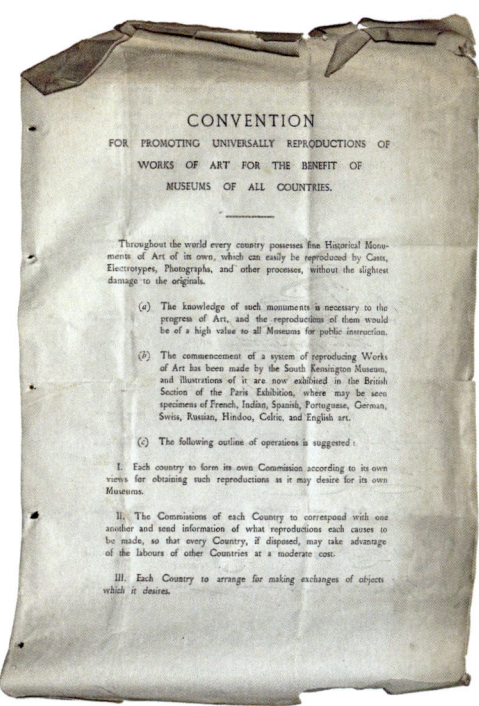

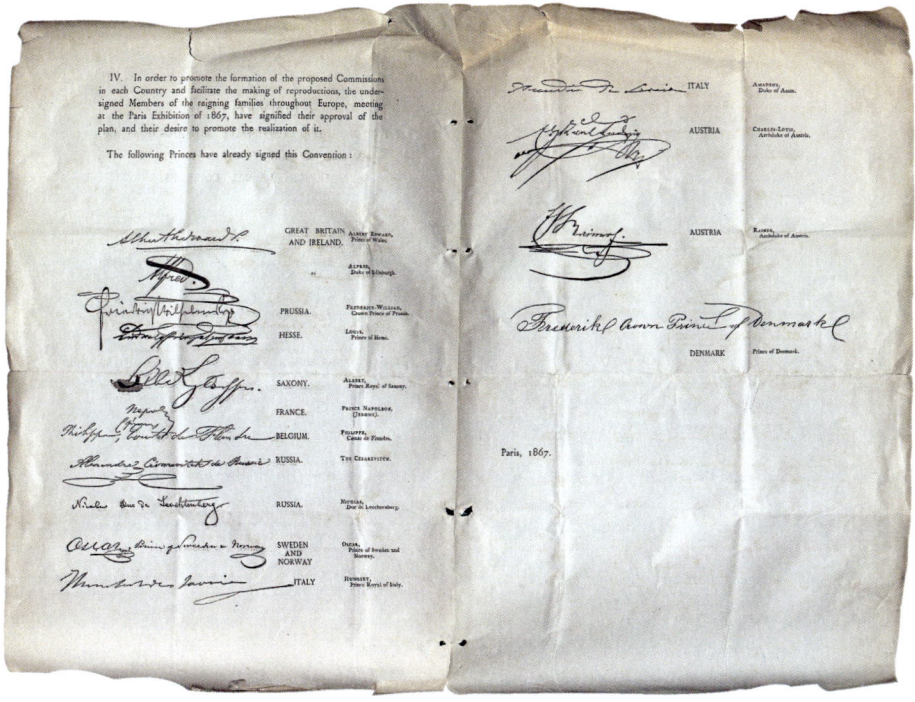

[Figure 1]

[Figure 2]

[Figure 3]

28

pieces of the Greek temple out of London and into an international cast market where they immediately became star objects and staples of every self-respecting cast collection across the world.[8]

That architecture easily gets lost in context is a lesson learned from the Quatremère-Canova correspondence. The idea that a completed building or a ruined structure loses its grandeur when seen in its place is wonderfully illustrated in the watercolor John Soane commissioned from his former student Henry Parke for his Royal Academy lecture devoted to the five orders of architecture [Figure 4]. The image depicts a Grand Tour tourist—impeccably dressed from top hat to delicate shoes—balancing on a ladder leaning towards the enormous Corinthian capital and entablature of the Temple of Castor and Pollux at the Roman Forum.[9] Armed with a measuring rod, he is completely dwarfed by the monument he is about to measure; a ruin anachronistically reconstructed on paper to its supposedly pristine state. We may wonder what the gentleman actually sees from this close-up, vertigo-evoking perspective. The view reminds us not only of the expenses and discomforts of travel, but also of the dangers involved in on-site monument inspection; in 1770 an architecture student was reported to have died falling from a ladder while ascending a monument at the Roman Forum.[10] Quatremère insisted that well-lit, neatly curated fragments domesticated in handsome galleries such as the Temporary Elgin Room, provided, by the power of imagination, totalities unavailable in situ. Fergusson, on the other hand, stated that scientifically displayed full-scaled reproductions presented historical totalities otherwise inaccessible. Both perspectives formed the basis for the exhibition and circulation of architectural plaster casts in the latter part of the nineteenth century.

Casts were offered from a plethora of sales catalogs issued from prominent European museums of antiquities. In addition, there were museums devoted to casts only, with their own workshops selling multiplied monuments, and a proliferation of plaster-casting companies, from Christiania to Cairo, run by *formatori,* mostly of Italian origin. From the Great Exhibition in London in 1851 and onwards, casts were often transferred to museums after having premiered at the World Exhibitions. The launching of national specimens into an international orbit of exhibition was crucial in the process of both redefining and inventing ancient, deteriorating structures as monuments. In this way, the vulnerability of originals in stone or wood was countered by their imitation in a far more ephemeral material. Monuments were preserved in plaster, so to speak, protecting them through publicity and canonization, and prompting the originals to be inscribed into discourses of preservation.

Within this busy cast industry and an increasingly trans-Atlantic trade in monuments, a peculiar phrase makes itself conspicuously manifest, namely the out-of-place topos that saturates the discourse on the plaster monuments, which I describe below.

In the mid-1930s, Eric Maclagan, the director at the Victoria and Albert Museum, confided that he found the full-scale Trajan's Column in his museum's Cast Courts a "monstrous perversion," "an incongruous white elephant," and "an anomaly as well as a prodigious inconvenience."[11] The monstrous perversion was produced in the 1860s, and dictated the height of the imposing skylit Architecture Courts when inaugurated at the then South Kensington Museum in 1873 [Figure 3]. Or, rather, half the column dictated the height; what was referred to as a "mammoth model" by contemporary press was cut in two in order to fit it into the gallery. The width of the space was given by another gigantic cast, the Pórtico de la Gloria from the Cathedral in Santiago de Compostela, manufactured in 1866 by Dominico Brucciani, master plaster caster at both South Kensington Museum and the British Museum.

Maclagan was not part of the tide that, in the first decades of the twentieth century, flushed huge collections of casts out of the galleries; in fact, he saved the Victoria and Albert Museum collection from destruction. It was this particular cast that troubled him, and the reason was not its size but its placement.[12] The problem was taxonomical, and related to the fact that the Roman monument was placed center stage in the gallery displaying Northern European and Spanish Gothic and Romanesque casts (among its closest neighbors are still three Norwegian Stave church portals). When characterizing the London Trajan's column as out of place, Maclagan was referring to a specific, local context. Nevertheless, he points to an emblematic condition at work in these collections of full-scale fragments, namely, the constant threat of the taxonomic order collapsing. Innumerable documents testify to this threat, which is inscribed into lists and catalogs by panicking curators and directors of rapidly expanding cast collections.

Planned by Eugène-Emmanuel Viollet-le-Duc and opened for the public in 1882, the Musée de Sculpture Comparée in Paris was explicitly based on Johann Joachim Winckelmann's theory on the periodical development of art. It aimed at displaying the advancement in French medieval and Renaissance architectural sculpture, contextualized by Greek and Roman casts as well as "sculptures étrangers." Both the concept and the displays in the enfilade galleries in the Palais de Trocadéro were founded on a rigorous art-historical scheme, encouraging comparison of stylistic developments, perfectly illustrated in three dimensions in the galleries. However, new acquisitions were a constant threat to the aesthetic theories upon which the collection was based. Heavy, fragile, basically immovable doorways and portions of facades were increasingly displaced as new monuments were included, bringing the perfectly curated casts out of place, a spatially unsolvable problem lamented by the director Camille Enlart in the 1911 *catalog raisonné*.[13]

Less taxonomical but equally spatial were the out-of-place problems arising during the planning of the Hall of Architecture at the Carnegie Institute in Pittsburgh. "If disposed of hastily, the Institute will obtain the most conventional of ready-made collections," a curator at the Museum of Fine Arts warned in 1905—at the time passionately fighting to get rid of the casts in Boston.[14] In hindsight, it is exactly the ready-made quality that makes the Pittsburgh collection so fascinating. Undisturbed by museum fashions, Andrew Carnegie was determined to have a grand collection of monuments installed in his hometown museum at the very moment when many museums where about to dismantle their cast collections. Most of the goods were ordered by mail from catalogs, making the collection reflect in interesting ways, the decreasing market of monuments as commodities.

For an empty plot between the full facade of the Romanesque church St. Gilles du Gard and the Erectheion Portico, the Carnegie director John W. Beatty wanted a Roman monument and settled for the Castor and Pollux temple. This was "an excellent choice" according to Camille Enlart, the director at the Musée de sculpture comparée, who advised Beatty on a number of matters and also supplied the Carnegie collection with several casts of French monuments. Enlart told Beatty that this is "the only Roman order, of which a complete proof can be made in Paris," and added, slightly surprisingly—given the immense size of the ruined monument—that the columns "adapt themselves very well to be placed in a museum." Thus, he recommends Beatty to place an order at the École des Beaux-Arts, where this cast hovered over the classical collection displayed in the school's Glass Courts.[15]

When eventually realizing that the colossal object couldn't possibly fit into The Hall of Architecture—designed as an inverted fantasy reconstruction of the Mausoleum in Halicarnassus—Beatty inventively decided to have the French cast of the Roman monument amputated quite brutally from below. "I will reply with all frankness," Enlart responded, "that this solution would seem to me a bad one." It "would be *out of place* in a museum of beautiful models," he writes, by now apparently mildly shocked by the adventurous American.[16] He does, however, politely advise on how to deal with the problem by showing fragments (of fragments) to "preserve the full value" of the monument, and suggests that the Carnegie collection swaps the Roman monument for "an angle of the Parthenon." One might wonder why the suggested cutting of the Roman ruin cast appears to be out of place, while an equally dismembered plaster portion of the biggest Doric temple ever built is seen to preserve the full value of the monument.

It was the Parthenon-as-exhibit that had inspired Quatremère to claim that, in architecture, a fragment is sufficient to reestablish wholeness and perfection. A well-mounted piece of a monument could enable the spectator to restore, in his imagination, order and wholeness, which means ultimately that a monument can only be fully grasped out of place. After all, James Fergusson's comparison of exhibited architectural fragments with collections of fingers or toes from sculpture, or eyes or ears from paintings, proved to become the curatorial basis for the display of lost totalities in the nineteenth-century cast museum.

[Figure 4]

[1] James Fergusson, "On a National Collection of Architectural Art," Introductory Address on the Science and Art Department and the South Kensington Museum, delivered on 21st December 1857, (London: Chapman and Hall, 1857), 4.

[2] Yve-Alain Bois, Denis Hollier, and Rosalind Krauss, "A Conversation with Jean-Louis Cohen," *October 89,* 1999.

[3] Fergusson, "On a National Collection of Architectural Art," 16.

[4] Ibid., 15.

[5] Ibid., 12, 14, 17.

[6] John Soane, "Crude Hints towards a History of my House in L[incoln's] I[nn] Fields," in Helen Dorey, ed., *Visions of Ruins: Architectural fantasies and designs for garden follies.* Exhibition catalog, (London: Sir John Soane's Museum, 1999), 69.

[7] Quatremère de Quincy, "Lettres écrit de Londres a Rome, at adressées à M. Canova, sur les marbles d'Elgin ou Les sculptures du temple de Minerva à Athènes," in *Considérations morales sur la destination des ouvrages de l'art, suivi de Lettres sur l'enlèvement des ouvrage de l'art antique à Athènes et à Rome* (Paris, 1836), 1836: reprint, Paris: Fayard, 1989. Author's translation.

[8] Ian Jenkins, "Acquisition and supply of casts of the Parthenon sculptures by the British Museum, 1835–1939," *The Annual of the British School at Athens,* Vol. 85 (Athens, 1990), 102.

[9] Soane's collection included more plaster casts of this temple than of any other building. Altogether, twenty-one casts of the Temple of Castor and Pollux were dispersed around his house, plus several scale models and a number of drawings, engravings, and paintings. For the casts, see Helen Dorsey, Appendix 3, "Catalogues of drawings, models and plaster casts from the Temple of Castor and Pollux, Forum Romanum, in Sir John Soane's Museum, London," in Kjell Aage Nilson, Claes B. Persson, Siri Sande, Jan Zahle, *The Temple of Castor and Pollux III: The Augustan Temple. Occasional papers of the Nordic Institutes in Rome,* 4 (Rome: L'Erma di Bretschneider, 2009).

[10] Frank Salmon, "'Storming the Campo Vaccino': British Architects and the Antique Buildings of Rome after Waterloo," *Architectural History, Vol. 38* (1995), 150.

[11] Everything on Maclagan is quoted from Diane Bilbey and Marjorie Trusted, "The Question of Casts," in ed. Rune Fredriksen and Eckhart Marchand, *Plaster Casts: Making, Collecting and Displaying from Classical Antiquity to the Present* (Berlin: De Gruyter, 2010).

[12] He did however suggest to cut the whole thing up and display— preferably somewhere else—the spiraling frieze in a manner that allowed for studying in detail the panels depicting emperor Trajan's victory over the Dacians, which is how the plaster panels from the column are displayed in the monument's home city, at the Museum of Roman Civilization in EUR.

[13] Camille Enlart, *Le musée de sculpture comparée du Trocadéro* (Paris: Librairie Renouard, 1911).

[14] Letter from Matthew Prichard to Mr. Longfellow, April 20, 1905. Hall of Architecture archive, Heinz Architectural Center library collection. Carnegie Museums of Pittsburgh.

[15] Letter from Camille Enlart to John W. Beatty, October 30, 1906. Hall of Architecture archive, Heinz Architectural Center library collection. Carnegie Museums of Pittsburgh.

[16] Letter from Camille Enlart to John W. Beatty, November 24, 1906. Author's italics. Hall of Architecture archive, Heinz Architectural Center library collection. Carnegie Museums of Pittsburgh.

Exhibitions, Objects, and the Emergence of Modernism in Germany

Wallis Miller

The international exhibit at the 1923 *Bauhaus Exhibition* started at the top of the stairs of the school's main building where models of projects by Walter Gropius and Mies van der Rohe welcomed visitors to the show [Figure 1]. According to Bauhaus historian Hans-Jürgen Winkler, Mies's models of his Concrete Office Building and Glass Skyscraper stood right at the stair landing, while Gropius's (his office's) model of the competition design for the Chicago Tribune Building stood opposite, "flooded with light from the stairwell."[1] Drawings and photographs of Gropius's design were displayed on the wall behind in a "free arrangement" with other designs. The exhibition continued in two rooms where the work of Gropius's office, his Bauhaus colleagues, and students was exhibited with work from Germany (including Erich Mendelsohn and Max Taut as well as Mies) and abroad: Holland (including Jacobus Oud), Czechoslovakia (assembled in part by Karel Teige), France (including work by Le Corbusier), Denmark (probably Knud Lonberg-Holm), and the U.S. (Frank Lloyd Wright). In addition, there was a section displaying photographs of industrial buildings, showing projects by Peter Behrens and Hans Poelzig alongside a selection of American grain silos.[2] (This was probably based on the photography exhibit, *Modern Industrial Buildings (Vorbildliche Industriebauten),* which Gropius had organized for Karl Ernst Osthaus's German Museum for Art in Industry and Trade in 1911–1914.) Overall, the international architecture exhibition showed new work—at Gropius's explicit request— and was, as Winkler put it, "the first point of consolidation after the war for the new generation."[3]

The Gropius and Mies exhibits set the tone for the exhibition not only because they appeared to stage a confrontation between the two architects, but because of the simple fact that models dominated the display. The Bauhaus section used the large plan drawing of the Bauhaus Siedlung by Farkas Molnár as a focus, but several models provided what Winkler called "plastic accents": among them, models of the Haus am Horn, constructed for the exhibition on a separate site; a mass-produced single-family house; Molnár's "Red Cube" house and a group of models showing possible variations of the Bauhaus Siedlung house. A model of the Kappe warehouse did the same for the displays showing the work by Gropius's office.[4]

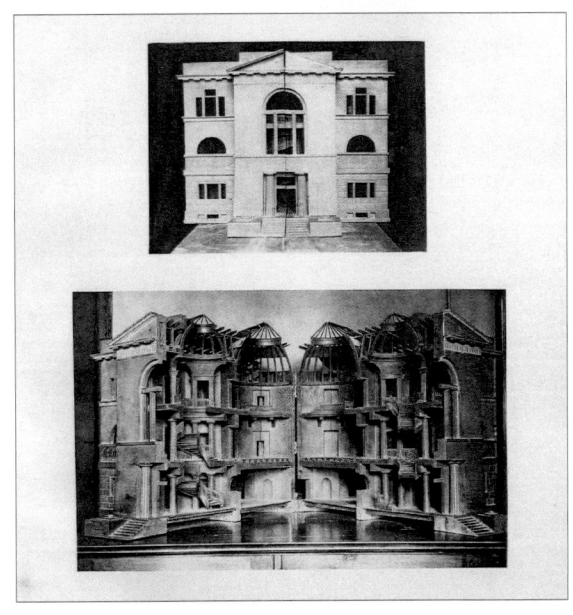

Models in an architecture exhibition are no surprise to our eyes. But their ubiquity at the 1923 exhibition was something of a novelty and part of an emerging trend in Germany and beyond, especially in exhibitions associated with the avant-garde, an issue that Oliver Elser has discussed in the essay for his exhibition *Das Architekturmodelle* held at the Deutsches Architekturmuseum in Frankfurt in 2012. Models were prominent, for example, at the exhibition *The Architects of the De Stijl Group, Holland,* which opened in Paris right after the Bauhaus exhibition had closed and in Gustav Platz's 1925 *Typen neuer Baukunst (Types of the New Architecture)* at the Kunsthalle in Mannheim. At the Bauhaus, the 1923 architecture exhibition was the second—albeit the more prominent one—that included models as a matter of course. The first, held a year earlier, had showcased the work of Gropius and his architecture office in a series of drawings, models—made of cardboard and plaster—and, most likely, photographs.[5]

In Berlin, too, the presence of architectural models at exhibitions of architecture had steadily increased after World War I. From 1919 until 1926 virtually every well known German architect associated with the avant-garde exhibited work with the Novembergruppe or the Bund Deutscher Architekten (the Association of German Architects), often but not always at the *Grosse Berliner Kunstausstellung* (the Great Berlin Art Exhibition, the successor to the Prussian Academy exhibition, since 1893). Many used models, for example: Peter Behrens and Hans Poelzig, Bruno Taut, Erich Mendelsohn, the Luckhardt Brothers, Gropius, and Mies, who exhibited the model of his Glass Skyscraper in 1922 and the models of his Concrete Country House and Concrete Office Building in 1923.[6]

The Berlin examples and, I would argue, the Bauhaus examples are part of a longer history of exhibiting architecture in the context of art, specifically at the Royal Prussian Academy exhibitions, where architecture had a constant presence since the academy's reestablishment in 1786. The Prussian Academy (Königliche Preußische Akademie der Künste) was the major venue in Berlin for exhibitions of architecture—specifically exhibitions of designs for new projects—until the mid-nineteenth century, when other venues emerged both in Berlin and outside the city: for example, the German sections of the World's Fairs sponsored by the Prussian and, then, the German government (and often organized by the Prussian Academy); the exhibitions at the Architekten Verein zu Berlin (Berlin Society of Architects) in the 1840s; and the architecture museum at Berlin's Technische Hochschule in 1874.

At the Prussian Academy exhibitions, architecture was exhibited as both an independent discipline and a subject for other works of art. The kind of object varied and its position changed, especially relative to sculpture and applied art. This was more than a logistical issue; it was an ontological one. Unlike painting, sculpture, drawing, and engraving, architecture never had a permanent home at the Prussian Academy exhibitions because its very nature—for example, architecture's changing relationship to building—challenged the taxonomies that structured the exhibition and, more generally, defined the arts. Architecture could be defined as a kind of object, a particular subject, the creation of an architect, or in terms of a specific position relative to the other arts. From this perspective, exhibitions can enrich our view of the theoretical discussions of architecture's definition—for example, architecture defined as art—and therefore contribute to our understanding of the emergence of modern architecture in Germany and elsewhere. In this context, models are good examples for consideration because their difficulties fitting into the art exhibition reflect these issues.

Indeed, architectural models had been present in the first Prussian Academy exhibitions but basically disappeared from them by 1800. The few models that were exhibited before then were of Berlin monuments under construction—as opposed to ideal projects—and designed by Carl Gotthard Langhans. In 1789, Langhans exhibited three models: a model of the Brandenburg Gate, showing off its classicism; one of the tower of the Marienkirche, showing off its Gothic style; and a third that showed off construction with the Dome of his Anatomical Theater.[7] In 1797, he exhibited the model of his design for the monument to Frederick the Great, which had won the competition and just received the King's approval for construction [Figure 2]. Heinrich Gentz's model of the New Mint was the last model of a new building exhibited as architecture for several decades; this was in 1800, just as the building was completed and two years after Gentz had exhibited nine drawings of the project.

The strange repetition in the exhibition of Gentz's design for the New Mint—drawings in 1798, the model in 1800—gives us some insight into the disappearance of models of buildings after the 1800 exhibition. The repetition is the result of exhibition taxonomies, which emphasized the difference between objects—the drawings and the model—rather than reinforcing the similarity of their content. And, for the taxonomies of the art academy, models were clearly a problem. Their allegiance was divided between the architect who designed their content and the craftsman who made the object. The academy catalog listed the New Mint model under Gentz's name, but the description attributed the model to one Herr Glatz, a royal carpenter; this was no doubt because Gentz viewed it, as he wrote elsewhere, as an example of "[Glatz's] skillful work."[8] While the academy's catalog entry and Gentz's comment revealed their respect for the model as an example of craftsmanship as well as of an architectural design, it also implied that the model's high degree of refinement challenged its identity as a work of architecture. This refinement and the undoubtedly high cost of the architectural models led to their undoing and, with a few exceptions, pushed them out of the architecture sections into the *Kunstindustrie* (literally, industrial art) section, or pushed them out of the academy exhibitions altogether in the first half of the nineteenth century.

There was no such ambivalence for architectural drawings in the first half of the nineteenth century. They easily fit into the taxonomy identifying architecture because they were regarded as a genre of drawing different from any other—the particular product of an architect's mind and often his hand. Consequently, drawings dominated the architecture section of the academy exhibitions as they already did the practice of architecture at the time. Along with the architecture section's almost exclusive use of drawings, the emphasis of its content shifted from buildings to ideal projects. This had interesting consequences for Berlin's new buildings in the 1820s, 1830s, and even 1840s, including Schinkel's major buildings. At this point, the new buildings started to be exhibited also as subject for paintings and engravings by well known artists, rather than merely as drawings and models made under the architect's own name.[9] Visitors had to wait a few decades for buildings and models to return to architecture.

It is no surprise that the public interest motivated the return of architectural models to the annual academy exhibitions following the example of the architectural exhibits at the world's fairs [Figure 3]. The models emerged with the fairs in the mid-nineteenth century when architects started to care about their popularity and governments were willing to support them. The German exhibition in the art section of the 1893 Chicago World's Fair contained only five models—compared to the two hundred sheets of drawings, mostly large perspectives—but the models clearly contributed to its great success. One in particular stood out: installed in the center of the court of the Palace of Fine Arts stood an enormous, spectacular plaster model of Paul Wallot's design for the soon-to-be-completed Reichstag (1884–94).[10] Its success in attracting attention more than justified the government's expenditure of 25,000 marks—around 150,000 dollars today—for shipping and insurance alone.[11] Like the models at the world's fairs and at the academy exhibitions in the late-nineteenth century, most of the models exhibited at the Berlin academy exhibitions during the second half of the nineteenth century represented monumental buildings because they were most meaningful to a general audience and there were large budgets available to pay for them.

When models returned to the architecture sections of the art academy exhibitions in the second half of the nineteenth century, they did not arrive alone but in the company of sculpture. Like the Reichstag model that would be shown at the 1893 World's Fair, the models represented public buildings at an impressive scale and degree of complexity. Many of the models were of churches. Their size and elaborate appearance echoed their noteworthy predecessors and played their traditional role as a means of communication: outside the exhibition, in order to communicate between architects and church officials and, now, inside the exhibition, to communicate between

[Figure 3]

[Figure 4]

architects and the public. Critics praised August Orth's 1:50 scale model for the Friedenskirche at the 1886 Prussian Academy's centennial exhibition for the way it exhibited the building's construction but also reminded readers of the artistic value of the object.[12] Several years later, Hermann Muthesius bestowed similar praise on the wooden model of St. Paul's Church in Munich shown at the Academy exhibition in 1894, mentioning the sculptor, F.X. Rietzler, as well as the architect, Georg Hauberrisser.[13] Muthesius reminded readers of the double role of models, explaining that wooden models were good ways to exhibit buildings, "even if they really were wood carvings," that is, works of art.[14]

This time, the convergence of different taxonomies did not get in the way. The association of models of buildings with sculpture did not isolate the models from architecture, as the association of models with craft had done. Instead, it ensured that models remained associated with architecture in the academy exhibitions and beyond in the twentieth century. The convergence of architecture and sculpture around 1900 drew on a history of overlapping taxonomies due to the academy's arrangements. Especially in the late-eighteenth-century exhibitions, works of architecture and sculpture shared the same exhibition spaces, and architects and sculptors collaborated or made parallel contributions to the same project, usually a monument. One hundred years later, the efforts of progressive artists before World War I and the avant-garde Novembergruppe after the war facilitated a rapprochement of architecture and sculpture, and, in turn, of architectural presentation models and the design process.

Architecture and sculpture moved closer in *The Architecture Exhibition of the City of Berlin,* a special section of the 1901 *Grosse Berliner Kunstausstellung.* Ludwig Hoffmann, the city building commissioner, filled twenty-two rooms with large plaster models of entire buildings and full-scale plaster mock-ups of ornamental details to showcase the latest designs for a range of new public buildings [Figure 4]. Berlin's economy was booming at the time and, as the scope of the projects and the installation indicated, the Berlin Stadthaus (the City Building Administration) had a budget to match. The models, some at 1:25 and even 1:10 for smaller buildings, and the full-scale mock-ups, along with some simplified architectural drawings and photographs, clearly catered to Hoffmann's public audience and convinced them that he was putting their tax money to good use.

The models and mock-ups suggested in different ways that there was a close relationship between Hoffmann's architecture and sculpture. The most obvious connection between the two lay in the resemblance of Hoffmann's installation of architecture to the installation of sculpture in the Musée de Sculpture Comparée in Paris, which gave Hoffmann's installation a definite air of monumentality. But the models and their installation also indicated that Hoffmann shared a design process with the various sculptors with whom he worked. That is, Hoffmann did not only collaborate with sculptors; his sketchbooks show that he thought like them. The sketches were accompanied by comments expressing his dissatisfaction with a profile that was "too deep," a silhouette that was "too high," or, in the case of the Baths of Diocletian, "appears very large." Occasionally, he expressed his approval: the Chigi chapel was "very good" and the Temple of Vesta "very clear."

Moreover, scattered evidence suggests that he designed like a sculptor, circling full-scale plaster models or even his own buildings under construction to judge the size, proportions, and location of details, sculpture, and profiles in changing light. For Hoffmann, the presence of his designs in three dimensions and the view of them from varying perspectives was definitive, directing changes to the drawings or, in the case of the Berlin Stadthaus, an eighteen-centimeter change to the dome of the building itself.[15] It is not clear whether he ever altered the models, but, following the examples of French architects such as such as Léon Vaudoyer and Charles Garnier, who designed with plaster models that had movable or detachable components, Hoffmann had craftsmen fabricate a model of the Leipzig Reichsgericht (Imperial Court of Justice) with a dome that he could raise and lower with a hand crank.[16] (This kind of model could have saved him some money if he had used one like it in Berlin.) Hoffmann's 1901 exhibition put his own way of working on display, if not the actual artifacts, by placing the models on pedestals that raised them to eye level in order to simulate the experience of seeing the building from the street and, in turn, to simulate the perspective that guided his approach to design.

At the *Grosse Berliner Kunstausstellung* in 1921, architecture and sculpture came even closer. The exhibition carried forward Hoffmann's approach and that of his immediate successor, sculptor-architect Hermann Obrist: the integration of plaster models into the architectural design process. At the exhibition, the similarity of the expressionist models produced by architects and sculptors, underscored by a few rooms containing the work of both, suggested that sculptors could design architecture and architects could make models.[17] Often using plaster or the new "Plasticine," plaster's synthetic clay cousin, sculptors and architects produced models that were explicitly architectural, characterized by irregular, scaleless forms.[18] For the architect Wassili Luckhardt, whose models were included in the exhibition, sculpture was not only architecture's equivalent, its technique became a springboard for an architectural design strategy. In the same year, Luckhardt called for architectural designs to emerge out of making models, specifically out of working with the modeling material.[19] Due to its integral role in the design process, the model, whether or not made by the architect, could be identified as a work of architecture and in this way find a place in the conventional academy taxonomy at the art exhibition.

But when visitors finally reached the top of the stairs of the Bauhaus building only two years later, they would have seen architectural models that apparently had nothing to do with sculpture or the art exhibition. Rational structure had replaced, or, in the case of Mies's Glass Skyscraper, challenged, the irrational forms of the expressionist models. But models still drove the design. Material provided the continuity between model and building as it had in the models exhibited at the *Grosse Berliner Kunstausstellung* in 1921 [Figure 5]. Around that time, many drawings of designs—exhibited or not—by architects such as Poelzig and the Luckhardt brothers, had portrayed buildings whose forms could only have been conceived of—literally or figuratively—in plaster; the forms emerged "out of the modeling material." The inaugural display of Mies's Glass Skyscraper model at the 1922 Novembergruppe exhibition confirmed that the relationship between model and form was not restricted to the use of plaster. Here the model was shown in a room full of watercolors, an installation that emphasized what they had in common: metaphorically speaking, both were made of light.[20] According to Mies, light, and not the mixed media out of which the model was constructed, was the rationale for the form of the Glass Skyscraper.[21] At the Bauhaus one year later, the Glass Skyscraper was joined by Mies's model of the Concrete Office Building. Their use of similar mixed media for different structural systems—concrete and steel—again emphasized the importance of light to the form of the models and, thereby, the designs. Opposite them stood Gropius's Chicago Tribune Tower model, whose plaster represented the concrete structure of the building.

In 1901, critics had started to sense the shortcomings of plaster presentation models. They criticized Hoffmann's plaster models for being too white and too abstract; because the models failed to indicate building materials, it was impossible to assess the designs.[22] But, in 1921, Luckhardt and several of his Expressionist colleagues had envisioned the abstract plaster as a building material. And at the 1923 exhibition, Gropius answered Hoffmann's critics with his tower model, which recast the typical plaster presentation model as a representation of a concrete building. Mies's two models stood opposite, recasting light as a modeling and, in turn, a building material, despite Gropius's alleged attempt to leave them in the dark. As the opening salvo to the exhibition, the models by Mies and Gropius underscored the close relationship between model and building. Their models, along with others in the exhibition (including some of Gropius's designs) and in the book that followed the exhibition, suggested, among other things, that the material characteristics of a model had become important aspects of modern building, for example, the sheer surfaces and color—sometimes the whiteness—of plaster and the newly introduced cardboard.[23] At the same time, the models and the book suggested something more conventional: that the envisaged characteristics of modern building shaped the models of their designs.[24]

[Figure 5]

The presence of models in the *Ausstellung Internationale Architekten* (International Exhibition of Architecture) at the Bauhaus was, on the one hand, due to a change in ideology that favored space, construction, and buildings. On the other hand, the institution itself was an important factor. Although histories include the Bauhaus as the modern incarnation of the German Art Academy, the Bauhaus was more than that: it was a radically transformed version of the academy, a product of the merger of art and applied art.[25] And this new version of the academy turned art's hierarchical system on its head by assigning architecture the most prominent position. The architecture exhibition signaled the change by welcoming visitors with models, a gesture that indicated a transformation of art's taxonomies as well. As they entered the exhibition, visitors encountered a confrontation of two modeling techniques: Mies's mixed-media models, whose purpose it was to shape light and the conventional plaster technique reinterpreted as concrete in the model of Gropius's tower. They saw splendid objects that not only served to present the architects' designs but also pointed towards the absence of the objects that architects sought to produce but could not easily exhibit: not models, but buildings.

[1] Klaus-Jürgen Winkler, "Die Architekturausstellungen in Weimar – 1919, 1922, 1923," in *Klassik und Avantgarde. Das Bauhaus in Weimar 1919–1925,* ed. Hellmut Th. Seemann and Thorsten Valk (Göttingen: Wallstein Verlag, 2009), 277.

[2] There were no Russian architects due to immigration problems. Ibid., 276–277.

[3] Ibid., 262. See also Barry Bergdoll, "Bauhaus Multiplied: Paradoxes of Architecture and Design in and after the Bauhaus," in *Bauhaus 1919–1933: Workshops for Modernity,* edited by Lea Dickerman and Barry Bergdoll (New York: The Museum of Modern Art, 2009), 50.

[4] Winkler, 278. Barry Bergdoll has pointed out that a striking number of axonometric drawings filled the exhibition. Along with the models, the axonometric drawings emphasized the three-dimensional character of the architecture, but, in contrast to perspective drawings, offered a new way to perceive it. Barry Bergdoll, "Bauhaus Multiplied," 50.

[5] See Winkler, 269. There was one more exhibition that may have contained models but the documentation does not exist: a version of the *Ausstellung unbekannter Architekten in 1919, reorganized* by Gropius, Bruno Taut, and Adolf Behne in the Museum am Karlsplatz in Weimar. See Winkler, 262–263.

[6] See, for example, the catalogs of the *Grosse Berliner Kunstausstellung* from 1921–1926.

[7] This and subsequent references to the Prussian Academy exhibitions between 1786 and 1850 are taken from the following source, unless noted otherwise: *Die Kataloge der Berliner Akademie Ausstellungen 1786–1850,* ed. Helmut Börsch-Supan (Berlin: Hessling, 1971).

[8] Heinrich Gentz identified the model as Glatz's "skillful work" in an article on the building published the same year the model was exhibited. Gentz, "Beschreibung des neuen Königlichen Münzgebäudes," *Sammlung von Aufsätzen und Nachrichten, die Baukunst betreffend,* 1 (1800): 22.

[9] In 1834 and 1842, the Bauakademie was portrayed in engravings attributed to various engravers rather than to Schinkel, the architect (although in the 1834 exhibition, Schinkel was credited with making the sketch on which the engraving was based).

[10] The model, at the scale 1:25, was made by the sculptor Berger from Berlin. Appelius, "Die Ausstellung Deutscher Architektur- und Ingenieur-Werke auf der Columbischen Welt-Ausstellung zu Chicago," *Deutsche Bauzeitung,* 27, 100 (16 December 1893): 613.

[11] Ibid., 614.

[12] F., "Von der Jubiläums-Ausstellung der Kgl. Akademie der Künste zu Berlin (Fortsetzung)," *Deutsche Bauzeitung,* 20, 82 (October 13, 1886): 490.

[13] *Grosse Berliner Kunstausstellung 1894. Katalog* (Berlin: Verlag von Rud. Schuster, 1894): 2144.

[14] Hermann Muthesius, "Die Architektur auf der Grossen Berliner Kunstausstellung," *Zentralblatt der Bauverwaltung,* 14, 25 (June 23, 1894): 257.

[15] Ludwig Hoffmann, *Lebenserinnerungen eines Architekten,* ed. Wolfgang Schäche (Berlin: Gebr. Mann, 1983), 125, 212.

[16] Ibid., 89. Vaudoyer put the Marseilles cathedral on rails, Garnier had his model of the Paris Opera fabricated as a set of exchangeable elements in order to modify their proportions, contours, and profiles. See Barry Bergdoll, *Léon Vaudoyer: Historicism in the Age of Industry* (Cambridge: MIT Press, 1994), 253 and Christopher Mead, *Charles Garnier's Paris Opera: Architectural Empathy and the Renaissance of French Classicism* (Cambridge: MIT Press, 1991), 150. It is unclear whether or not Hoffmann's model was made of plaster.

[17] In his review of the 1921 *Grosse Berliner Kunstausstellung,* critic Walter Lehwess commented that the Novembergruppe exhibited sculpture and architecture, in particular models, in the same room "in a sisterly way." Walter Lehwess, "Architekturschau im Moabiter Ausstellungspalast," in *Stadtbaukunst alter und neuer Zeit,* 2,7 (1921): 108.

[18] Eva Afuhs and Andreas Strobl, ed. "Erste Grundlagen zu einem Fragmentierten Werk," in *Hermann Obrist, Skulpture|Raum|Abstraktion um 1900.* (Zürich: Scheidegger & Spiess, 2009), 27–43.

[19] Wassili Luckhardt, "Vom Entwerfen," Stadtbaukunst alter und neuer Zeit, 2,11 (1921): 169–70, excerpt reprinted in *Brüder Luckhardt und Alfons Anker,* Achim Wendschuh, ed. (Berlin: Akademie der Künste, 1990), 184. Wolfgang Pehnt echoed Luckhardt's claim when he wrote that "the majority of ... [Wassili Luckhardt's] designs ... emerged from the modeled form," in *Die Architektur des Expressionismus* (Stuttgart: Hatje, 1973), 101.

[20] For an extensive discussion of the Glass Skyscraper Model see Spyros Papapetros, *On the Animation of the Inorganic* (Chicago: The University of Chicago Press, 2012), 251-256.

[21] Mies Van der Rohe, [Hochhäuser], *Frühlicht,* 1,4 (1922): 122–124, excerpt reprinted in Fritz Neumeyer, *Das kunstlose Wort* (Berlin: Siedler, 1986), 298.

[22] See, for example, P.W., "Feuilleton. Die Architektur auf der Kunstausstellung," *Vossische Zeitung* (August 2, 1901).

[23] *Internationale Architektur,* Bauhausbücher 1, edited by László Moholy-Nagy, Walter Gropius (München: Albert Langen Verlag, 1925).

[24] The point that the plaster models directly influenced the character of modern buildings is an extension of Mark Wigley's argument about Le Corbusier's House at Vaucresson concerning the influence of the drawing on the model and, in turn, on the design of the building. According to Wigley, "[t]he building is made to conform to the idealistic model that had in turn been made to conform to the original elevation." See Mark Wigley, *White Walls, Designer Dresses* (Cambridge: MIT Press, 2001), 194. It is befitting that Le Corbusier intended to exhibit photographs of the model—not the building—of the house at Vaucresson (and of the Maison Citrohan) at the 1923 exhibition of International Architecture at the Bauhaus. (Bauhaus Archiv, Berlin).

[25] See Ekkehard Mai, *Die deutschen Kunstakademien im 19. Jahrhundert. Künstlerausbildung zwischen Tradition und Avantgarde* (Köln: Böhlau, 2010), 367–370.

[Figure 1]   *Ausstellung internationaler Architekten* [Exhibition of International Architects], Bauhaus, Weimar, Summer 1923. Left: Mies van der Rohe: Models of the Glass Skyscraper and the Concrete Office Building. Right: Walter Gropius and Adolf Meyer, model of the competition design for the Chicago Tribune Tower. Courtesy of Bauhaus-Universität Weimar, Archiv der Moderne and Brandenburgisches Landesamt für Denkmalpflege und Archäologisches Landesmuseum, Zossen, Bildarchiv.

[Figure 2]   Heinrich Gentz, "Die Münze in Berlin" [The Berlin Mint], Model shown in the 1800 exhibition of the Royal Prussian Academy of the Arts. Reproduced from: Adolf Doebber, *Heinrich Gentz ein Berliner Baumeister um 1800* (Berlin: Carl Heymanns Verlag, 1916), Plate 21.

[Figure 3]   Exhibition of German Architecture in the 1893 *World's Columbian Exhibition* in Chicago with Paul Wallot's model of the Reichstag. Reproduced from *Unsere Weltausstellung: eine Beschreibung der Columbischen Weltausstellung in Chicago, 1893* (Chicago: Fred. Klein Company, 1894), 513. Courtesy of the Newberry Library, Chicago.

[Figure 4]   Architecture Exhibition of the City of Berlin at the *Grosse Berliner Kunstausstellung* (1901) showing models of Ludwig Hoffmann projects, including the Märkisches Museum (center). Reproduced from: Hans Schliepmann, "Die Architektur auf der diesjährigen Grossen Berliner Kunstausstellung," *Berliner Architekturwelt,* Vol. 4 (1902): 121, image 154.

[Figure 5]   Wassili Luckhardt, *Denkmal der Arbeit* (ca. 1920), from top to bottom: model, pencil sketch, charcoal drawing. Reproduced from Matthias Schirren, "Die Brüder Luckhardt und der architektonische Expressionismus—Ideologisches, Experimentelles und Monumentales," *Brüder Luckhardt und Alfons Anker,* Schriftenreihe der Akademie der Künste, vol. 21 (Berlin: Akademie der Künste, 1990), 40. Image courtesy of Akademie der Künste, Berlin.

Campo Urbano, Como, 1969

Romy Golan

On September 21, 1969, forty artists, joined by musicians, architects, art critics, local firemen, electricians, and the public, took over the northern Italian city of Como, as well as part of its lake, with a series of interventions that went on from the early afternoon into the night: *Campo Urbano: interventi estetici nella dimensione collettiva urbana.* Initially announced through a distribution of leaflets, the action and its resulting photobook were coordinated by the historian of art and architecture Luciano Caramel; Ugo Mulas, one of Italy's best photographers, known for his cinematic photoreportages of the Venice Biennales; and Bruno Munari, a generation older, whose career began in the 1920s as one of Italy's most experimental graphic designers.

Campo Urbano came on the heels of a series of sorties—what the artist/critic Piero Gilardi called "mostre aperte"—that illustrated the reorientation of contemporary art practices towards the dematerialization of the art object and the extramural trespassing of the artifact into its surroundings.[1] The closest precedent—though the Italians managed to avoid trivializing their interventions into retinal divertissements and gadgetry—was *A Day in the City* orchestrated by the recently disbanded French Groupe de Recherche d'Art Visuel (GRAV). Another was *Con/tem/l'azione* on December 4, 1967, in which the Turinese artist Michelangelo Pistoletto sent one of his Minus Objects, a large ball made of newspaper, rolling out of the gallery and through his hometown's famed arcades. A few months later, Pistoletto himself went into the streets of small provincial towns to perform impromptu theatrical pieces with fanciful props and neo-medieval clothes, with a troupe of artists he called Lo Zoo. That summer of 1968, in Amalfi, Germano Celant convened an international cast of artists for *Arte Povera+Azioni Povere,* three days of actions, performances, and debates that spilled from the town's old arsenals into the streets. What distinguishes *Campo Urbano* from its precedents is the way it used the architecture of Como as its container and frame.

Although many late-1960s event-based artistic interventions used the printed page as their documentary platform, the *Campo Urbano* photobook is unique. Printed full-page, the photographs alternate between contact sheets, bird's-eye views, and panoramic shots, with many of the images rotated vertically to create a jolting collage effect and with some actions spilling across multiple pages. The shifts in spatial and temporal registers capture the way the photographer, the artists, and the public move across the city to partake in events that often took place simultaneously in different locations. At Munari's direction, some of the images printed from Mulas's black and white negatives were bathed in a solution of metallic cerulean blue, making them reflective and difficult to read, simulating an act of erasure. Nothing could be more presentist and event-based than this photobook, without which no trace of that day would remain, shot with a single handheld Olympus camera. And yet I believe that the images and their layout were intended by Caramel, Munari, and Mulas to trigger a series of associations with earlier Italian art and fleeting episodes from a still-unwritten history of an art of participation —attempts to collapse art and life by both the avant-garde and the neo-avant-garde.

[Figure 1]

Caramel's choice of the word *campo,* rather than *spazio urbano,* came from "Teoria del campo: corso di educazione della visione," a class taught by Attilio Marcolli, a Milanese architect, at a technical school in nearby Cantù. Marcolli's eponymous book, a classroom primer, was illustrated with myriad diagrams to demonstrate the progression of four types of vision: from geometric to gestaltic to topological to phenomenological and the application to town planning.[2] One of the diagrams, for example, invites the eye to follow dots traversing, dispersing, and reassembling, but still recognizable as a distinct group. Marcolli's book was in many ways a throwback to the gestaltic experiments of the 1950s, a moment when the organization of experience became the main issue in the redefinition of a socially engaged art. The book had traction because its diagrams seemed readily transposable from the page to the ongoing "movimenti di piazza," the dozens of student and worker demonstrations that were taking place in almost every city in Italy. By early 1969, this agitation had finally reached the politically conservative city of Como, sheltered until then by the fact that it was not a university town.[3]

[Figure 2]

The interventions of *Campo Urbano* began in the early afternoon. At 3 p.m. on Via Tommaso Grossi, a short distance from the center of town, the group Art Terminal tried unsuccessfully to remove the derelict iron gate of the city's orphanage, in collaboration with its young occupants. Half an hour later, a number of actions began in different parts of the Piazza del Duomo. The ex-Nucleare group painter Enrico Baj and his collaborators, wearing mock uniforms bedecked with medals, staged *Segnaletica orizontale,* a simulated political coup in which, using a roller designed to paint pedestrian crosswalks, Baj painted a huge Italian flag on the pavement in front of the Broletto, a medieval building adjacent to the cathedral that had been Como's original town hall [Figure 3]. Pamphlets were flung from the balconies and tricolored posters distributed to crowds massed below, while a band played mock military tunes. Then came *Riflessione* (Reflections) by the architect Mario Di Salvo and the conceptual artist Carlo Ferrario, a duo from Como, who lined a series of mirrors at the foot of the Duomo, effectively unhinging, as it were, the edifice via myriad reflections, and forcing their fellow citizens to think, as I will argue, their relationship to the town's most iconic monument [Figure 1]. Inside the Duomo, a tape recorder concealed beneath a mirror in a cement well shaped like a baptismal font emitted fragments of music and almost inaudible political slogans recorded during a recent street demonstration. Meanwhile, Munari invited adults and children up to the tower to fold little bits of paper and launch them downward. The various shapes circled like toy airplanes, floating at different velocities and on different trajectories, visualizing the resistance of the air. Gianni Pettena's uninvited intervention, titled *How come everyone has chosen the main square?,* violated Como's most stately square by stringing laundry on clotheslines between two lampposts smack in front of the Duomo [Figure 2]. This reminder of the working class— unsightly and yet eternally picturesque—brought an image of Italy's periphery into the city center and metaphorically washed the dirty linen of local and national politics out in the open. At 4:20 p.m., moving the action from the square to the narrow medieval adjoining streets, Grazia Varisco, formerly a member of the Milanese collective Gruppo T, lined up cardboard boxes on Via delle Cinque Giornate, in *Dilatazione spazio-temporale di un percorso,* a mock barricade that forced a passerby to meander down the street [Figure 5]. Ten minutes later, Marcolli (the author of *Teoria del Campo)* and Annarosa Cotta produced *Colore-Segnale,* a semiotic intervention along another commercial street, Via Boldoni, extending fifty meters down to the Piazza San Fedele. Offering an alternative to the garish commercial signage of these thoroughfares, Marcolli posted simple crepe paper signs color-coded to identify merchants, as in bygone times: red for butchers, green for fruit venders, and so on. At 5:15 p.m., the Milanese architect/designer Ugo la Pietra "liberated" (as he put it) the city's main commercial artery, Corso Vittorio Emanuele, from its economic compulsion by constructing a wooden tunnel covered with opaque black plastic to block the pedestrians' view of the street's shop windows. At 6:30 p.m. came an *intermezzo* in the form of a musical intervention: *Suonando la città.* Giuseppe Chiari, a Florentine composer connected to Fluxus, and the mezzo-soprano Franca Sacchi, stretched electric wires down from the windows of the Broletto and tower across the piazza to produce a gigantic harp. Connected to microphones and loudspeakers, the sound installation included car sirens, two dishwashers, and a blender. After whistles, tambourines, and harmonicas were distributed to the public (this was the most popular and raucous intervention of that day), the Comaschi were invited to "play" (suonare), quite literally, their city.

The night was reserved for more poetic interventions by former members of the Paduan and Milanese collectives Gruppo N and Gruppo T, artists who had made their mark with kinetic objects but who had since shifted to creating immersive environments shaped by the manipulation of light. At 9 p.m., Dadamaino (Eduarda Emilia Maino) took Como's inhabitants to the lake—a site largely ignored, she said, in the everyday life of the city. She dispersed phosphorescent plaques of polystyrene foam across its surface, animating the normally placid expanse of water. Having long debated what to do, Edilio Alpini, Davide Boriani, Gianni Colombo, and Gabriele De Vecchi finally decided to designate a special perimeter of the Piazza del Duomo at 9:15 p.m. for *Tempo libero: struttura temporale in uno spazio urbano.* This title plays on the word temporale, which means both "temporal" and "rainstorm" in Italian. The three artists enlisted local firemen and electricians to commandeer the city's hydrants, producing an artificial storm while loudspeakers emitted taped sounds of falling rain and projectors cast bluish green lights interrupted by flashes to simulate lightning striking the wet pavement [Figure 6]. The

[Figure 3]

[Figure 4]

synchronized action lasted exactly fifteen minutes. As soon as it was over, Munari began to project his polarized lights onto white umbrellas which had been distributed to the public and which acted like screens. The day ended with a noisy debate between the artists and the public in a crowded room of Como's town hall, which went on past midnight.

While *Campo Urbano's* organizers had sought sponsorship from the municipality, the Tourist Agency, the Chamber of Commerce, and other local and state institutions, that very action actually highlighted the reality of constant regulation in a country like Italy, known for observing few rules. The verdict in the mostly conservative local press the next morning was harsh: "Expensive games by a bunch of artists yesterday in town. Carnival atmosphere and Belated Dada Antics," read the headline in the *Corriere della Provincia:* "a futile and patronizing attempt by a bunch of avant-garde artists to spark electricity in the air of a provincial town on a sleepy Sunday afternoon."[4] Reporting on the event for *Casabella,* the critic Germano Celant dismissed *Campo Urbano* as "tourist art" scheduled to coincide with summer pilgrimages around the Bel Paese.[5] The misgivings expressed in *Domus* by a less partisan critic like Tommaso Trini, who had actually participated in the event, were even more substantial. The full-page photograph of Di Salvo and Carlo Ferrario's *Riflessione* spelled out Trini's theme even before one read his article's title: "Towards Theatre." His meaning was clear: Como's historical center had been used as a stage set, and the actions looked as if made expressly for the camera.[6]

These reviews were written in the present tense. A different temporality—the temporality of the flashback and the eclipse—informs the photobook. In it we encounter one of the first instances of the "afterlives" of the quasi-mythical Parisian events of May 1968, photographs of which—the police dispersing protesters with tear gas and water cannons in front of the Panthéon, for example, or the Paris Stock Exchange at night, which they seized and tried to set on fire—became iconic almost as soon as they were shot. As if sifting through an imaginary photo archive, the *Campo Urbano* photobook harkens back to unrealized projects such as the "constructed situation," titled "The World as Labyrinth," which was described by the French and Dutch Situationists in the fourth issue of their journal in 1960.[7] The project would have involved a three-day urban drift in the center of Amsterdam in coordination with a micro-*dérive* in two galleries of the Stedelijk Museum. The latter would have comprised—as did *Free Time* by Gruppo T—a coordinated system of rain, artificial fog, and wind; the passage of the participants and the public through different thermal and light zones, including an obstacle (a tunnel of *Industrial Paintings* made by the Italian Giuseppe Pinot-Gallizio); and a sound piece (noises and random words emitted by a battery of megaphones). Ultimately canned by the Situationists—no doubt because it was spectacular and involved a broad public—"The world as Labyrinth" was also one of the few constructed situations described and thus "documented" by the SI (Situationists International), a group whose aversion to detailed documentation stemmed in part from their fear of being imitated and having their projects "reified."[8]

The photographs of *Campo Urbano* also evoke the most memorable, if saccharine, sequences of Vittorio De Sica's *Miracle in Milan,* released in 1951. A rare example of "fantastical neorealism," the film takes place in the shantytowns that sprang up as southern immigrants were expelled to the outskirts of Milan. One of the film's final scenes, replete with technical tricks, shows the migrants protecting themselves from powerful jets of water—pumped from canisters by police at the behest of the capitalist developers—with a canopy of umbrellas, opened and pivoted in unison. As if by magic, the water appears to flow back into the canisters by reverse motion. In the final shots, corny but iconic, the migrants gather on the Piazza del Duomo and fly over Milan on broomsticks borrowed from the city's sweepers.

Structured as a series of flashbacks within flashbacks, the photobook takes us to earlier events known to us either through extant photographic documentation or by other means. One such event depicted in the book took place in Paris on the afternoon of April 14, 1921 when the poet André Breton launched that year's Dada Season by taking his friends on an excursion to the Church of Saint-Julien-le-Pauvre near the Latin Quarter, where his anticlerical declamations drew a hundred listeners in spite of persistent rain—an event for which only two photographs survive. Another earlier "campo" event, whose only material relics are the pamphlets themselves, comes next in the book: on April 27, 1910, Filippo Tommaso Marinetti and his Futurist cohorts hurled from the Campanile in the Piazza San Marco in Venice 800,000 copies of their manifesto, titled *Contro Venezia Passatista,* which decried the Serenissima as the decrepit queen of the Adriatic, that great Italian lake, enfeebled by centuries of wordly plea- sures. By distributing his pamphlets throughout Europe to request support for his interventions (including one on the stage of the Teatro La Fenice), Marinetti secured—for a moment—Italy's position at the cutting edge of an international avant-garde.

There was one square, however, that *Campo Urbano's* participants avoided: the Piazza del Popolo— formerly the Piazza Impero—which contained Como's principal architectural landmark, Giuseppe Terragni's Casa del Fascio of 1936, one of the key monuments of Fascist rationalist architecture. After the war, the former Fascist headquarters became the center of operations of the Guardia di Finanza, the state agency that deals with financial crime and smuggling. When I interviewed Caramel and asked why they had avoided this location, he brushed my question aside, claiming that Terragni's building wasn't relevant at that point in time.[9] And, yet, it turns out that, exactly a year earlier, a large conference on Terragni and his architectural legacy—specifically, from the time of his death in 1943 to 1968—had taken place in Como. Both Caramel and Di Salvo had spoken at this event.[10] Caramel lectured on Terragni and abstract painters from Como, a topic that would continue to preoccupy him for the rest of his career. Caramel and Di Salvo also contributed essays for the local periodical, *Quadrante Lariano,* which devoted, in advance of the conference, a special issue on Terragni and his circle in Como. The cover of the special issue, featuring the Casa del Fascio, directly quoted an earlier and much more famous magazine, the October 1936 monographic double issue of the supra-modernist/supra-Fascist architecture journal *Quadrante,* likewise dedicated to the Casa.[11] In that issue, Terragni had hopefully declared: "With the building of the Casa del Fascio, provided by the city's regulatory plan, it is possible today in Como to imagine the not-far-off realization of the 'fascist city.'"[12] Two photographs chosen by Terragni to illustrate that issue would rank among the best-known images of Italy during the *Ventennio* (Mussolini's twenty years in power). The first was Terragni's lineup of the facades of Como's medi- eval tower, the Duomo and the adjacent Brolotto together with the Casa del Fascio. The technique of photomontage was used to signal that this (partly unrealized) project was part of a total redesign of the Piazza dell'Impero and was intended both as an extension and substitution for the Piazza del Duomo. The second photo, doctored to make the crowd look bigger, more integrated, and univocal, showed hundreds of Comaschi standing in front of their brand new Casa on May 5, 1936, awaiting a broadcast- ing of the Duce from the Piazza Venezia in Rome [Figure 4]. Next to it Terragni wrote:

> The moving quality of the work is no longer the rhetorical figure with spade or pick
> on his shoulder and the sun behind him. It resides rather in acknowledging the
> thousands and thousands of black-shirted citizens amassed in front of the Casa
> del Fascio to hear the voice of their leader announce to Italians and foreigners the
> advent of Empire.[13]

Campo Urbano was, as contemporary reviewers concurred, by contrast a carnivalesque, dispersed, and plurivocal event. It flashed back to historical liberatory moments, including Baj's fictional coup against the State, the very antithesis of the Fascist rally illustrated in *Quadrante* in 1936. The organizers and the artists involved in *Campo Urbano* sought to eclipse the city's Fascist past. If they had gone to Terragni's piazza, they would have been caught up in it.

[Figure 6]

[1] See *Fuori!: Arte e Spazio Urbano 1968–1976,* Silvana Bignami and Alessandra Pioselli eds., (Milan: Museo del Novecento, 2011).

[2] Attilio Marcolli, *Teoria del campo: corso di educazione della visione,* 2 vols. (Florence, Sansoni, 1970/1972) "Studenti in Piazza a Como," supplement *Quadrante Lariano* 2, No. 7 (Como, February 1969).

[3] See Guido Crainz, *Il paese mancato. Dal miracolo economico agli anni ottanta* (Rome: Donzelli, 2003).

[4] "Il costoso gioco di alcuni artisti: *Campo urbano*—aria di sagra e trovate Dada (un pò in ritardo)," *Corriere della Provincia* (Como, September 22, 1969)

[5] Germano Celant, "Arte turistica," *Casabella* no. 342 (November 1969): 6–7.

[6] Tommaso Trini, "L'estensione teatrale/Towards theatre," *Domus,* no. 480 (November 1969): 48–51.

[7] "Sur l'empoi de temps libre" and "Die Welt als Labyrinth," *Internationale Situationiste,* no. 4 (Paris, June 1960): 111–115.

[8] See Claire Bishop, *Artificial Hell: Participatory Art and the Politics of Spectatorship* (London: Verso, 2012).

[9] Interview with the author, Venice, July 23, 2013.

[10] It took place on September 14–15, 1968 to mark the 25th anniversary of the architect's death. See "Atti del convegno di studi L'eredità di Terragni e l'architettura italiana 1943–68," *L'Architettura* 15, no. 163 (May 1969): 1–52.

[11] See Mario Di Salvo, "Cesare Cattaneo; oltre il razionalismo," *Quadrante Lariano* 1, no. 3 (May–June 1968): 51–55; Luciano Caramel, "Terragni e gli astrattisti comaschi," ibid., 1, no. 5 (September–October, 1968): 43–53 and *Quadrante* no. 35–36 (October 1936).

[12] "Giuseppe Terragni, "La costruzione della Casa del Fascio a Como," ibid: 5–27. English translation in Thomas Schumacher, *Surface and Symbol: Giuseppe Terragni and the Architecture of Italian Rationalism* (New York: Princeton Architectural Press, 1991).

[13] Ibid. See also David Rifkind, *The Battle for Modernism: Quadrante and the Politicization of Architectural Discourse in Fascist Italy* (Vicenza: Marsilio, 2012).

Immersive Environments

Exhibitions Against Architecture: The Trigon Biennale in 1967 and 1969

Paula Burleigh

For the occasion of *Ambiente/Environment,* the 1967 Trigon Biennale in Graz, artists from Austria, Italy, and Yugoslavia were invited to the Künstlerhaus to create installation-based environments, which were then arranged by local architects Günther Domenig and Eilfried Huth [Figure 1].[1] This essay argues that the layout of *Ambiente/Environment* could be read as a prototype for a megastructure, in that it modeled a city contained within a single expansive architectural form. And yet, while the exhibition's design gestured towards the totalizing qualities of a megastructure, *Ambiente/ Environment* also mounted a critique of both architecture and the architect in that the exhibition's director, Wilfried Skreiner, as well as Domenig and Huth, the architect-designers, effectively argued for a more symbiotic relationship between architects, urban planners, and the public. Furthermore, the major leitmotifs among Trigon 1967's artist-created environments were *anathema* to architecture in their resistance to materiality, fixity, and visibility. In other words, Trigon '67 was defined by architecture's omnipresence and dissolution, oppositional tendencies that existed in productive tension with one another. That tension was fragile, however, which became apparent in the subsequent Trigon Biennale in 1969, intended to conceptually build on *Ambiente/Environment.* By way of a coda, this paper briefly examines the 1969 Trigon, which witnessed the collapse of the delicate tension engendered by *Ambiente/Environment* between architecture and its critique.

From 1963 to 1991, the Styrian federal government sponsored the Trigon Biennale, which showcased contemporary art from Austria, Italy, and Yugoslavia.[2] *Ambiente/Environment,* the 1967 exhibition's title, suggested the diffusion of objects into environments: most works in the show were constructed as immersive installations, in addition to several large sculptures, all of which were then staged as a series of encounters facilitated by the architects Domenig's and Huth's organizational

[Figure 1]

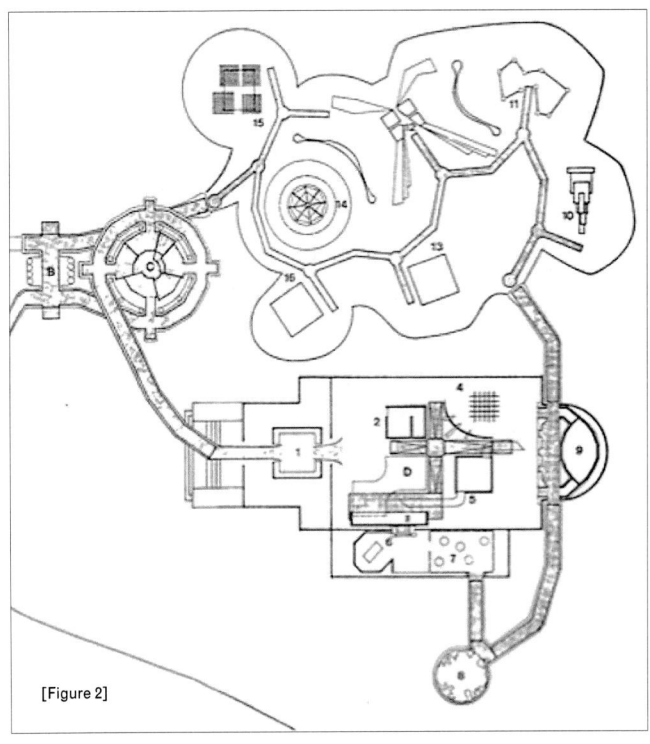

[Figure 2]

schema, to which I will return in detail. Director Wilfried Skreiner worked with two commissioners, from Yugoslavia and Italy, respectively, to select sixteen artists from the three countries to design artworks responding to the broad theme of "environment." As Skreiner indicated in his essay for the exhibition's catalog, artists were to "create a new *Gesamtkunstwerk* outside of medium-specificity, which [would] point toward a new concept of space."[3] Further, Skreiner argued that sculptors and painters were as well, if not better, equipped than architects to invent innovative habitable spaces that would revitalize the city's urban fabric.[4] Consequently, architects were conspicuously absent from an exhibition that was loosely architectural, setting the stage for a critique of conventional methods of modernist architecture.

Participation was key to *Ambiente/Environment.* Many of the Trigon's artists, including Enzo Mari, Ivan Picelj, Vjenceslav Richter, and Gianni Colombo, were associated with the New Tendency, an international network of artists who conceived of art as a platform for perceptual research.[5] Typically, these artists used modest technologies including light projections, mirrors, and reflective industrial materials to experiment with visual effects. Responding to Umberto Eco's analysis of the open work, the New Tendency emphasized the integral role of viewer participation in the artwork's completion. In the context of the Trigon, participation was inflected with an urban dimension, in that Domenig, Huth, and Skreiner envisaged the visitors' active role in the exhibition—climbing sculptures or feeling their way through disorienting environments—as a metaphor for increased public agency in the creation of future urban spaces.

The most radical example of viewer agency on display was Milan-based Luciano Fabro's empty, floor-to-ceiling white room, in which the visitor was meant to simply imagine her own design for a new kind of space. In Fabro's white room, architecture was literally a blank slate onto which the viewer could project will or fantasy, suggesting that the experience of architecture was highly subjective. While Fabro's room was the most extreme example, other artists worked to draw out the subjective nature of spatial and architectural experience. In Vienna-based artist Marc Adrian's *Oval Room in Black,* for example, he radically destabilized the space by painting the walls black and contriving the appearance of false walls through mirrors onto which intentionally absurd images and text were projected. By creating a space that defied visitors' attempts to form a coherent picture of their surroundings, Adrian wrote that the work highlighted the subjective, personal nature of experience in the modern city, which was similarly incomprehensible.[6] Thus, both Adrian's work and writing questioned the modernist commitment to rationality in architecture and urban design, as well as underscoring the exhibition's urban metaphors espoused by Skreiner in the catalog.

Like Adrian, Florentine artist Gianni Colombo's work, *Spazio Elastico,* undermined the conventional stability of architecture.[7] In a darkened room, the artist made space tangible through a cubic, modular structure of white nylon threads, loosely suggestive of space-frame architecture. Attached motors made the nylon cube constantly expand and contract. Similar to Adrian's installation, Colombo orchestrated the rapid projection of light onto mirrors, which distorted the cube and its movements through short and intense flashes of light, generating afterimages that overlapped with the actual nylon threads. Out of the environments exhibited in the Trigon, those by Adrian and Colombo were the most intense in their sensory assault on the viewer, rendering the environment unstable and illusory, which radically destabilized the viewer's conception of space. Other artists employed similar techniques, but to less disruptive effect: Rudolf Pointer dimmed the lights and projected images throughout a room that was, disorientingly, covered from floor-to-ceiling in multicolor designs, symbols, and texts; Oswald Oberhuber made a humorously absurd analogy between architecture and the body by designing the interior of his structure to look like a giant, open mouth; and Miroslav Šutej's environment was a mélange of textures made of inflatables and Astroturf, with large plastic flowers sitting on the ground and strings of ping pong balls hanging from the ceiling.

Separate from the artists invited to create environments, Skreiner commissioned the local architecture firm Planunsgruppe Graz, comprising Günther Domenig and Eilfried Huth, to design the layout and superstructure of *Ambiente/Environment.* As the exhibition plan indicates, there were three major areas in the exhibition: the environmental installations inside the Künstlerhaus, the sculptural works on the lawn, and the entrance pavilion designed by Domenig and Huth, all of which were connected by an elaborate network of pathways [Figure 2]. The organic curvature of the exhibition's outdoor component offset the rational geometry of the Künstlerhaus ground plan, and, indeed, Domenig's and Huth's layout effectively superseded that of the existing museum. Because of the pathways snaking through the museum, ushering viewers from one discrete environment to the next, the structure of the Künstlerhaus played little to no role in either the visitors' movement through the show or her experience of the exhibition-as-environment. In an interview with the architects filmed by Ferry Radax for a documentary on the making of *Ambiente/Environment,* Huth showed a three-dimensional model of the exhibition plan in which the Künstlerhaus was reduced to a schematic wire outline, clearly subordinate to the more detailed models for artist environments and the connecting passageways. In the film Huth explained, "The wire form is an abstraction of the Künstlerhaus, which we are trying to abstract and dematerialize through these passages."[8] Indeed, the Künstlerhaus was subsumed by the larger exhibition network, with Domenig's and Huth's entrance pavilion serving as the visitors' first and last contact point with the show.

The architects' entrance pavilion consisted of plastic, spherical tubing set amidst an irregular grid of steel scaffolding, which echoed the juxtaposition of the organic and the geometric evident on the exhibition plan. Inside, visitors followed a spiraling catwalk to an open "information room" in the pavilion's center, where they could peruse catalogs and exhibition maps. From there they followed a covered path, which led to the environments in the Künstlerhaus, eventually guiding them out to the lawn and then back to the entrance. The pavilion was covered in a type of plastic normally used in landscaping to protect from inclement weather, but, inside, visitors could see a model of the uncovered pavilion [Figure 3]. The presence of the model emphasized the way the pavilion functioned as an image in its own right—the pavilion image appeared in several forms in the exhibition's catalog, including graphic renderings of the scaffolding [Figure 4]. Reading the graphic as architecture, it has neither facade nor interior, only an interplay between material and negative space, reminiscent of the space frame architecture that was common in megastructural planning in the 1960s, with which Domenig and Huth were both involved. Concurrent with their work on the Trigon, the two architects were collaborating on *Überbauung Ragnitz* (1963–1969), a megastructural project developed for the nearby city of Ragnitz, the form of which comprised a tetrahedral space frame infrastructure designed to support clustered spatial cells for living.[9] A major advantage of the space frame was its capacity for extension and growth, capacities that Domenig and Huth evoke in the images of scaffolding, suggesting a fragment of an infinitely extensible structure. Similarly, the catalog displayed photographs of the pavilion from above in order to emphasize its spiral form, which served as an apt metaphor for the capacity of infinite, organic expansion. In sum, both the pavilion's spiral and scaffolding gestured toward the adaptable, flexible architecture of the megastructure.

According to its most incisive critic, Reyner Banham, a megastructure contained a dominant and monumental supporting frame, subordinate and flexible containers for habitation, and an overall layout that could grow along with the city's population.[10] Significantly, the city's inhabitants would not feel alienated from the surrounding architecture because, in theory, they would have creative agency to shape, design, and generally manipulate their individual housing units. Thus, the design and arrangement of the various habitable containers would lie beyond the control of the megastructural architect whose primary concern was the city's skeletal infrastructure. There would, accordingly, be an egalitarian distribution of creativity; indeed, the creative agency of the urban dweller had become a priority for Domenig and Huth in the years immediately preceding *Ambiente/Environment.* For example, in an essay published in the magazine *Bauen + Wohnen* just before the Trigon's opening, Domenig and Huth argued that in future cities individuals should be responsible for manually shaping the character of their living spaces. How this was to be achieved wasn't clear, but as to its purpose, they wrote: ". . . personal contribution is the starting point for new creativity and production of thoughts. It will bridge the gap of misunderstanding between art and mass population will."[11] I would argue that the megastructural

[Figure 3]

[Figure 4]

architect's necessary willingness to cede some degree of authorial control, as well as the democratization of architecture through a collective production model between architect and urban dweller, were both essential to the meaning and significance of the 1967 Trigon. While Domenig and Huth designed the exhibition's infrastructure, the contributing artists functioned as the model city's inhabitants, and, crucially, as its amateur architects.

Two years later, for the occasion of the 1969 Trigon Biennale, Skreiner aimed to build on the legacy of Ambiente/Environment with an exhibition that dealt more explicitly with architecture. Titled Architektur und Freiheit, the show featured twenty-seven projects submitted to Skreiner's open call to design a hypothetical city that would exist in the year 2000.[12] Projects were exhibited in a variety of ways, including traditional architectural models, film projections, and large-scale sculptures. Like the 1967 Trigon, there was a discernible polarity between the exhibited projects, between architecture that was omnipresent and architecture that was, in effect, disappearing.

The most extreme example of architecture's disappearance was the Austrian architect Hans Hollein's pill, the ultimate diffusion of architecture as built environment into pure sensory experience. Once ingested, the pill would supposedly generate "unusual sensory experiences," the precise nature of which Hollein did not describe. The pill didn't appear in the galleries, thus playing no role in the visitors' experience of the space, but the purchaser of the exhibition's catalog would find a small white tablet in a laminated pouch affixed to a page opposite Hollein's manifesto-like discussion of architecture as, simply, everything. While Hollein's reduction of architecture to a pill, with an emphasis on psychological effect, was consistent with the '60s culture of psychotropic drug use (although Hollein was specifically inspired by medications for agoraphobia), he was also thinking about the dematerialization of architecture in terms of the new media and information culture. Citing the ubiquity of media such as television, Hollein argued that the built environment was on its way to extinction: ". . . it seems almost unimportant whether or not the Acropolis or the pyramids physically exist, as the majority of the masses will never experience them personally, but rather through other media—their role relies completely on information technology."[13] He went on to argue for a new kind of architecture that is scaled to the body and activated through technology, pointing to examples like the telephone booth, fighter pilot helmets, and space suits.[14]

Hollein's belief in the power of technology to transform architecture into pure information was echoed throughout Architektur und Freiheit. For example, Coop Himmelb(l)au exhibited Soul Flipper, an apparatus for the head by which the wearer could transmit communicative signals into space. Independently of the architect-generated projects, visitors were invited to record their impressions of the show into a rudimentary computer system, which then projected the recordings throughout the gallery space. Thus, thoughts became ambient noise, information became environment.

As opposed to these essentially invisible architectures, there were numerous models for both megastructures and giant metropolises, including the Yugoslavian artist Predrag Ristic's Student Megopolis 2000, which he described as a modern-day realization of the Tower of Babel, and the sprawling model for Spinal City submitted by Domenig and Huth. In contrast to the 1967 iteration, the works displayed in 1969 rarely emphasized the role of the city dweller, and, relatedly, few of the works were participatory. Tellingly, critical reactions to Architektur und Freiheit were ambivalent at best. A review in Casabella, for instance, argued that the exhibition presented "mostly authoritarian solutions to today's urban problems," and further, that there was no relationship to speak of between the theme of freedom invoked in the show's title and the works on display.[15] One could argue that even radical propositions like Hans Hollein's architecture pill deprived the body of agency by proposing that the individual who swallowed the pill would be part of an immersive environment over which he or she had little control, and from which there was no physical or mental escape until the pill's effects wore off. As Craig Buckley has argued in relation to Hollein's pill, as architecture was made smaller, it also became more pervasive and total.[16]

This paradox of architecture that disappears only to be everywhere meant that there was less tension between architecture's omnipresence and dissolution than in the 1967 Trigon—instead, the two collapsed into one another. However, not everyone was oblivious to this collapse, which is evident in the Florence-based group's *Continuous Monument,* which debuted at the 1969 Trigon.[17] Superstudio, which included Adolfo Natalini, Christiano Toraldo di Francia, and Piero Frassinelli, exhibited a room-sized model that corresponded, on a much smaller scale, to the plans for an architecture that would in theory traverse the globe, which they described in the exhibition's catalog [Figure 5]. The *Continuous Monument* was all facade with no discernible interior; in drawings it loomed over older cities and sliced through rural environs, and in *Architektur und Freiheit,* it coated the walls of one room and bifurcated the gallery space.[18] Superstudio situated the *Continuous Monument* as the apex of an historical tradition of monuments from antiquity, including Stonehenge, the Egyptian pyramids, and the Great Wall of China.[19] In this way, the *Continuous Monument* engendered a strange tension between its invocation of the pre-modern or archaic monument and a capitalist architectural language evoked by its gridded surface resembling a curtain wall, the gridded surface of which was effectively a wall of non-signification. Simultaneously transparent and reflective, it was form without content, meant to facilitate the flow of information and capital in a late-capitalist world order.

In *Architektur und Freiheit,* architecture was pushed to the brink in its negation of materiality and fusion with the body. Whereas a main argument of Trigon '67 was the necessity for the individual to participate in constituting the urban fabric in concert with the architect, in Trigon '69 passivity was back, as the viewer simply ingested a pill or donned a helmet in order to assimilate with a reality constituted through new technology. As Superstudio's contribution suggested, architecture was moving dangerously close to a totalizing environment devoid of meaning. Amidst many more earnest proposals for future cities, as well as an increased integration of technology and architecture, it was Superstudio's *Continuous Monument* that was most portent of the future in its irony and detachment.

[Figure 5]

1 Thanks to the Neue Galerie Graz at the Universalmuseum Joanneum for generously providing access to their archives relating to the Trigon exhibitions, and granting permission for reproduction of images here. Also, my sincere thanks to Lisa Dietrich, who, unless noted otherwise, has completed all of the German translations.

2 Styria is a *Bundesland* or state in the southeastern region of Austria. For a discussion of the art-world dynamic among the three countries, as well as the development of the Trigon Biennale, see Herwig G. Höller, "Overcoming the Bulwark: Graz as a Platform for Art from Eastern and Southern Europe," *Umelec* 13, no. 2 (2009): 28–33.

3 Wilfried Skreiner, *Ambiente/Environment. Trigon 67. Italia-Jugoslavija- Österreich* (Graz: Neue Galerie am Landesmuseum Joanneum, 1967). n.p.

4 Ibid.

5 The term *New Tendency (Nove tendencije)* derived from a series of three eponymous exhibitions held in Zagreb between 1961 and 1965. As Jack Burnham wrote of the loosely defined movement in 1968, the artists exhibiting under the rubric of the New Tendency were linked by "[t]he feeling . . . that lyricism was passé if not dead." Groups associated with the New Tendency included Group Zero in Germany, Gruppo T in Italy, and G.R.A.V. in France, among others. See Jack Burnham, *Beyond Modern Sculpture: The Effects of Science and Technology on Sculpture of This Century. (*New York: George Braziller) 247–262.

6 See text by Marc Adrian in ed. Skreiner, *Ambiente/Environment* catalog entry no. 9, n.p.

7 The most critically acclaimed work in the 1967 Trigon, Colombo's was the only work in *Ambiente/Environment* that would have a significant afterlife. Colombo recreated *Spazio Elastico* the following year for the Venice Biennale, where it won a prize. *Spazio Elastico* was recreated much later, in 2003, for the occasion of *Einbildung: Das Wahrnehmen in der Kunst,* which was the first exhibition housed in the newly erected Kunsthaus Graz. In the exhibition's catalog, the curator Peter Pakesch wrote of Colombo's *Spazio Elastico* that it was, "one of the most spectacular contributions to Trigon '67, the singularly epochal exhibition of new art of the 1960s, which made a huge impact in Graz and abroad, not least because of this particular work. In the following years, the exhibition came to be regarded as the key event that marked the beginning of an intense exploration of contemporary art at the Neue Galerie am Landesmuseum Joanneum." See ed. Peter Pakesch, *Einbildung: Das Wahrnehmen in Der Kunst* (Cologne: Werlag der Buchhandlung, 2003), 27. Indeed, *Ambiente/Environment* seems to have marked a major turning point for Graz in its introduction of a radical avant-garde, as was evident in the lively debates over the exhibition's validity as art that took place in the local press.

8 Ferry Radax, *Trigon Graz,* 16 mm, 1967.

9 In Radax's filim *Trigon Graz,* Huth shows the interviewer a model for their concurrent megastructural project, *Überbauung Ragnitz,* after discussing their model for the exhibition *Ambiente/Environment,* creating thus a suggestive connection between the two.

10 See Banham's introduction in Reyner Banham, *Megastructure: Urban Futures of the Recent Past* (London: Thames and Hudson, 1976), 7–12.

11 Günther Domenig and Eilfried Huth, "Propositionen," *Bauen + Wohnen* 5, 1967: 183.

12 Skreiner, Wilfried et al., *Italien, Jugoslawien, Österreich: Dreiländerbiennale Trigon '69 : Architektur und Freiheit.* (Graz: Neue Galerie am Landesmuseum Joanneum, 1969).

13 Hans Hollein, "Vision oder Wirchlichkeit," in ibid.

14 Ibid.

15 Giorgio Tagini, "Graz Trigon 69," *Casabella,* no. 342 (November 1969): 7. That the idea of Freiheit, or freedom, was not carried out to the fullest potential was, to some degree, acknowledged in Skreiner's catalog introduction, when he noted that only seventy projects were submitted due to the last-minute call for participation. Additionally, Skreiner noted that the exhibition's jury only gave out seven of the ten possible cash prizes, and some participants were chosen because "they presented significant contributions even if they did not deal with the theme of architecture and freedom."

16 Craig Buckley, "From Absolute to Everything: Taking Possession in 'Alles Ist Architektur,'" *Grey Room,* no. 28 (July 1, 2007): 108–22, 117.

17 For a detailed account of the *Continous Monument* and other works by Superstudio, see Peter Lang, William Menking, and Superstudio (Group), *Superstudio: Life without Objects* (Milano/New York: Skira, 2003).

18 Fernando Quesada provides a useful physical description of Superstudio's installation at the 1969 Biennale. See Fernando Quesada, "Superstudio 1966–73. From the World without Objects to the Universal Grid," *Footprint (1875–1490)* 5, no. 1 (March 2011): 23–34; 26.

19 See "Superstudio" in Skreiner, *Italien, Jugoslawien, Österreich: Dreiländerbiennale Trigon '69 : Architektur und Freiheit.*

Between Image and Apparatus: *Structures Gonflables,* April 1968

Craig Buckley

> The world of inflated objects has invaded the museum of the city of Paris. The
> visitor is received in the grand entrance hall by an enormous rubber rocket, resting
> obliquely, it stretches from the basement to the parapet of the second floor mezza-
> nine. The ceilings are encumbered with helium-filled balloons, pearlescent planets
> floating above our heads, reminding us of a universe in a state of levitation. Here
> is a category of forms entirely different from the static stone walls that enclose the
> museum—a dynamic world held together by the difference of pressure between
> inside and outside.

Jacques Michel, *Le Monde*

Published in the newspaper *Le Monde* in March of 1968, these lines described the impression of entering *Structures Gonflables,* an exhibition at the Museum of Modern Art of the City of Paris organized by
the group of architects, sociologists, and urban planners known as Utopie. Less an elegant entrance
than an invasion, inflatables took over the museum without yet being quite at home within it.[1] There was
a certain drama to the ill-fitting relationship, which Utopie seemed to relish, from the two-story rubber
rocket leaning sideways in the entrance hall, to the placement of a dirigible such that it occupied nearly
the entire volume of a room. For the *Le Monde* journalist, these objects represented a new "category of
forms," but they also announced something grander: "Today a new generation is being born, one that
covers construction, architecture, furniture, and even sculpture; air is now 'consumed' on an aesthetic
level." While heralded as a drastic transformation, inflatable architecture was not exactly new in 1968.
The idea itself can be traced back centuries; the first architectural patents date from the time of WWI,
and the rise of inflatable pavilions was already well developed by the 1950s. How then to make sense of
the reviewer's impression that in entering the exhibition he had entered something of a new world?

[Figure 1]

[Figure 2]

[Figure 3]

What was changing at this moment, I would argue, is something like the exhibition value of pneumatics. *Structures Gonflables* was the first large-scale exhibition of pneumatic objects in France, but it was also the first instance in which the Museum of Modern Art of the City of Paris had shown technical, military, commercial, and architectural objects rather than artworks [Figure 1]. The exhibition thus registers a larger cultural shift with respect to both the museum and to what constitutes an architectural exhibition. The exhibition value of pneumatics does not relate only to the literal exhibition of inflatable objects in a museum. The use of pneumatics in architecture during the decade of the 1960s was increasingly bound up with exhibitions, from structures that Victor Lundy designed for the traveling *Atoms for Peace* exhibition to the numerous air-supported pavilions at *Expo '70* in Osaka.[2] Could it be that, for a younger generation of architects and artists in latter half of the 1960s, pneumatics appeared as a technology designed for reproducibility, not so different from printed images? Part of the appeal of pneumatics was that they could be made in potentially unlimited copies, copies that could be directly assembled, taken apart, and disposed of by users themselves. It is not for nothing that a group like Utopie, highly invested in making use of cheap means of reproduction like offset lithography, would also be interested in pneumatics. If inflatables were "designed for reproducibility," they were also closely linked to a particularly plastic conception of the image, of a world in which matter had been more totally given over to the shaping powers of human imagination. With its dense collisions of pneumatic devices, *Structures Gonflables* assembled a three-dimensional image of pneumatics, an experience that *Le Monde* described as immersive—to visit the exhibition was not to survey a collection of things, but to be plunged into a different "world," a "universe" in a "state of levitation" [Figures 2-3]. Such a universe was not held together by cement, joints, or bolts, but by a more immaterial play of forces. What was exhibited was not strictly architecture, but the making perceptible of something that typically eluded visible form, from flows of air to the equilibrium between different pressures. As Jacques Michel remarked: "today, even air is consumed on an aesthetic level."[3]

The exhibition provides an opportunity to read this immersive rhetoric somewhat against the grain, for if *Structures Gonflables* concerned immersion, inflation, and flotation, it also emphasized structure, material, and apparatus. If the exhibition aimed to present visitors with an overwhelming image, the group's interest in pneumatics was also tied to questions of assembly and industrial production, part of an effort by a group of architects, urbanists, and sociologists to theorize the place of architectural practice within a highly industrialized, consumer society. They also aimed to rethink traditions of structure within the École des Beaux-Arts, an institution where the architects had trained, itself on the verge of a historical implosion that spring in 1968.

Utopie, a group of architects, urban planners, and sociologists who collaborated for roughly a decade beginning in 1967, included the architects Jean Aubert, Isabelle Auricoste, Jean-Paul Jungmann, and Antoine Stinco, sociologists Jean Baudrillard and René Lourau, assistants of Henri Lefebvre at Nanterre, and urban planners Catherine Cot and Hubert Tonka.[4] The importance of structure to the group can be seen in the way they frame the status of assembly, a shift highlighted by their use of the verb *démonté* (disassembly or dismantling). The term recurs at a number of points in the group's writings, most extensively in a text titled "Architecture as a Theoretical Problem," published in the midst of the dissolution of the Beaux-Arts in May and June of 1968. Describing the challenges faced by a new theorization of architecture, they sought to "[first] dismantle the economic, political, social, and cultural manifestations of architecture, and in a second movement attempt to penetrate subjective appearances and ideological illusions in order to comprehend architecture's role and status as the result and product of a society."[5]

The verb *démonter* lends itself to a range of potential readings. Something that is *démonté* has been taken down, like an object removed from its case, or, even more violently, like a statue knocked from its pedestal. *Démontage* equally recalls the broader circulation of the prefix *dé* in artistic and intellectual culture in France at this moment, such as Raymond Hains's use of *décollage* to describe his practice of exhibiting torn billboards and advertisements from Parisian hoardings, or the Situationist International's use of the term *détournement* to theorize the strategic misappropriation of everyday materials. Yet *démonter* appears distinct from these senses. Neither a knocking down, or conspicuous tearing of image's surface, nor a deliberate program of misuse, it concerns the intricate task of disassembly. This distinction linked pneumatics to questions of demountable construction, but also allowed them to look at ideology as though it were a problem of structure, whose affects could be arrested and understood by taking it apart.

The effort to dismantle what they called the "manifestations of architecture" was also an effort to theorize architecture differently, one that required dislodging certain definitions centrally ensconced in the lexicon of the former Beaux-Arts school. Architecture, they argued, could not be understood as a "work of art, a creation, or a synthesis," nor did it suffice, as certain militant ex-Beaux-Arts slogans would have it, to define architecture as "a service to the people" or "a political act."[6] In contrast to these definitions, the group's interest in disassembly was part of an effort to comprehend "the moments of transformation of a commodity called architecture in the course of its production at the heart of French society." Such a rhetoric of disassembly supported an architectural interpretation of lightweight, demountable construction as appropriate to the advanced mechanization and accelerated urban transformations that also characterized the age, yet it also involved a theoretical process of deciphering mass imagery and mass discourse by taking them apart, one that sought to come to grips with a changing practice of architecture in a postwar consumer society that was itself increasing ephemeral and uncertain.

It was on returning from the exhibition in Paris in 1968 that the historian Reyner Banham published perhaps his best-known text on inflatables: the article "Monumental Windbags."[7] Banham, much like the critic from *Le Monde,* saw the mania for inflatables as part of a historical rupture, one fueled by a fortuitous confluence between postwar advances in plastics technologies and a generational shift in attitude. For Banham, it was precisely the immersive and responsive quality of pneumatic enclosures that was so different and so appealing. They were evidence of the waning of what he called the "bad, old school of Platonic abstraction" and the rise of "the direct-participation, real-space, real-time, involvement-aesthetic," the convergence point between new materials and new media. It was a point driven home by Banham's recollection of being fully immersed within a transparent pneumatic dome inside a BBC television studio, an experience that was "more truly like [being in] the skin of a living creature than the metaphorical 'skin' of say, a glass-walled office block." Such a description calls to mind Banham's own naked silhouette collaged into the drawings of Francois Dallegret's Power-Membrane House only a couple of years earlier, in which the historian fantasized about being immersed within a lightweight, transportable "standard-of-living" package, capable of dispensing with the mass and bulk of conventional enclosures while catering perfectly to every creature comfort.[8]

Banham's formulation is suggestive for the way it combines a technological shift—"advances in plastics"—with a new condition fully defined by exhibition value; a pneumatic dome that both exhibits its contents and transmits those images through the mass media. Yet, the radical break that Banham asserts also obscures lines of continuity with previous traditions. It is significant that Utopie's interest in pneumatics and disassembly emerged within a particular segment of the École de Beaux-Arts, the studio of Édouard Albert, where Aubert, Jungmann, and Stinco met as students. A pioneer in steel construction, Albert's teaching drew together a particular twentieth-century lineage of lightweight architecture, including unorthodox structures like the Tour Croulebarbe (1961), a tower constructed from an innovative, lightweight tubular steel structure that also holds the distinction of being the first skyscraper for housing in Paris. The Albert atelier included hundreds of students, and was also open to external teachers, an opportunity that Aubert, Jungmann, and Stinco took to invite David Georges Emmerich, a specialist in tensile construction and demountable building systems, to help advise their thesis projects.

Structures Gonflables extended such lines of inquiry, yet it also complicated them, something that made the exhibition different from the immersive media experience highlighted by Banham. Photographs of the installation show spaces as dense and heterogeneous as the elements arranged on Utopie's pages, including everything from hovercrafts to aircraft tires, emergency life rafts, weather balloons, inflatable kinetic sculptures, decompression chambers, dirigibles, Andy Warhol's Mylar clouds, high-altitude pressure suits, and more. Configured within an apparatus of demountable scaffolding, the pneumatic objects appear to perform their lightness, at times appearing in mid-air. Supporting such provisional encounters was a distinctly un-pneumatic apparatus of metal scaffolding; holding up this "universe in levitation," it served as a type of orthopedic for the three-dimensional image. This armature also deployed a dense layer of technical information in the form of panels that snaked through the exhibition space. On the one hand, these recall the relationship of object and information used in commercial exhibitions, yet, at the same time, the panels occupy an ambiguous position. Unlike commercial exhibitions, the panels did not carry texts supplied by the manufacturers. Nor did the panels offer standard interpretive museological texts. Instead, they served as something between a three-dimensional tack-board and a draft for a catalog, compiling brief historical genealogies, offering technical specifications such as materials, operating pressures, manufacturers, dimensions, and availability, and conveying glimpses of the objects deployed in the world.[9] If the panel armature physically supported the immersive effect, it also punctured it, calling for a different type of attention from the reader, one that referred such pneumatic devices back to a larger apparatus of industrial production.

The relationship between objects and panels also points to the place of such an architectural exhibition within the larger shifts taking place in French museum culture at this moment. The exhibition was able to enter the institution due to a newly formed initiative, Animation Recherche Confrontation (ARC), headed by Pierre Gaudibert. ARC sought to open up the museum, moving from a strict emphasis on art to an expanded engagement with popular education, which included an effort to reflect on the culture of industrial society and "the aesthetics of everyday life."[10] A full decade before the opening of the Centre Pompidou—and a year before the founding of the Centre de Creation Industrielle—there were very few places in which such an exhibition could be mounted. The manner in which the *Structures Gonflables* seized the exhibition value of pneumatics as an opportunity to think about the relationship between industrial society and the aesthetics of the everyday object was an intellectual problem that anticipated the programs that emerged in these institutions.[11]

Deciphering the cultural logic implicit in the everyday object was a concern at the heart of Jean Baudrillard's 1968 book *The System of Objects,* a book developed during the period he collaborated with Utopie.[12] Postwar consumer culture, Baudrillard argued, could no longer be grasped at the level of the individual object, but had to be understood in terms of relationships within a larger system of objects, one in which inessential differences amongst things were more thoroughly "systematized by the production process." A key example was the proliferation of industrial styling, first pioneered by automotive industries and expanded in the postwar period to an entire range of consumer goods. Adapting a structuralist framework akin to the one Roland Barthes had used to decompose advertising and fashion, Baudrillard looked to understand the dialectical interaction between a dynamic and unpredictable structure of technological development, on the one hand, and a cultural structure that arrested, organized, and codified such technics into systems of form, on the other hand. Adding a new dimension to Karl Marx's concept of commodity fetishism, Baudrillard posited not a relationship turned on its head, so much as an object internally divided, one whose external surfaces performed in a manner largely determined by the signifying agendas of advertisement and communication rather than according to logic of its internal mechanical structure. If the outsides of objects were alarmingly discontinuous from their internal workings, their increasingly minute design enunciated a compensatory rhetoric of control, promising an ability to manipulate forms of power that lay, in fact, ever more thoroughly beyond human grasp.

Baudrillard's theory of the system of objects intersects the exhibition in a particular way. The installation strategy suggested less a sequence of developments than a host of unresolved collisions, the field of pneumatics appearing as one whose disposition had not been entirely determined, a still heterogeneous set of technical possibilities lying at the limits of architectural culture, and thus still lacking anything like a coherent code. In this sense, it was less an example of the systematic coordination

[Figure 4]

[Figure 5]

of objects than a breach or blind spot within it. Laying claim to their teacher Henri Lefebvre's slogan "all technology at the service of everyday life," the group sought to envision other uses for such technics, which carried the promise of disrupting the reigning order of things. Not unlike the contemporaneous emergence of forms of cheap and changeable standardization in Pop music or fashion, for a brief moment pneumatics promised a similarly radical instability, a vector for accelerating the decomposition of inherited cultural codes by connecting them to the unpredictable effects of an emerging technology.

Reaching outside of architecture to other technical fields was also a means of challenging the symbolic frontiers that marked the edges of the discipline. The pneumatic designs developed during the same years by Aubert, Jungmann, and Stinco provide a glimpse of how the architects negotiated this liminal zone. Emphasizing low-cost, mass-production units, their designs were neither the low-pressure skins mentioned by Banham, nor were they quite inflatable substitutes for existing furniture types. Developed with the manufacturer SCIFA, they offered the user not only the ability to blow up or deflate at will, but the flexibility to interchange and rearrange the parts in order to mount different forms. As visible in the detail, the same repertoire of parts could be used for an enclosure, a partition, a bed, or a seat—less a system of objects than an object as system [Figures 4-5].

In the pages of its journal, Utopie developed techniques for dispersing and dismantling the forms of coherence structuring media images, and with pneumatics such a project confronted an object that was both seemingly open to appropriation yet also strangely resistant to it. Composed of welded sheets of plastic or rubber, pneumatic structures depended on the minute integrity of every single inch of their seams, a pressurized system in which even the minutest discontinuity carried the threat of leakage, deformation, and collapse. In the group's designs for furniture, and even more so in this design for a temporary exhibition environment, such discontinuities were multiplied. Pneumatics are used to exhibit a structural idea and to test its limits—a single high-pressure tube was repeated, to allow for demountability and to create a system that could continue to be self-supporting even when subject to deformations. Here, the insistence on dismantling redirected the more amorphous plasticity of the pneumatic image towards a taut geometrical logic of structure; at once drawing on and exacerbating the constructive tradition of figures like Emmerich and Albert. What Banham had summarized as a combination of disaffection for "official modern architecture" and an enthusiasm for do-it-yourself technology, can be seen in these cases as the site of deeper contradictions. If such pneumatic structures appeared as a means for a more radical dismantling of architecture's attachment to values of durability and permanence—becoming an apparatus subject to flexible, open ended disassembly—they also drew architecture closer to a logic of the commodity that emphasized ever greater disposability. Disposability can be understood here in the familiar sense of something designed to be used up and thrown out, but it can also be seen as something more thoroughly conceived as adaptable to multiple and changing dispositions, capable of molding itself to the logic of a *dispositif.*

In their insistence on openness and disassembly, such structures could be seen as counter-images to a cultural system which members of the group saw as increasingly closed in on itself. Baudrillard's system of objects was one effort to describe this more total closure, yet even it was never totally secure. As he pointed out, the system of objects was also a "systematization of fragility." Citing the ephemerality of fashion, the febrility of objects designed to fall apart, the repetition compulsions incited by serial production, and the ever more rapid passages between satisfaction and disillusion, a specter of disassembly haunts Baudrillard's system of objects.

> [O]nce assembled and mounted the components of the technical object imply a certain coherence. But such a structure is always vulnerable to the human mind . . . . The hierarchy of elements can be dismantled at any time, and those elements made interchangeable within a paradigmatic system that the subject uses for his self-narration. The object is discontinuous already—and certainly easy for thought to disassemble.[13]

In such a scenario, it is not only the object that is taken apart, but also something of the subject. Articulated amidst the political and theoretical turbulence of the end of the 1960s, the rhetoric of disassembly absorbed conflicting forces, refusing both the traditional fixity demanded of architecture and the programmed fungibility of styling, wagering on a more profoundly unstable interaction between technics and culture. Skeptical of architecture as an instrument of direct action in the immediate wake of May 1968, they were equally wary of a reactionary return to the compositional security of the Beaux-Arts. Not insignificantly, this more radically dismantled architecture was tied to a faith in theoretical construction. In this sense, the effort to seize the exhibition value of pneumatics not only made visible the normally unseen flows of air, and balance of pressures, but looked to make visible the disparate components of the technological apparatus of which pneumatics were a product. The literal instability of pneumatic structure can be seen as a vehicle for the larger intellectual project of disassembly, one that sought to render architecture's identity unstable by taking it apart, to reflect on the workings of architectural production in order to question how disciplinary limits were drawn.

[1] Jacques Michel, "Le monde dynamique des structures gonflables," *Le Monde,* March 14, 1968.

[2] For an overview of pneumatics in architecture and design, see Marc Dessauce, ed. *The Inflatable Moment: Pneumatics and Protest in '68* (New York: Princeton Architectural Press, 1999) and Sean Topham, *Blow-up: Inflatable Art, Architecture and Design* (Munich: Prestel, 2002).

[3] Michel, "Le monde dynamique des structures gonflables."

[4] The group's eponymous journal *Utopie: Sociologie de l'urbain* appeared from 1967 to 1978. For selected translations see Craig Buckley and Jean-Louis Violeau, eds. *Utopie: Texts and Projects 1967–1978* (Los Angeles: Semiotext(e), 2011).

[5] Hubert Tonka, Jean-Paul Jungmann, Jean Aubert (Signed Utopie), "Architecture comme problème théorique," in *L'Architecture d'aujourd'hui* 139 (September 1968): 81–92. "Architecture comme problème théorique" was an expanded version of "Architecture as a theoretical problem," published in *Architectural Design* (June 1968), 255. The appearance of the text in *Architectural Design* prior to its expanded form in *L'Architecture d'Aujourd'hui* testifies to the important connections between groups in different cities at this moment. The text would be reprinted in pamphlet form as *Des raisons de l'architecture* in early 1969, to address the milieu of the ex-École des Beaux-Arts in the midst of its reorganization.

[6] Ibid, 81.

[7] Reyner Banham, "Monumental Windbags," *New Society* 290 (April 18, 1968): 569–570.

[8] Reyner Banham, "A Home is not a House," *Art in America* (April 1965); reprinted in *Clip-Kit: Studies in Environmental Design* (1966), n.p.

[9] The catalog that was produced for the exhibition compiled much of this technical information. See Utopie, eds. *Structures Gonflables* (Paris: Musée d'Art Moderne de la ville de Paris, 1968). The ambition, according to Tonka, was to assemble for pneumatics the equivalent of the *Manufacture française d'armes et cycles de Saint-Etienne,* a product catalog not unlike the early catalogs of Sears-Roebuck in the United States.

[10] *See Musée d'Art Moderne de la ville de Paris: la collection* (Paris: Paris musées, 2008).

[11] Tracing this impact is beyond the scope of this short essay. Lefebvre and Baudrillard's writings can be found in the early exhibitions and publications of the CCI. See, for instance, *Matériau, technologie, forme* (Paris: Centre du Création Industrielle, 1974) as well the journal *Traverses,* founded in 1975.

[12] Jean Baudrillard, *Le système des objets* (Paris: Gallimard, 1968); *The System of Objects,* trans. James Benedict (London: Verso, 1996).

[13] Ibid., 110.

E.A.T. in Osaka: Transducing Technology

Mark Wasiuta

In his essay, "Photographic Recording of Some Optical Effects," Billy Klüver, former Bell Labs engineer and president and co-founder of the artist and industry matchmaking enterprise, Experiments in Art and Technology (E.A.T.), is grasping at a description of some of the perceptual and optical disturbances encountered in the disorienting, fog-enveloped, electro-acoustically programmed installation, the *Pavilion,* that E.A.T. had been commissioned to design and manage for PepsiCo., Inc. at the 1970 Osaka World Exposition:

> For a viewer moving around on the floor the optics are nonparaxial, resulting in spherical aberrations and astigmatism ... We shall use the term 'real' to describe images that appear between the viewer and the Mirror and the term 'virtual' to describe images behind the Mirror. These definitions are necessary to deal with the ambiguity that arises from multiple reflections, where, for instance, a virtual image of an object can result in a real image.[1]

Perhaps attuned to the descriptive limitations of his dry, technical assessment of vision and compound reflection, in another text Klüver shifts idiom, from astigmatic optics to the aesthetics of immersion and indeterminacy of experience:

> The *Pavilion* was a living responsive environment ... The space in the Mirror was gentle and poetic, rich and always changing ... We discovered new and complicated relationships every day ... the visitor became part of the total theatre experience. Anything that one did in this environment was beautiful.[2]

Klüver's difficulty in describing the installation is symptomatic of the *Pavilion's* fate and E.A.T.'s aesthetic practice more generally. The oscillation between a vocabulary of absorbing perceptual experiences and mechanisms of vision hints at the imbrication between engagement and instruction that colors E.A.T's emerging TV bias. When the *Pavilion* opened in 1970, such shifts in idiom and terminology were well practiced by Klüver. The project had been the primary fixation of the entire E.A.T enterprise for the previous sixteen months, and the most visible demonstration of its capacity to assemble artists and engineers, aesthetics and technology into novel alignments. With his definition of E.A.T. as a "transducer between art studio and industrial laboratory" able to communicate the problems of artists through the vocabulary of engineers, Klüver alludes to the signal conversions that characterized the Osaka project and that coordinated E.A.T. projects in general, both conceptually and technically.

Through his experience with electron beam lasers at Bell Labs, this lexicon of signals and exchanges would appear to Klüver as the most apposite descriptors of the social assembler that E.A.T. aspired to become, able not only to translate art into electronics, but also able to co-process seemingly incompatible social and cultural codes. Indeed, Klüver declares from the outset that E.A.T. was less motivated to bring together art and technology than to explore "the possibilities of human interaction."[3] Seeking the investment of industry and corporations in this arena was the natural outcome, according to Klüver, of the trend within industry to shift from "products to functions," and of industry's increasing involvement in the "environment and society."[4]

As Klüver's attention to these signs of epochal industrial and cultural transformation suggest, the Pepsi pavilion was incubated within the late-1960s hothouse of advanced technologies, strategies for social interaction, and, especially, media environments. In competition for the Osaka project against the media collective USCO (The Company of Us) and the *Electric Circus*—the New York intermedia-oriented nightclub and occasional hangout of The Grateful Dead and The Velvet Underground—Klüver astutely recognized that E.A.T's loose organization and possibly incomprehensible range of activities might place it at a disadvantage. By 1970, E.A.T. projects encompassed more than one hundred categories of experimentation, from high-voltage coronas to electroluminescence and from anti-gravity machines to the "reorganization of language."[5] To skew the contest in his favor, Klüver wagered on the cultural capital of the museum. He led the Pepsi delegates to Swedish curator Pontus Hultén's 1968 exhibition at the Museum of Modern Art, *The Machine as Seen at the End of the Mechanical Age,* that staged a selection of art and technology projects from an E.A.T.-organized competition. The implication was that the breadth of experimental exuberance on view at MoMA would be integrated into one immediate experience that would satisfy the demand to appeal to a "Pepsi Generation," Pepsi's advertising slogan for a youth consumer base attuned to and touched by the cultural, industrial, and mediatic shifts on which Klüver's enterprise was also fixated. Alan Pottasch, by 1968 president of Pepsi Japan, had devised the slogan for the American market in the early 1960s as a means of appealing to youth, to "community," and to "the people side of what is happening today."[6] These vague invocations of social transformation were strangely resonant with Klüver's description of E.A.T's interest in human interaction.

Well before E.A.T.'s involvement, Pottasch had hired Takenaka Komuten Construction and architect Tadashi Doi to design and build a faceted dome to house the Pepsi pavilion. Pottasch initially envisioned the structure as a bandstand for international rock concerts. Robert Breer, one of the E.A.T. artist members, referred to it as a "Buckled Fuller" dome, alluding to what he saw as its ersatz geodesic geometry. It was this design that E.A.T. inherited, along with the commission, and which their project sought to disguise.

Although, in the end, the pavilion's popular success would prove elusive, through its inclusion in *Arthropods,* Jim Burns's 1971 survey of design futures, as well as through the 1972 E.A.T. publication, *Pavilion,* the project is still easily identifiable through the double erasure of the building's contorted shell. From the exterior, the *Pavilion* was obscured by a cloud of fog drifting from a network of nozzles wrapping the skin and, from the inside, the shell was masked by an inflatable mirrored hemisphere whose fugitive and destabilizing optical effects, and the spectral apparition of "real" bodies in space, Klüver is struggling to concretize in the passage cited earlier.

Along with sixty-five engineers, consultants, and other collaborators, the principal components of the project were authored by five E.A.T. artists: the exterior fog system was designed by Japanese artist Fujiko Nakaya with Mee Industries; a team of motorized "Floats" roving the building's terrace were designed by Robert Breer; "Suntrak," a system for redirecting solar light rays was conceived by Frosty Myers; the *Pavilion's* electronic sound-modifier console was designed and engineered by David Tudor with Gordon Mumma; and the installation of the interior reflective dome was directed by Robert Whitman.

[Figure 2]

[Figure 1]

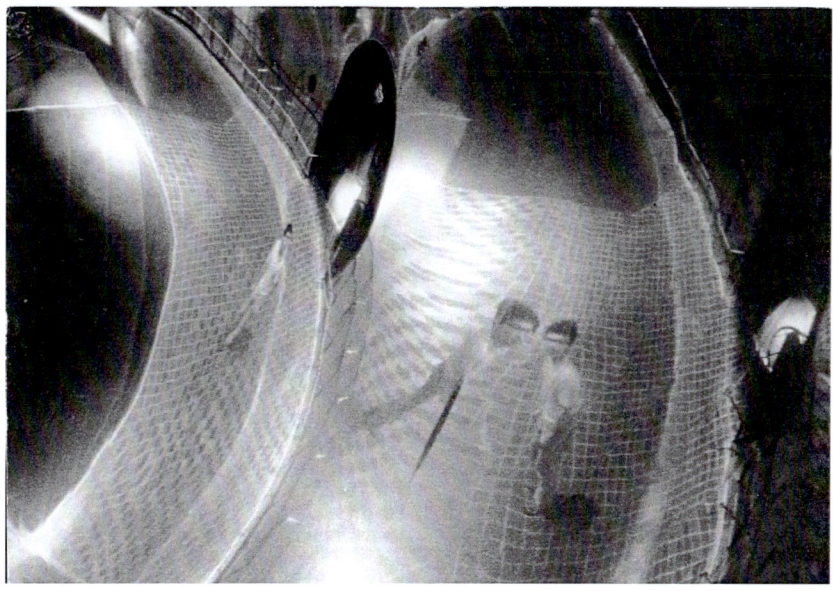

[Figure 3]

Walking through Nakaya's fog, past Breer's "Floats," and Myers's "Suntrak," visitors would enter the pavilion through a tunnel in which they were given a clear plastic electronic handset. With this they passed into the penumbral space of the so-called "Clam Room," an environment intended to "absorb previous impressions," and to prepare visitors for their ascent to the reflective dome above.[7] Equipped with speakers and receivers, the handset would pick up sound transmissions from the floor of the dome room that had been segmented and treated with a variety of textures and materials. Each segmented "zone" would transmit a loop of environmental sounds. Standing in the Asphalt zone, for example, one would hear squealing brakes, or a Harley-Davidson motorcycle, while the Grass zone transmitted the sound of frogs, cicadas, and turkeys gobbling. The dome was surrounded by an array of lights and thirty-seven speakers, all connected to the control console and the recording archive, which managed the environmental sound loops, and through which the invited artists would manipulate lighting and sound as "live programmers." Through live programming, the E.A.T. team claimed, "sound vibrations will cause a reaction to the body—and visual images will open the mind."[8] These acoustic and lighting effects were enveloped by the hemisphere and its reflective surface. Standing at the center of the dome—the "egocentric position"—viewers would see themselves reflected infinitely in every direction.

Reviewing the *Pavilion* for the art journal *Studio International,* critic Gene Youngblood expanded on its total perceptual impact:

> One is able to view actual holographic images of oneself floating in three-dimensional space in real time. The effect is utterly indescribable. One is overwhelmed with a sense of vertigo. One is unable to walk in a straight line since the slightest motion sends phantasmagoria of color and light whirling insanely about the environment.[9]

As this hallucinatory apparatus was being realized, Klüver exercised a deft control over ever-erupting chaos, placating Pepsi with assurances that E.A.T. was interested in them, not art, reinforcing E.A.T.'s commitment to the corporation while simultaneously securing total independence for the artists working on the *Pavilion.* The coordination of interests and agendas was managed on two distinct rhetorical and conceptual communicative tracks.

Despite this appearance of agility, however, a scant four weeks after the launch of the Osaka Expo, Pepsi dismissed E.A.T., severing Klüver and his team's association with the *Pavilion.* While guards hired by Pepsi escorted E.A.T. members away, the punch tapes that directed the acoustic and light programming, along with David Tudor's sound archive of crickets, birds and waves—the core acoustic database—were smuggled out of the *Pavilion,* effectively lobotomizing its electronic, environmental controls. For the next three weeks, Tudor and Mumma's sound console instead played, "It's A Small World," PepsiCo's theme song for its UNICEF pavilion at the 1964 New York World's Fair, overriding whatever remained of the *Pavilion's* soundtracks. Needless to say, the substitution of a Disney jingle for the acoustic scores and manipulations of the Tudor console by La Monte Young, Anne Halprin, and the other twenty-four artists selected by E.A.T. to activate the *Pavilion,* was not the transduction of signals Klüver had envisioned.

Although baffling to Klüver, the abrupt termination of the contract was in fact a manifestation of the instability of E.A.T.'s posture, and exposed a symmetry of disorientation: Klüver, off-balance within the corporate patois of public relations; and Pepsi lost within the spectral space of the mirrored dome. Assessing the challenge posed by these conditions, only weeks after the Pepsi debacle and now back in New York City, E.A.T. announced a symposium on "Esthetics." Attempting to account for the difficulty of orientation and communication in precisely such situations, Klüver's symposium brief diagnosed a slippage among conflict, aesthetics, and environment:

> As the commitment to the conscious development of the environment increases, there is a greater need for experimental open-ended projects to develop procedures for action in this area . . . Many of the most disruptive and difficult conflicts that arise in these open-ended, multi-disciplinary working situations can be traced to personal or professional esthetic biases. These esthetic commitments are usually . . . disguised . . . as something else (economic, political, technical, cultural and psychological, etc.).[10]

On the one hand, then, the "failure" of the *Pavilion* comes down to a conflict that appears through a disguise of aesthetic biases. Yet, on the other hand, it is equally likely that, chiasmatically, economic, political, and technical biases are suppressed within the aesthetic. It is the ambiguous boundary between these two—or multiple territories of conflict cutting across the *Pavilion*—that Klüver's symposium ultimately reflects on.

One primary source of conflict can be traced to the exhibition conventions of the Osaka World Exposition. John Pearce, a recent graduate of Yale School of Architecture was hired by Klüver to coordinate the production of the E.A.T. artists' projects and to manage the *Pavilion's* installations. He had recently left Davis-Brody, the architectural firm designing the U.S. national pavilion, disaffected by a project that he saw degenerating into a banal didactic exhibition of disconcertingly lifeless astronaut mannequins, lunar modules, and other objects that cited national accomplishment. From Klüver and the E.A.T. artists Pearce inherited the notion that the Pepsi project would be "anti-expo." Not only did the *Pavilion* eschew conventional displays, images, and objects, where the U.S. pavilion fixated on crowd flow in an effort to direct visitors to see, "as much 'America' as possible," the E.A.T. design was to release visitors from any form of temporal regulation and directional control.[11]

The nonlinear, aleatory encounter with the *Pavilion's* perceptual effects was positioned against the management of experience and attention. A visitor to the *Pavilion,* Klüver explained, would, "discover relationships and forms of interaction," or "choose his own experience and determine his own environment."[12] Asked what the Pepsi pavilion meant, a Japanese press agent responded that it meant nothing. This surprisingly blunt assertion countered E.A.T's more evasive approach. E.A.T.'s sly refusal of program and signification concealed the more aggressive intention of opposing the narrated, expository media of the fair and its didactic exhibition devices. Yet, following Klüver, the goal was not to dismantle Pepsi's public identity but, rather, to reinscribe a corporate message of engagement within forms of experimental electronic sound performance that would simultaneously resist the direct communicative imperatives of public relations and advertising.

Recalling the theme of conflict raised by the "Esthetics" conference, the conflict that could be found here was located within this double stance and the indeterminacy of such concepts and their related terminology. Notions of engagement, interaction, and immersion become the activators of the *Pavilion* and the counter-logic to the Osaka World Exposition that motivated the project conceptually, socially, and aesthetically. Yet, at the same time, they remained the anodyne descriptors of a comfortable corporate wish for public involvement.

A related ambiguity colors the *Pavilion's* aluminum-coated bubble itself. If E.A.T. intended to subvert the rules of engagement of the exposition, its inflatable similarly offered a deviation within Osaka's pneumatic landscape. The apotheosis of inflatables, the Osaka fair trembled with a ubiquitous soft pneumatic architecture supported by positive air pressure. But, taking a different pneumatic approach, the *Pavilion's* reflective skin was secured by a perimeter vacuum of negative pressure, replacing the animated, gasping volatility of conventional inflatable structures with the inert silence of a vacuum that assured optical precision.

[Figure 4]

[Figure 5]

コシノ・ジユンコ女史のデザインになるペプシ館ホステスのユニフオーム。

[Figure 6]

While this pneumatic mutation may have been driven by technical exigencies, the result placed the E.A.T. inflatable at the uneasy encounter between two distinct economies of experimentation and social action. The first tests for the *Pavilion's* inflatable dome were conducted on a soundstage at MGM studios in Los Angeles. The prototype was fabricated by the architectural collective Envirolab. However, anxious that the junior office could not achieve the optical standards required, Klüver shifted production to the firm G.T. Schlajdehal, a military contractor and manufacturer of the inflatable PAGEOS (Passive Geodetic Earth Orbiting Satellite) satellite. The E.A.T. bubble then not only inverted the pneumatic logic of air pressure, but at the same time redirected the recent lineage and cultural encoding of the inflatable. On the West Coast of 1960s America, despite their early military origins, inflatables were most firmly identified with a collectivist ethos and with notions of a counter-cultural nomadism. With E.A.T.'s dome, the terms of experimentation shift from those practices at the advanced edge of the profession and its political registers, to the terrain of product development and technical objects.

A further complication of the status of the inflatable dome suggests a link between the disorientation of perception and electronic transmission. Klüver and E.A.T. co-founder Robert Rauschenberg commonly referred to the *Pavilion* as an "invisible environment," a phrase that echoes the title of Marshall McLuhan's essay, "The Invisible Environment: The Future of an Erosion." The invisible environment McLuhan is famously addressing is televisual. Undetected, he claims, its electromagnetic conditioning and manipulation of sensory thresholds alters behavior, cognitive processes, and "the outlook and experience of a whole society."[13]

Absent film, multi-screen projection, or video, the immersion within the Pepsi pavilion's spectral hallucinations was optically and technically distinct from the perceptual saturation of late-1960s visual media and television environments. Yet, the interior of the *Pavilion* was, at least materially, the interior of a satellite: reflective, optically enclosed, but calling up the network of message relays, airspaces, and electromagnetic territories that preoccupied McLuhan. If this televisual inscription seems tendentious, or merely an accidental remainder of its fabrication, this would not discredit its acuity for Klüver. Shortly after the Osaka project had opened, he offered E.A.T.'s services to the Space Research Institute at the University of Tokyo, referring to the *Pavilion* as evidence of E.A.T.'s expertise with inflatable relay antennae and telecommunications satellites.[14]

Nor is it surprising that Klüver would be considering the televisual dimensions and possibilities of the Osaka project. Concurrent with the Osaka Exposition, E.A.T. had initiated a series of alternative broadcasting ventures in which artists would provide television program content, aligning E.A.T.'s appropriation of television with its earlier experiments connecting artists to mechanical and electronic technologies, and placing E.A.T. in dialogue with a range of video and TV practices, from Raindance Collective to TVTV and Videofreex.[15] At the same time, in light of the possibilities television suggested, E.A.T.'s TV mission bifurcated. Along with its more familiar artist collaborations, Klüver envisioned a different developmental role for E.A.T. Competing most intensely for Klüver's attention during the design of *Pavilion* were E.A.T.'s efforts on the Anand Project, an educational broadcast network for rural India. In its educational service mode, E.A.T. was looking past engagement with artists' projects, as represented by E.A.T.'s earlier experiments with video relays, the *E.A.T. Cookbook,* or exhibitions by others, such as the seminal 1968 exhibition, *TV as Creative Medium,* at the Howard Wise Gallery, in New York. Instead, the collective searched for models in the proposed public educational television network for El Salvador and in the Children's Television Workshop, the production company that conceived and produced *Sesame Street* with research funds from the U.S. Government and the Ford Foundation. In these models, as for E.A.T's Anand Project, the televisually impoverished and the underdeveloped were overlaid and read as isomophoric. Collectively, these projects seem to translate McLuhan's assertion that the "environment is a teaching machine made of electric information," into literal pedagogical precepts.[16] For example, the directors of the Children's Television Workshop suggested that "basic concepts of number and shape," taught through the television environment, "would close the gap between disadvantaged and middle class children."[17]

This correlation among television, education, perceptual engagement, and impoverishment registers in a series of E.A.T. projects and proposals from the same period. In his "Outline for Article On The Role of The New Technology In The Ghetto," to cite one example, Klüver argues that the provision of local TV antennae, signal amplifiers, and a network of closed-circuit televisions, with a camera in each apartment, would lead to new forms of education and literacy as well as to accelerated social and technical involvement. Moreover, such involvement would allow the "street intelligentsia" to be saved from "deterioration" and would provide an alternative to "political extremism." Finally, Klüver adds, "The ghetto represents a model for less developed nations."[18] This range of E.A.T. proposals postulated a coordination between new channels of communication and development for the politically, financially, and technically underserved regions of cities and nations, while cementing a relationship between perceptual integration through technology and political integration through the possibility of televisual instruction.

While arguments for global development through telecommunications and advanced technology were hardly unfamiliar in the late '60s—one only has to think of R. Buckminster Fuller and Stewart Brand, among many others—Klüver's placement of the political, economic, and technical under the authority of aesthetics seems ever more striking in this context. One could even say this compels us to reconsider what aesthetics is, or how it appeared for Klüver and E.A.T. at this moment, and in the *Pavilion*. The formulation that "everything looked beautiful" might not get close enough. Indeed, a better guide may be Klüver's dissection of the astigmatic optics, the confusion of real and virtual image, and the implications for engagement.

At the very least, it is at this juncture of aesthetic bias, technologies of engagement, and modes of instruction that the *Pavilion* represented a more dire crisis for E.A.T. It was perhaps less consequential that Pepsi rejected as too obscure E.A.T.'s programming and electronic sound environment than it was that the pavilion seemed unable to involve visitors as anticipated. If the *Pavilion* was meant to liberate visitors by dislocating perception from managed experience, to open up new forms of interaction, and to hint at an immersive mode of perceptual instruction distinct from the narrative didactic model of fair exposition, the population of Expo attendees seemed unprepared for this option. This is evident from the following excerpt of an awkwardly translated, unidentified review in a Japanese magazine:

> Pepsi Pavilion which is located near Expo Land is entirely uninteresting. The visitor receives a small handset like a telephone receiver at the entrance. Upon leaving the tunnel the visitor enters empty Dome Room. He hears music by the handset. The pavilion was announced like the following: Many new possible experiences for the visitors themselves in Pavilion. But visitors went out quickly without showing any interest. In the evening, they have few visitors. And only the extremely short skirts of the hostesses attract our attention, which was designed by Junko Hoshino. The reputation is worst of all pavilions.[19]

Questions of engagement through immersion also troubled the televisual operations that E.A.T. was engaging by 1970. Implicated in this pursuit were not only the conditioning effects of the invisible environment, but also related issues of global imbalances, technologies of distribution, as well as an array of other economic, political, and cultural conflicts inscribed within the aesthetic biases of television and its open-ended environment. If these questions registered through E.A.T.'s conception of education and informational imbalance in proposals such as the Anand Project, a further attenuation of E.A.T.'s televisual engagement could be found on New York's Upper East Side, where, in 1970, the American Foundation on Automation and Employment had established *Automation House* as a center for collective bargaining and job training, and as a forum in which, "social and political issues would be thrashed out, recorded and broadcast."[20]

Original plans for *Automation House* called for the insertion of an elaborate technical armature. An electronic receptionist would greet visitors, after which projections and screens would offer them directions, information, or distraction, delivered via ever-changing floor patterns. In its auditorium, all walls would also receive projections, and seats would rotate, enabling visitors to turn freely to more easily view the images and information surrounding them. An array of television cameras would pan and tilt, allowing events to be recorded for projection and playback in other rooms. "A visitor," the author of the plan explains, "would distinctly realize that his mental processes must be accelerated," and "that large demands are being placed on his senses."[21] *Automation House* was a total instructive media environment in which visitors, perhaps workers with jobs rendered insecure by automation, would be exposed to the latest audiovisual teaching devices. Mediatized demand on the senses mapped directly onto perpetually heightened perceptual engagement and accelerated education. In this space, television was archival system, feedback loop, and transforming agent of work and perception, automating not labor, but the reception and absorption of information as a form of instructional conditioning.

Perhaps not surprisingly, *Automation House* was also the site of E.A.T.'s new offices and the setting for several new E.A.T initiatives. Early plans suggested a further complicity between instruction and aesthetics. The brief for *Automation House* announces that, "the technical equipment lent to artists aligned with E.A.T. would make it the finest living and kinetic art gallery in the world."[22] While *Automation House* would assume an active role for E.A.T.'s Projects Outside Art, I mention it here more to suggest that even if it provides a model of the densely mediatized image environment that the *Pavilion* appeared to distance itself from, it also hints at a pervasive educative undercurrent that also figured in E.A.T.'s conception of perceptual engagement.

In his "A Genealogy of Video," Paul Ryan, video artist and theorist, uses "surface" and "system" to distinguish early practices of video activism that infiltrated or dislocated the conventional broadcast apparatus from those practices that directly manipulated television images, sequences, and temporalities.[23] Viewed globally, E.A.T.'s televisual bifurcation, its doubled television aesthetics, straddles both sides of Ryan's schema. And while, at first view, the Pepsi pavilion appears to take another stance, refusing an explicit relation to the systems and surface of Ryan's description, something of both surface and system and something of E.A.T.'s televisual preoccupations seem to leak back into it. Not only did Klüver read the network of television distribution and its telecommunications relays inscribed within the skin of the inflatable, the confusion of real and virtual bodies appears as a peculiar analog to the simulacral terrain of televisual space, and as a parade of ghostly apparitions that recall the hazy and absorbing image of McLuhan's low-resolution, coldly mediatized television set.

As do the *Pavilion's* spectral bodies, the aesthetic biases of the *Pavilion* seem to refract and multiply— from the optics of beautiful reflections and astigmatic vision to engagement, immersion, and televisual transduction. Klüver's formulation that the *Pavilion* would be a device for "non-ordinary human perception" may have been its undoing for Pepsi and fair attendees, eager for more ordinary perception and absorption. Though Klüver dismisses such complaints as merely disguised aesthetic bias, his insight that this bias is encumbered by conflict and a range of economic, technical, and political filters suggests another type of refraction, and a messier transduction, in which corporate communications might not easily translate into experimental practices and back again. What might have looked like nothing, or emptiness, or the consequence of giving too much license to the *Pavilion's* artists, was itself the refraction of the modes of perceptual engagement and instruction that infiltrated E.A.T. and its emerging TV aesthetics. This emptiness, surprisingly saturated with communicative effects, calls up the shift from objects to functions that Klüver had identified as well as real and virtual economies, real and virtual notions of educational asymmetry and instruction, uneven modes of production, concomitant notions of global development, and a vertigo of conflicts, communicative impasses, and signal noise.

[Figure 7]

[Figure 8]

[1] Billy Klüver, "Photographic Recording of Some Optical Effects," in *Pavilion,* eds. Billy Klüver, Julie Martin, Barbara Rose (New York: E.P. Dutton, 1972), 247.

[2] Billy Klüver, "The Pavilion," in *Pavilion,* eds. Billy Klüver, Julie Martin, Barbara Rose (New York: E.P. Dutton, 1972), x.

[3] *E.A.T. News,* Vol. 1, No. 2 (1967), 4.

[4] Billy Klüver, typed notes for *E.A.T. News,* Experiments in Art and Technology Records, 1966–1993, Special Collections, The Getty Research Institute, Los Angeles.

[5] Typed notes for *E.A.T. Activities Report,* Experiments in Art and Technology Records, 1966–1993, Special Collections, The Getty Research Institute, Los Angeles.

[6] Calvin Tomkins, "Outside Art," in *Pavilion,* eds. Billy Klüver, Julie Martin, Barbara Rose (New York: E.P. Dutton, 1972), 107.

[7] Elsa Garmire, "An Overview," in *Pavilion,* eds. Billy Klüver, Julie Martin, Barbara Rose (New York: E.P. Dutton, 1972), 174.

[8] Typed description of the *Pavilion,* Experiments in Art and Technology Records, 1966–1993, Special Collections, The Getty Research Institute, Los Angeles.

[9] Gene Youngblood, "The Open Empire," *Studio International,* vol. 179, no. 921 (April 1970), 178.

[10] Typed announcement for *Esthetics* conference, June 10, 1970. Experiments in Art and Technology Records, 1966–1993, Special Collections, The Getty Research Institute, Los Angeles.

[11] John Pearce, "An Architect's View," in *Pavilion,* eds. Billy Klüver, Julie Martin, Barbara Rose (New York: E.P. Dutton, 1972), 256.

[12] *Draft Statement on Descriptive Trip Through the Pavilion,* Experiments in Art and Technology Records, 1966–1993, Special Collections, The Getty Research Institute, Los Angeles.

[13] Marshall McLuhan, "The Invisible Environment: The Future of an Erosion," *Perspecta 11,* Vol. 11, (1967), 166.

[14] Letter from Billy Klüver to Dr. Minora Oda, Space Research Institute, University of Tokyo, April 10, 1970. Experiments in Art and Technology Records, 1966–1993, Special Collections, The Getty Research Institute, Los Angeles.

[15] A proposal by artists Ed Ruscha and Mason Williams, for the *E.A.T. Cookbook,* a program E.A.T. conceived as the vehicle for artists' television projects, offers insight into the format Klüver imagined: "A movie filmed entirely in a car in which a girl would pick up a hitch-hiker and talks non-stop to him on subjects such as politics, earthquakes, pollution, etc. The content would be factual and humorous."

[16] Marshall McLuhan, "The Invisible Environment: The Future of an Erosion," 164.

[17] The Mayor's Advisory Task Force on CATV and Telecommunications, *A Report on Cable Television and Cable Telecommunications in New York City* (New York, 1968), 2.

[18] Billy Klüver, *Outline for Article On The Role of The New Technology In The Ghetto.* Experiments in Art and Technology Records, 1966–1993, Special Collections, The Getty Research Institute, Los Angeles.

[19] Typed translation of unidentified review of the *Pavilion* from a "Japanese magazine." Experiments in Art and Technology Records, 1966–1993, Special Collections, The Getty Research Institute, Los Angeles.

[20] Letter from Theodore Kheel, *Automation House* president, to architect Thomas Lehrecke, describing programming requirements of *Automation House,* August 13, 1968. Experiments in Art and Technology Records, 1966–1993, Special Collections, The Getty Research Institute, Los Angeles.

[21] *Communications and Information Systems Description.* Experiments in Art and Technology Records, 1966–1993, Special Collections, The Getty Research Institute, Los Angeles, 5.

[22] Ibid., 13.

[23] Paul Ryan, "A Genealogy of Video," *Leonardo* Vol. 21, no.1 (1988), 40.

Public
Encounters

Theo Crosby's Environment Games, 1956–1973

Simon Sadler

Curating Conflicts of Interest

The central figure of my essay is Theo Crosby. He is at once well known to us, and yet barely known to us at all. He is known to us as the co-founder of the celebrated Pentagram design consultancy, which produced the poster for the Yale symposium; he is known to us as the technical editor of *Architectural Design* magazine from 1953 to 1962 during its transformation, under Monica Pidgeon, into one of the most progressive forums in the world; and as a formidable architectural impresario in postwar London. Some may even know him as a creator of the revived Globe Theatre in London. But when I mentioned to an eminent UK colleague that I'd decided to tackle Crosby for this symposium, my colleague told me he'd just disposed of one of Crosby's diminutive books to make more space on his shelf. Such was my colleague's sense of Crosby's contribution. He asked me whether my interest in Crosby represented a change of heart about a figure over which I'd expressed righteous indignation following his question-able 1990s alterations to the Barbican Centre in London. As an architect, I now recall, Crosby struck me as a dilettante: he was driven, but he completed no solo major building project.[1]

Crosby appeared, instead—even according to one of his admirers—to be a "mother hen,"[2] busying himself with the postwar vanguard art and architecture scene in London, which is the main subject of this essay. I wonder, though, whether Crosby was more than a mother hen figure. Crosby's curatorship of a series of key exhibitions from the mid-1950s to the early 1970s was, rather, an act of stealth archi-tecture, I'll argue here. Beyond being a canny editor or enthusiast, Crosby was an architect-curator who elevated curatorship to the level of modernist heroism in an era which, he seems to have intuited, was edging beyond modernist heroism into what we would now recognize as postmodern quietism. Sensing the imminent loss of a unifying project in the arts, and at the same time the opportunity which that presented for a stimulating pluralism, his exhibitions tried to imagine future communities without identity—communities of creators and audiences that did not depend on core affinity. Community would be instead played out through unavoidable conflicts of interest.[3]

The "Pessimist Utopia"

This is the ethos represented formally and ideologically in his exhibitions, and never more clearly than in his final major show, *How to Play the Environment Game* of 1973 [Figure 1]. We might not know this, though, since the show is as overlooked as its author, it would seem: London's Hayward Gallery, which hosted the *Environment Game* before it went on a national tour, can today find no installation shots of it, an anomaly which the archivists are at a loss to explain. Certainly the show appears dowdy compared to the thrilling vanguardism of its forerunners, *This is Tomorrow,* and *The Living City,* which Crosby curated in 1956 and

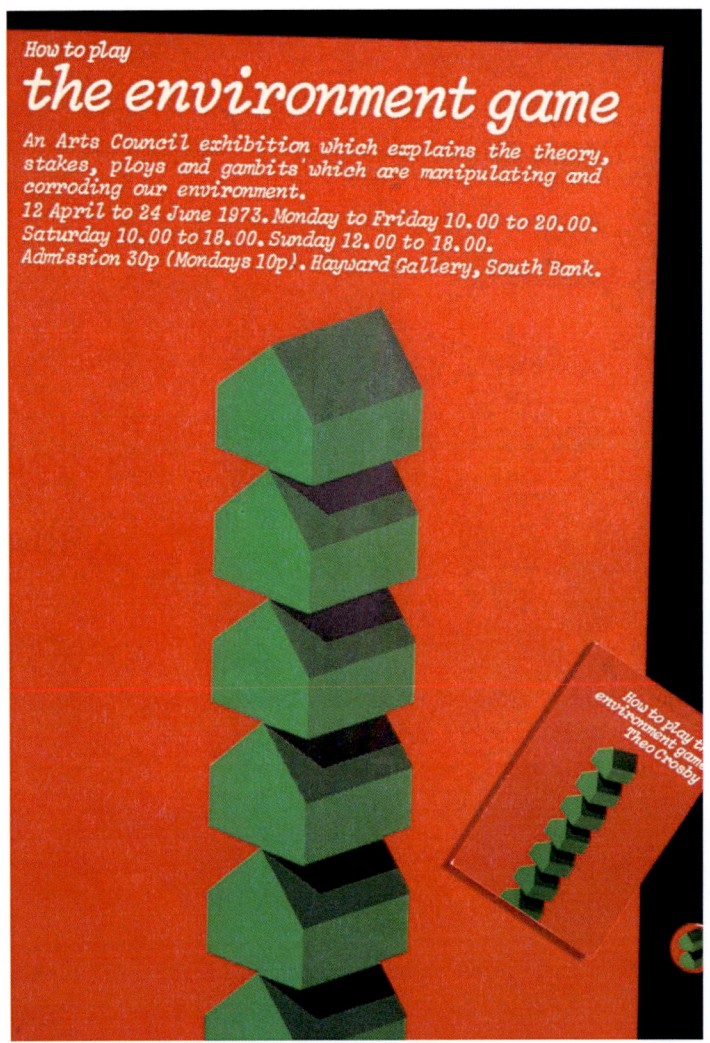

[Figure 1]

1963, respectively. The *Environment Game* might be a forgettable turn away from vanguardism, though I see it more as the confirmation of Crosby's long-running program of depicting communities as though caught in a perpetual "environment game."[4]

In the *Environment Game,* Crosby presents a methodical guide to the interacting forces that make the built environment—design, capital, planning, technology, history [Figure 2]. As though in a very good undergraduate course with exceptional visiting speakers—like Joseph Rykwert, Andrea Branzi, Peter Cook, and former government minister Lord Kennet, who provide texts and panels for the exhibition and accompanying book—Crosby explains the Modern Movement alongside the forces arrayed *against* its transformative ambition. At one level it's a typical early 1970s lament for the loss of modernism—his job, Crosby once said, was "clearing up the mess after the Modern Movement,"[5] an assignment which would include, in this case, giving the eulogy for Archigram, the legendary vanguard group which he had helped launch with the *Living City* exhibition ten years earlier. Indeed, the *Environment Game* is a gateway to postmodernism in so far as it announces the loss of a planned or unitary future. Whereas 4,750 visitors per week[6] crammed into the confines of the Whitechapel Gallery in the fall of 1956 to find out what *Tomorrow* looked like, only 500–600 visitors per week came to the expanses of the Hayward Gallery in 1973, where Crosby withdrew any fixed image of the future.

Crosby replaced architectural projection with a projection of the visitor herself or himself, as an advocate, campaigner, complainant—as an interventionist or cultural entrepreneur much like Crosby himself. Crosby called now for the "pessimist utopia," which he outlined as "the possibility of regeneration through social and administrative means rather than construction."[7] The "pessimist utopia" pursued consultation, land use and building controls, preservation, generous building budgets, open space, public transport, human scale, and a sense of ownership.

The "Joint Work" After Modernism

In other words, Crosby was seeking the mechanism for the resolution of environmental conflicts of interest. His laundry list for the pessimist utopia actually sounds a lot like the environmental governmentality of the welfare state, which provided the postwar consensus upon which British architecture was based, and which had its founding and popular image in the 1951 Festival of Britain. But Crosby was attentive to another emerging consensus point of view: that the architecture of the welfare state was by and large homogenizing, and instituted top-down. All three exhibitions under review in this essay—*This is Tomorrow,* the *Living City,* and the *Environment Game*—instead offered bottom-up pluralism.

Thus, the pessimist utopia of 1973 was completely consistent with a core curatorial ethos that had carried Crosby through the 1950s and 1960s. What *changes* for each show are the immediate trends in art and architecture circulating through Crosby's immediate circle. In 1956, Crosby's friends in the Independent Group meetings at the Institute of Contemporary Arts (including his flatmates Alison and Peter Smithson)[8] provided the most exciting installations at *This is Tomorrow.* In 1963, the curious group of architects that Crosby was managing in an office at Taylor Woodrow Construction assembled the *Living City* and soon became known as the Archigram group. By 1973, Crosby understood that the action was moving to community activism. Regardless of these changing trends, though, Crosby's utopia is consistently pessimistic across all three shows—pessimistic in the sense that there is no single core image, nor mandate, nor style, nor ethos, nor technique, nor object—while remaining utopian nonetheless: there will be a future, each show decrees, and it will be jointly constructed, and the exhibition is its rallying cry and organizational tool. And architecture—as spectral as it is in all the exhibitions—is the *thing,* the "matter of concern," the metaphor and synecdoche, that organizes and articulates and processes the pessimist utopia, bottom-up.

One might dispute that my emphasis on ideological continuity suppresses the formal differences and changing visitor experiences between the shows and, by extension, the fluctuating architectural futures they project. The switch from techno-utopianism to historicist-utopianism is certainly dramatic when the

Living City and *Environment Game* are considered side by side. In fact, in 1963, the same year that he curated the *Living City* in London, Crosby traveled to New York to meet the woman he described as "a prophet of sanity,"[9] Jane Jacobs. A decade later and his pessimist utopia is aggressively preservationist—"Accept and delight in the past for its disruptive, its poetic, role in the present," he asks, as he promotes the place-making of unique urban identities and the training of a new generation of public artists.[10] We can without exaggeration say that Crosby's hope was that the metaphorical making of cathedrals, in the sense once understood by the Arts and Crafts and the early Bauhaus, are still possible after the decline in the prestige of single-agenda, manifesto-driven modernisms. Crosby comments at the *Environment Game* in 1973 that "The madness that once built cathedrals lingers on only in the architect,"[11] and he pleads the case for public art and sculptural enrichment of architecture in an era lost to industrial culture.

But then this sentiment oddly resonates with Lawrence Alloway's introduction to *This is Tomorrow* in 1956. *"This Is Tomorrow,"* announced Alloway some seventeen years before the *Environment Game,* "is an exhibition to prove a point. Leading British artists and architects of the younger generation have pooled their talents to prove that the ability of painters, sculptors, architects and designers to work harmoniously together did not die out with the cathedral builders or the Georgian interior decorators . . . but is flourishing still."[12] The style employed—be it techno-utopian or historicist-utopian—is wholly subsidiary to the Crosbian ambition to resurrect traditional relations of urban production, relations which are being reinvented at the exhibitions. Moreover, these relations answer the question of how to build the cathedral of the future, *bottom-up*—without the divine God of the medieval cathedral, without the metaphysical god of the modernist grid, without the demi-god of the welfare state planner or director.

We can count three key ways that these exhibitions spirit up the immanent god of the joint work to dictate their physical form. The first is through their encouragement of "guild-like" collaborations and alliances. *This is Tomorrow* marshals thirty-eight participants into twelve collaborative clusters, each teaming an architect with colleagues from art, design, and criticism. *Living City* brings together the future Archigram team around the immediate practical problem of assembling the complex, crumpled-geodesic structure that houses the exhibition: "We learned to weld," Archigram's Peter Cook would recall of the experience, "we learned to glue, we learned to fix switches."[13]

Note here Cook's memory of *making* things, of craft, which was the second way in which the exhibitions encouraged the spirit of cathedral building in the very age of repetitive, standardized, and prefabricated built production which the *Living City* was optimistically exploring. From 1947 to 1958 Crosby spent his evenings studying sculpture at the Central School of Arts,[14] where he met several of the artists that took part in *This is Tomorrow.* An insistence on faktura, so obvious in, say, Group 8's cylinder-and-cross structure at *This is Tomorrow* (by James Stirling, Michael Pine, and Richard Matthews) extends even to the anonymity of the *Environment Game,* where the bland panels, apparently subcontracted by Crosby to the commercial vendor Aerofilms, are tied together by neat elastic joints, which serve as the mark of the architect's craft and are obsessively detailed in Crosby's archive [Figure 4].

All Crosby's exhibitions thus preview the revival of a dialectics of making—dialectics between artists and architects, ornament and structure, serial production, and craft. Crosby positions Group 1 of *This is Tomorrow*—when he teams up with William Turnbull, Edward Wright, and Germano Facetti—as the entry and exit to the exhibition, because "by using simply and directly certain materials which we consider constituent elements in current production" visitors would then be introduced to the idea that the built environment is the result of permutation—as much serendipitous as planned—that becomes the cathedral-like sum greater than its parts. By the time he curates the *Environment Game,* Crosby is presenting little more than a stock-taking, an inventory of environmental components.

That public dialectic of making—through guild-like organization, faktura, and permutations—asserts the third consistency of Crosby's shows, which is the group construction of meaning. The exhibitions are insistently colloquial and dialectical—between participants in the shows, and between participants and their public. *This is Tomorrow* drew on information theory, *Living City* on existentialism, and

[Figure 2]

[Figure 3]

[Figure 4]

the *Environment Game* on game theory, to explain how environmental meanings and messages are formed without recourse to a single author. The looping of information structured the shows. *This is Tomorrow* arranged its sections in a circuit of competing dioramas. *Living City's* existential thematic sections morphed into so-called "gloops." The *Environment Game* assumed the form of an unfolded dossier. We might think of the shows as miniature cities—explicitly in *Living City's* effects of urban simulation, more metaphorically in *This is Tomorrow,* where the arrangement of the participants into little "neighborhoods" reconciled the pluralism of British modernism following the collapse of the unitary aesthetics sought in the grids of the MARS group (the English section of the Congrès Internationaux d'Architecture Moderne (CIAM)) and in the picturesque of the Festival of Britain. Both the grid and the picturesque can be detected in *This is Tomorrow,* but the show as a whole adheres to neither. It instead promotes a workshop format to which new tendencies can be invited, most notoriously Pop.[15]

This collegial quality again has the effect of summoning the god of community, training its visitors to look, to think, to question, to complete the shows' communicative loops, and then to continue the work instigated by the exhibitions into the making of the city beyond: London in the first place, but also the provincial cities to which the *Living City* and the *Environment Game* were dispatched. The *Environment Game* ended with checklists of community organizations beseeching its visitors to become urban activists. *This is Tomorrow's* Group 12 guarded against the risks of sterile "learned responses" promoted by the expand-ing regime of contemporary communications, expounding instead the model of the "tackboard"—"a convenient method of organizing the modern visual continuum according to each individual's decision." The mission was to instigate a general and, above all, *indeterminate* urban democratic surround:[16] to turn the once dreamy daytrippers of the Festival of Britain into the mature political and consumer players of the environment game.

Exhibiting the Paradox of Architecture

The exhibition format meant that the architect-curator did not have to surrender his influence over architecture's "Others" that are ever lodged in the vernacular, in the economy, in information [Figure 3]. These factors external to design were instead made into allies, folded into the very understanding of what architecture is, expanding architecture's reach, through assertively popular and accessible exhibitions, into a totality that was otherwise ever further from the architect's grasp—ever receding from the optimistic utopias of MARS and the Festival of Britain. Through curatorship, Crosby was able to retain the authority of Le Corbusier's hovering hand (I am thinking of the famous 1925 photograph of the Plan Voisin model), even though Crosby had no model at which to point—only tackboards, effects, collages, inventories, history lessons.

But this hunting for the communal center, as capitalism is unleashed in the late 1970s from the rela-tive constraints of the planned mixed economy and welfare state, drags Crosby's project ideologically ever rightwards. His attempt to forge a metaphoric Arts and Crafts in the 1950s and 1960s succumbs to an almost literal Arts and Crafts project in the 1970s and 1980s, leading to his controversial 1990–1993 tenure as professor at the Royal College of Art (previewed, appropriately enough, in his 1976 Lethaby lecture at the college),[17] and to his retention as an architectural advisor to Prince Charles. Crosby's pessimist utopia evolves during its ascent to power—from the margins of the Whitechapel Gallery to the centrality of the Hayward Gallery and then membership of Prince Charles' retinue. An archaic guild culture would merge into a Thatcherite enterprise culture. The community, which Crosby in 1973 wanted to see expand into a general environment, is condensing by 1974 into the charming microcosm of his Globe Theatre project, which Crosby initially assigned, remarkably, to Archigram's Ron Herron.

My finding is that Crosby starts out with the supposition that architecture is a kind of paradox, in its bid to unify totality without suppressing its constituent parts and actors, and that Crosby simply found ways of *exhibiting* that paradox: not so as to debunk architecture, but to make it into a means of interpreting the present and projecting a communal future.

[1] Peter Rawstorne, "Obituary: Professor Theo Crosby," *The Independent,* Thursday, 15 September 1994.

[2] Rawstorne, *op. cit.*

[3] Alan Powers, "Crosby, Theo (1925–1994)," *Oxford Dictionary of National Biography,* Oxford University Press (September 2011). [http://www.oxforddnb.com/view/article/54828, accessed 16 July 2013].

[4] Theo Crosby, *How to Play the Environment Game* (Harmondsworth: Arts Council of Great Britain and Penguin, 1973), 7.

[5] Powers, *op. cit.,* quoting *The Architects' Journal,* 204, 1996, 26.

[6] Total attendance of *This is Tomorrow* was c. 19,000, which would equate to c. 4,750 per week during the four weeks the exhibition was open (August 9–September 9). Source: Florence Ostende, ed., document compiled to support the lecture "This is Tomorrow," by James Lingwood, at the Museu d'Art Contemporani de Barcelona, October 19. 2009.

[7] Crosby, *op. cit.,* 64.

[8] Crosby and the Smithsons were flatmates in Doughty Street sometime in the late 1940s–early 1950s. See Powers, *op. cit.*

[9] Crosby, *op. cit.,* 64.

[10] Crosby, *op. cit.,* 86.

[11] Crosby, *op. cit.,* 239.

[12] Lawrence Alloway. "This is Tomorrow: At the Whitechapel Art Gallery, August 9–September 9, 1956" (press release for the exhibition), in Bruce Altshuler, ed., *Salon to Biennial: Exhibitions That Made Art History,* Vol. 1, 1863–1959 (New York: Phaidon Press, 2008) 366, and quoted in Ostende, *op. cit.* For a call for the unification of the arts echoing Alloway and Crosby, see too David Lewis, "Introduction 3," in *This is Tomorrow,* exhibition catalog (London: Whitechapel Art Gallery, 1956), n.p.

[13] Peter Cook, "A Quickstart Introduction to the Archigram Group," in Archigram, ed., *A Guide to Archigram 1961–74* (London: Academy, 1994, 6–11), 10. Dennis Crompton writes in an e-mail to the author, 19 September 2013, that "The process after those early sketches by Peter and the lot of us talking about how to make it happen was that I made that wire-frame model so that the whole construction was based on two standard triangles. One equilateral and the other a 90-degree one with sides based on the measurements of the other one. At the time we were working with Theo on the Euston Station project (unbuilt, what is there was by others, but that is another story!). Our offices were in the old Euston hotel so there was lots of work space for us to use in the evenings. The frames were made out of standard electrical conduit which I welded together. Meanwhile the others were cutting the fiber board infill panels and papering both sides before adding the collages (some at Euston and the rest at the ICA)."

[14] See Powers, *op. cit.*

[15] Group 12 referred to their piece as their "stand," as though it was an exhibit at a trade show or supermarket, in pointed contrast to the high modernism of Groups 5, 7, 9, 10, and 11. The "neighborhood" model, combining pluralism within a unitary whole, might be compared to the first published Situationist map, also 1956, which depicted the city as both unitary and split.

[16] Compare with Karl Popper's vision of the "open society," an influential evolutionary model of social democracy promoted from the London School of Economics. Compare too with Fred Turner's description of the "democratic surround" of postwar U.S. liberalism in exhibitions like *Family of Man:* see *The Democratic Surround: Multimedia and American Liberalism from World War II to the Psychedelic Sixties* (Chicago: University of Chicago Press, 2013).

[17] The Lethaby Lecture was published as Theo Crosby, *The Pessimist Utopia* (London: Pentagram, 1976).

The Contested Subject: The *Greater Number* at the 1968 XIV Triennale of Milano

Federica Vannucchi

More than architectural photographs, models, interiors and buildings, the XIV Triennale of Milan, held in 1968, exhibited an ideological construct. Its curator, architect Giancarlo De Carlo, dedicated the venue to the *Grande Numero* (Greater Number). Based on a concept first introduced by Michel Écochard while he was Director of Public Works in Morocco, *Le plus grand nombre* (The Greatest Number) represented the promise of solving the disorderly—anarchic, in Écochard's words—growth of North African cities by using modern construction methods to house the growing population.[1] Presented in the 1953 Congrès International d'Architecture Moderne (CIAM) meeting at Aix-en-Provence by ATBAT-Afrique (the African branch of Atelier des Bâtisseurs), *habitat pour le plus grand nombre* (habitat for the greatest number) became central to the housing problem throughout the Team 10 discussions.[2]

From that point on, De Carlo slowly transformed *Le plus grand nombre* into a personalized conception. As a side effect of a broadening mass production, De Carlo's greater number insisted on the need to enlarge the number of individuals participating in the decision making regarding the built environment. But, besides its architectural translation, De Carlo's conception voiced a political vision: that of opening the governmental arena to a greater number of individuals and their divergent positions. This process would eventually challenge the very principle of parliamentary democracy—the delegation of sovereignty to representatives.[3] Following his anarchist convictions, for De Carlo the dialogical process leading to decisions of public interest was in fact central to the personal evolution of the individuals both participating in and affected by those resolutions.[4] And yet, within the Triennale exhibition complex, how could the opening of the governmental arena to the greater number of individuals—De Carlo's ideological drive—be communicated?

De Carlo was assertive about the relationship between architecture and ideology. He stated that architects should design following their "ideological background," that was "the moral, political, rational, utopian pattern from which we derive both theoretical directives and architectural forms."[5] Yet, "ideology" was certainly a multifaceted, historically charged, and at times abused term at the end of the 1960s in Italy. When the Triennale finally opened to the public on May 30th, 1968, the unexpected happened [Figure 1]. The exhibition was contested by a group of students criticizing—rather than prizing—the Triennale for being an ideological product: it was the compensatory outcome of an intellectual class unable to come to terms with its ineffectiveness.[6] After erupting in the Palazzo dell'Arte, the students formed an assembly and declared their occupation of the Triennale. De Carlo asked the assembly to perform the role of the Study Center, the committee dedicated to the Triennale organization and headed by De Carlo himself. The Milanese architect wanted the students' assembly to "transform the chaotic character of a general dissent in a system of ideological and political choices, whose aim was to formulate a strategy" for the Triennale reformation.[7] For the students, however, enacting the Study Center meant complying with bourgeois false consciousness. Far from finding common agreement, the assembly ultimately did not direct its disparate voices towards a coherent proposition for the institution's renewal.[8]

Through the work on exhibit, De Carlo had purposely aimed to present an array of different voices virtually in dialogue on a single theme: the "greater number." Arata Isozaki, Aldo Van Eyck, Shadrach Woods, the Smithsons, George Nelson, Archigram, György Kepes, and Hans Hollein, among others, expressed their responses to the theme via their installations. But the greater number was first, and most extensively discussed and enacted within the Study Center. Innumerable meetings and exchanges with the invited architects proved how De Carlo's Study Center utilized the Triennale as a sophisticated thinking mechanism for discussing, re-forming, and testing the conception of the chosen theme. The engaged, at times confrontational, exchanges among the members of the Study Center embodied the very inaction of De Carlo's greater number: the forming of a collective voice to discuss differences through an active dialogical participation.

At the same time, those meetings were responsible for the transformation of the theme. During these exchanges, the concept of the greater number registered as a significant mutation from De Carlo's original understanding. Initially, the Study Center discussed the greater number as the massive quantity of objects produced by a consumption-based economy and their inclusion in the human environment. The conception then evolved into the large amount of people affected, and also empowered by the new means of production; and finally the greater number became a methodological tool for processing and controlling large quantitative problems. In its various iterations, De Carlo's aim for collective agency was continually tested. And yet, as exposed in the Triennale's final arrangement, the greater number proved inadequate to offering the students a means to elaborate their collective voice. The Study Center dialogical process was not extended to the students' assembly. After all, the contestation proved the fragility of De Carlo's attempt to transform an ideological predicament into an expositional paradigm.

My essay aims to problematize the use of an exhibition complex—the Triennale—to expose a political vision, that of enlarging the governmental arena to include a greater number of individuals. In this regard, the Triennale's actual display is understood only as the final—albeit most eloquent—phase of a complex institutional apparatus. I will focus specifically on what took place prior to and behind the scenes of the exhibition, the transformation of the "greater number" concept through the Study Center's dialogues. The final aim of this examination is to explain why the dialogical form of the exhibition setting finally failed in the hands of the students' assembly, where it instead might have found its most effective political form; and secondly, to understand how this failure affected the architectural debate at large.

On the evening of March 11th, 1966, members of the Study Center met once more at the Palazzo dell'Arte to discuss the forthcoming XIV Triennale. The Study Center had convened religiously for the last two years, but now was a time of concern. The architects Giancarlo De Carlo, Aldo Rossi, Marco Zanuso, the painter Pasquale Morino, the sculptor Carlos Ramos, and the graphic designer Albe Steiner, together with the committee secretary Tommaso Ferraris, could no longer avoid answering the most urgent question: was the exhibition to be organized around a central theme, or was it meant simply to expose the latest architecture and industrial design products and avoid making any overarching statement?

Behind this question, the Study Center's members expressed radically different understandings of architecture. The discussion unfolded around a disciplinary problem: on one side, architecture was to be understood through its physical manifestations, and through the urban conditions that had converged to create it. On the other side, architecture was comprehended in its projective value, as the answer to current problems, relegating the physical manifestations of architecture from premises to outcomes. The difference was at once methodological and conceptual.

Rossi voiced the first camp. He was opposed to a central theme, which he criticized for being overly abstract. The exhibition should display physical products or reproductions of existing buildings—in his words, *fatti reali* (real facts).[9] From the analysis of "real facts," the exhibition audience would extrapolate architectural problems and solutions. Within this frame, architecture had to be treated autonomously, related to its centuries-long history but not affecting nor affected by the immediate contingency of social relationships. Consistent with his communist affiliation, Rossi extended historical materialism to architectural analysis. Zanuso differed from Rossi's view. He advocated for the adoption of a central theme, which was how large quantities of industrial products had affected the *ambiente umano* (living environment) creating networks of production, accumulation, distribution, and usage. Directly addressing Rossi's concerns, he specified that "a more tight relationship among objects, functions, and environment will allow the architect to overcome the misunderstanding of the autonomous character of the object."[10] In conversation with the CIAM meetings of which he had been a member, "environment" for Zanuso meant a "habitat, a context formed by elements mediating the individual's relationship with the surrounding space."[11] In other words, environment included man-made objects which mediated the relationship between man and space.

Reacting to Zanuso's words, De Carlo stated that the architectural object did not simply affect the abstract, in his view, environment, but the organization of the contested territory, the ground of economic and political disputes.[12] Moreover, De Carlo enlarged the problem from simply being concerned with objects to what he called a "totality." He announced that "the program of the next Triennale could be the architecture for the 'Greater Number.' [...] It is no longer an action towards an object but towards a totality."[13] The XIV Triennale theme was finally conceived.

While the "greater number" was first proposed by De Carlo, it was Zanuso who provoked its discussion. The theme was prompted by Zanuso's understanding of mass production and its effects on the human environment. In the exhibition, the greater number of industrial products—in their potential and problems— was overly represented. The storage system for kitchenware by Libero Greco and Sergio Rizzi summarized the quantitative aspect of mass production and its storage requirements. A similar quantitative argument was expressed by Joe Colombo's mobile bar and Pierluigi Spadolini's *Meeting Point for the Collective* consisting of reflective mirrors.

Equally centered on the greater number of objects, and overtly critical of the standardized repetition it implied, filmmaker Saul Bass and designer Herb Rosenthal exposed rows of drawers [Figure 3]. Emphasizing their obsessive replication, piles of drawers created a narrow, disproportionately tall space where Bass's film, entitled *Thoughts on Creativity,* was projected. Yet, when the viewer opened the

[Figure 1]

[Figure 2]

[Figure 3]

[Figure 4]

[Figure 5]

drawers, he would have found all sorts of different, unexpected contents. As a demand for creativity, Bass and Rosenthal pointed to the individual's need to overcome the flattening effect of mass production.

In the March meeting mentioned above, Zanuso referred to the greater number of industrial products, De Carlo instead referred to a totality—more precisely, to "an action towards a totality." He further explained that:

> By the greater number we mean the contemporary system of human needs which has assumed proportions never before experienced in history. The growth of these proportions is motivated by the propagation of democracy, the dissemination of wealth, the increase of social mobility, the growth of production.[14]

In De Carlo's words, the greater number referred to the ever-growing population who had access to mass production, but also—and equally important—to the increasing number of individuals participating in public decisions, as democratic systems require. However, the greater number was not simply an analytical tool (for instance, descriptive of how mass production had radically changed the urban territory), but also—and especially—a projective model. If mass production had, in fact, witnessed the birth of the greater number of people, De Carlo carefully distinguished the greater number of individuals from mass society. While the society of the masses was a given datum, the participation of the greater number of individuals to the organization of public affairs was a point to be conquered.[15]

Organization was a key concept in De Carlo's understanding of the greater number, which he shared with Team 10 colleague Shadrach Woods. When invited to participate in the Triennale, Woods wrote to De Carlo, exposing his conception of the theme: "Dear Giancarlo, in the two months and a half in which the Triennale will last, the world urban population will grow by approximately nine million."[16] The Triennale organizers cited Woods for his work on organizational systems. The Study Center defined the latter as "organized chaos," urban organization of complex services based on a spatial and temporal flexibility. Together with artist Joachim Pfeufer, Woods designed the installation entitled *Urbanism as Collective Problem*.[17] The installation used a diagrammatic language to express the centrality of organization [Figure 2]. What was to be organized was not merely the matter of the city, but also—and primarily—unquantifiable human actions such as thoughts and stimuli. These, together with space, time, matter, and energy, represented the main objects of organization. These latter categories could be organized to guarantee food, cultivation of the body, control of the environment, and the construction of shelters, but also the more ethereal cultivation of the mind, the practicing of relaxation and fulfillment of self-expression. Moving outwards, the final part of the diagram was dedicated to how different patterns of organization corresponded to different urban structures. In other words, an organizational system produced an urban form.

Woods and Pfeufer's installation provided the closest answer to De Carlo's definition of the architecture for the greater number: "the conception of new typologies and new forms of organization for the human environment."[18] At the same time, it affirmed the ideological understanding of the architecture of the greater number: if architecture consisted of an organizational problem, and forms of social organization were political in nature, then architecture was inherently political.

Mutatis mutandis, the final explanation of the greater number, the one included in the exhibition catalog, acquired a broader, and yet more generic meaning. The greater number had become a methodological process able to quantify large-scale phenomena, as hinted by the selection of the six posters advertising the venue. It was a process aimed to collect, classify, analyze, and interpret phenomena in numerical data. The catalog mentioned Gerolamo Cardano's *Liber de ludo aleae* (Book of Dice for Playing) as the antecedent of modern statistics and Siméon Denis Poisson's *Recherches sur la probabilité des jugements* (Researches on The Probabilities of Judgments) as its first theorization. Poisson, in fact, described his new science in 1838 as the *loi des grands nombres* (the law of great numbers).[19]

However, as an operative system, the greater number was finally utilized as an organizational strategy applied mainly to the exhibition's final presentation, rather than to the architectural problems that the exhibition itself tried to address. The organization of the introductory spaces titled *Errors, Information, and Prospective* exemplified this shift [Figure 4]. The three rooms exposed, respectively, the negative consequences, information, and latest inventions produced by the society of the greater number. The tidily framed and carefully edited tripartite system did not leave space for alternative paths, which had been fundamental to De Carlo's realization of the greater number. The ideological—even militant—tension original to De Carlo's conception had dissolved: the Triennale introductory space looked like a series of controlled vitrines.

The Triennale's evolution into a vitrine was best expressed by De Carlo and film director Marco Bellocchio's room dedicated to the students' uprisings [Figure 5]. As a reproduction of the contestation, rubble occupied the center of the room, and photographs of marching students hung on the walls. Once the Triennale was occupied, this room was finally— and yet ironically—filled with its actors. But in its original idea—in its staged suspension, the absence of action and especially the absence of dialogical confrontations—the space brings to mind Rossi and De Carlo's discussion two years prior. Back to where we started, in the Study Center, Rossi had argued for representing architecture through physical manifestations, while De Carlo supported an exhibition that could enact an ongoing discussion about an architectural conception. The recording of De Carlo's voice in these early meetings proves that the XIV Triennale failed for being unfaithful to its very premise: in the final exhibition, action turned into stillness, into a static representation. Having lost its point of departure, the greater number became an ambiguous statement. Occasionally, the Study Center's debates—the unseen—erupted and became visible in the exhibition. These eruptions, however, were more likely demonstrations of the Study Center's positions, instead of points of interrogation.

Aftermath

After all, the occupation represented a debacle for De Carlo's conception of the *grande numero.* But it also contributed to the escalation of the emerging neo-rational group *Tendenza,* represented in the Milanese context by Aldo Rossi, Massimo Scolari, and Giorgio Grassi. In fact, while Rossi resigned in 1966 from the Study Center due to disagreements with De Carlo, he went on to curate the Architecture-City section in the following 1973 Triennale, advocating for an autonomous language of architecture.[20] After De Carlo's effort, Rossi's Triennale was greeted as a return to order.[21]

1 As explained by Vanessa Grossman, Écochard introduced the term in 1950 while delivering a lecture on the inauguration of the Institut Technique Français du Bâtiment et des Travaux Publics du Maroc, in Michel Écochard, "Urbanisme et construction pour le plus grand nombre, conférence donnée le 10 février 1950 à la Chambre du Commerce et de l'Industrie de Casablanca," *Annales de l'Institut technique du Bâtiment et des Travaux Publics* 148 (1950), 5. Vanessa Grossman, "Michel Écochard and the Invention of the Greatest Number," unpublished. See also, Jean-Louis Cohen and Monique Eleb, *Casablanca: Colonial Myth and Architectural Ventures* (New York: Monacelli Press, 2002); Monique Eleb, "An Alternative Functionalist Universalism: Ecochard, Candilis and ATBAT-Afrique," in *Anxious Modernisms Experimentation in Postwar Architectural Culture,* edited by Sarah Williams Goldhagen and Réjean Legault (Cambridge, MA: MIT Press, 2000), 55-74.

2 At Aix-en-Provence, Victor Bodiansky, Georges Candilis, Michel Écochard, Henri Piot, and Shadrach Woods presented their research in Morocco with the name, "Habitat du plus grand nombre Grid." *Contribution à la Charte de l'Habitat: CIAM 9,* Aix-en-Provence, 19–25 juillet 1953 (Boulogne-sur-Seine: [s.n.], 1953).

3 As De Carlo clearly stated, while commenting on his project for Rimini's new urban plan (1965–69). Giancarlo De Carlo, Special Issue: "Rimini secondo De Carlo," in *Parametro* 39–40 (1975), 50.

4 In his anarchist education, De Carlo cited the importance of figures such as Vernon Richards, Colin Ward, and John Turner but also Peter Kropotkin, Patrick Geddes, Frederick Law Olmsted, and Lewis Mumford. Giancarlo De Carlo and Franco Buncuga (eds.), *Conversazioni con Giancarlo De Carlo: Architettura e libertà,* (Milano: Elèuthera, 2000), 65.

5 Giancarlo De Carlo, "Team 10 Meeting, 25–26 Feb. 67, Parigi," in Max Risselada and Dirk van den Heuvel, *Team 10: 1953–81, in search of a utopia of the present* (Rotterdam: NAi, 2005).

6 In this case, the students used the term ideology as "false consciousness" as described by Marx and Engels in *The German Ideology* and named by Georg Lukács at the beginning of the twentieth century. For the reasons motivating the students' protest against the Triennale, see Carlo Guenzi, *Casabella* 325 (1968) 82–85.

7 "… la chiarezza e la determinazione necessarie a trasformare gli elementi confusi di un dissenso generale, in un sistema di scelte ideologiche e politiche che potesse servire da sostegno a una strategia." [Author's translation] Giancarlo De Carlo, "Una 'scalata' contro la cultura del sistema," L'Unità, June 12, 1968, 8.

8 The students occupied the Triennale until the police's intervention on June 8th. In disagreement with the police action, De Carlo resigned from his position. "La polizia interviene a Milano per sgomberare Triennale e Cattolica," L'Unità, June 9, 1968, 2.

9 Aldo Rossi, "Triennale di Milano, Arch. Aldo Rossi – Schema della relazione per un incontro internazionale discussa con il Centro Studi della Triennale." On 28–29 September 1965, Rossi revealed his program at an international meeting called to define the XIV Triennale's overall organization. Archivio Storico della Triennale di Milano.

10 "Una più stretta relazione fra oggetti, funzioni, e ambiente potrà infine dar luogo al superamento degli equivoci dovuti ad una accentuazione dei caratteri autonomi dell'oggetto." [Author's translation] Marco Zanuso, "Programma per la mostra di industrial design alla Quattordicesima Triennale." Riunione della Commissione di Centri Studi dell'25/2/1966. Archivio Storico della Triennale di Milano.

11 "… habitat, cioè, quel tal contesto di elementi che stabiliscono il rapporto dell'individuo e lo spazio che lo circonda." [Author's translation] Marco Zanuso, Riunione della Commissione di Centri Studi dell'21/3/1966. Archivio Storico della Triennale di Milano.

12 The use of territorio in substitution of ambiente was certainly central to De Carlo's argument. Whereas both indicated an extension beyond the urban delimitations, ambiente held an abstract dimension, whereas territorio was concrete and at the same time implied the question of possession. Simply, the Italian word ambiente derives from the Latin ambiens from the verb ambire: to go around. The Italian territorio instead comes from the Latin territorium: formed above a support, also territor means possessor of land; territorium is formed by terra: land, and –torium which derives from –tor, –torem: which signify "own by an agent." Riunione della Commissione di Centri Studi dell'11/3/1966. Archivio Storico della Triennale di Milano.

13 "… il programma che si potrà trattare alla Triennale è l'architettura per il 'grande numero' … Non è più un'azione rivolta ad un'oggetto, ma a una totalità" [Author's translation] Giancarlo De Carlo, Riunione della Commissione di Centri Studi dell'11/3/1966. Archivio Storico della Triennale di Milano.

14 "Per grande numero si intende il sistema contemporaneo delle esigenze umane che ha assunto ampiezze mai viste nella storia del mondo, in seguito al diffondersi della democrazia, all'espansione del benessere, all'incremento della mobilità sociale, all'accrescimento della produzione." [Author's translation] Giancarlo De Carlo, Verbale della riunione del Consiglio di Amministrazione della Triennale di Milano (31 ottobre 1966). Archivio Storico della Triennale di Milano.

15 "Il problema è quello di sollecitare attività creative anche in quelle classi che finora non erano mai state chiamate a collaborare, particolarmente perchè il problema della massa deve essere sostenuto dalla

consapevolezza e dalla partecipazione del grande numero di persone operanti all'interno della società." [Author's translation] In Verbale della riunione del Consiglio di Amministrazione della Triennale di Milano (3 luglio 1967). Archivio Storico della Triennale di Milano.

16 "Cher Giancarlo, Dans les deux mois et demi que va durer la Triennale la population urbaine mondiale va croître de ca. 9 millions, soit la population de Milano tous les 15 jours. Est-ce intéressant à démontrer, dans l'introduction à l'expo?" [Author's translation] Shadrach Woods to Giancarlo De Carlo, 14 September 1967. Archivio Progetti, Università Iuav di Venezia, Giancarlo De Carlo.

17 For an accurate reconstruction of the Triennale installation, see Paola Nicolin, Castelli di carte: La XIV Triennale di Milano, 1968 (Macerata: Quodlibet Studio, 2011). Also, Paola Nicolin, "Beyond the Failure: Notes on the XIVth Triennale," in Log 13-14 (2008), 87–100.

18 "Si può affermare che la domanda più pressante che la società oggi pone all'architettura e al design sia quella della invenzione di nuove tipologie e nuove forme appropriate alle nuove esigenze organizzative ed espressive dell'ambiente umano? [...] Si può credere che dalla loro capacità di rispondere a questa domanda dipenda l'avvenire dell'architettura e del design come attività strutturali (non accessorie o tributarie o surroganti) nel contesto più generale delle discipline sociali?" [Author's translation] Centro Studi Triennale di Milano, "Linee programmatiche per la Quattordicesima Esposizione redatte dalla Commissione di Centro Studi Giancarlo De Carlo, Pasquale Morino, Carlo Ramos, Alberto Rosselli, Albe Steiner, Marco Zanuso." Triennale Program, November 1966. Archivio Storico della Triennale di Milano.

19 Quattridicesima Triennale di Milano, (Firenze: Centro Di, 1968), 25.

20 Aldo Rossi, letter to the Giunta Esecutiva, 4 July 1967. Archivio Progetti, Università Iuav di Venezia, De Carlo–atti/038.

21 This research started with my first archival visit in the summer of 2009 at the Archivio Storico della Triennale di Milano, and at the Archivio Progetti, Università Iuav di Venezia. I would like to thank the archivists, in particular Tommaso Tofanetti, Claudia Di Martino, and Elvia Redaelli in Milan and Riccardo Domenichini, Rosa Maria Camozzo, and Francesca Sardi in Venice. This essay also benefited from the consultation of Shadrach Woods' papers at Drawings & Archives, Avery Architectural and Fine Arts Library, Columbia University. Christine Boyer, Jean-Louis Cohen, and Spyridon Papapetros have been constant guides for this research. Lastly, I would like to thank Vanessa Grossman and Alicia Imperiale for our discussions on the Greater Number.

[Figure 1]   Giancarlo De Carlo and Gianni Emilio Simonetti at the entrance of the XIV Triennale of Milan (1968). Photograph by Cesare Colombo. Courtesy of the author.

[Figure 2]   Shadrach Woods and Joachim Pfeufer, Illustration included in Woods and Pfeufer's installation "Urbanism as Collective Problem" at the XIV Triennale of Milan (1968). In Shadrach Woods and Joachim Pfeufer, Stadtplanung geht uns alle an: Urbanism is Everybody's Business; Urbanistica come problema di interesse collettivo, (Milano: Hoepli, 1968).

[Figure 3]   Saul Bass and Herb Rosenthal, "The Problem of Creativity in the Society of the Great Number," installation view of the XIV Triennale of Milan (1968). Courtesy of the Archivio Fotografico, © La Triennale di Milano.

[Figure 4]   Giancarlo De Carlo, Alberto Rosselli and Gruppo MID, "Information," installation view of the introductory space to the XIV Triennale of Milan (1968). Courtesy of the Archivio Fotografico, © La Triennale di Milano.

[Figure 5]   Giancarlo De Carlo, Marco Bellocchio and Bruno Caruso, "The Protest of the Youth," installation view of the XIV Triennale of Milan (1968). Courtesy of the Archivio Fotografico, © La Triennale di Milano.

Towards Paper Architecture: Tallinn and Moscow

Andres Kurg

"Paper architecture" was the name used in the Soviet Union in the 1980s to describe a body of work that countered inflexible building regulations and norms by using imaginative drawings, symbols, narration and allegory, and saw graphic work as its end result. Criticizing the monotony and anonymity of the industrially produced city, practitioners of paper architecture emphasised architecture as part of the cultural sphere rather than construction industry, and used publications and exhibitions as the media for disseminating their ideas.

Gaining international recognition as a movement during Perestroika in the late-1980s, this approach was often seen as a withdrawal from official design practice, understanding withdrawal through the dominant dichotomous model of oppression versus resistance, where the all-powerful state was countered by an escape to private life.[1] Further underlined by the postmodern critique in the West, paper architecture was seen as a turn away from rationalist and collective values.

I am following a different trajectory for describing the paper projects and argue against the notion of withdrawal, proposing instead an active dialogue with the transformations of the late-1970s and 1980s, and a desire to engage the public, through exhibitions. Their practices were intertwined with official institutions and often grew out of them; their work repeatedly interpreted earlier iterations of modernization, and several of the works could be read as a deterritorialization of, rather than escape from, the prevailing modernism. I will look at two groups of architects that worked almost in parallel in Tallinn and Moscow in the 1970s and '80s, and whose broadened notion of architecture went on to have significant repercussions on the process of redefining the profession.

Tallinn

On May 22, 1978, the *Architectural Exhibition 78,* comprised of fourteen architects-artists-designers, opened in the foyer of the Academy of Sciences Library in Tallinn [Figure 1]. Although the premises for the exhibition were officially organized through the youth section of the Union of Estonian Architects, the show differed from the usual survey exhibition by presenting the work of a group of architects who shared a similar educational background (all had attended the State Art Institute in

121

[Figure 1]

[Figure 2]

Tallinn), as well as a critical attitude towards existing architectural practices. The participants used the exhibition as a platform for presenting their rejection of the standardization of building practices and modernist urban planning and to launch a dialogue about architecture's role in the cultural sphere. Leonhard Lapin, one of the initiators of the exhibition, retrospectively wrote:

> In 1978 we presented "pure ideas," as our aim was to show architecture as an independent form of art, a manifestation of the spiritual, but also as an independent and influential feature that played a part in social processes.[2]

This coexistence between a desire for the autonomy of architecture (pure ideas) and its engagement (playing a part in social processes) was characteristic of the works in this exhibition, as well as the various individual preferences of its participants, and the other practices of the so-called Tallinn School throughout the 1970s.

Parallel to their work in the design office of the collective farm construction company, KEK, several architects in this group published polemical articles in the cultural press on urban issues and the built environment, discussing these topics in a style and manner quite different from previous pragmatic modes of writing. The critique and dissolution of Soviet architectural practices corresponded to wider public dissatisfaction with large-scale, system-built housing that went hand in hand with the emerging discourse about the alienation caused by these prefabricated suburbs.

The exhibition of 1978 was in many ways a culmination of this critique, displaying projects that directly addressed the prefabricated suburbs and also, occasionally, utopian proposals for redeveloping cities. The exhibition was divided into two, with photographs of built works hanging near the entrance on a white wall, and projects and conceptual proposals placed on high stands lined up along the glazed foyer.

The exhibited works were, formally, surprisingly different from one another, and because the participants did not make any prior agreements on content, the divergent approaches of individual members were occasionally quite pronounced. For example, Harry Shein showed allegorical black-and-white photomontages of the prefabricated housing areas in Tallinn with a corpse and a vandalized car in front of a partly ruined panel house that had either accidentally collapsed or had intentionally been left to collapse [Figure 2]. This dystopian street scene could have been documenting an image seen after a revolt (e.g., the Paris riots of 1968), or the degeneration of the area itself (in the author's own interpretation, the corpse was an alcoholic sleeping on the street). In a completely different direction, Tõnis Vint's works for *Mandala house* used floors to represent different phases of the meditative path. One of the central works in the Academy of Sciences exhibition, in terms of the attention it garnered and its political relevance, was Lapin's *The City of the Living—The City of the Dead,* which ironically commented on the mono-functional housing districts where public areas were usually left unfinished after the apartment blocks had been put up [Figure 3]. The project placed a cemetery in one of these empty public courtyards in the micro-districts of panel houses, which usually served as car parks or areas for people to walk their dogs. Here, however, garages became tombs, and bodies were buried in cars. The area was also meant to function as a children's playground. In this way, as one exhibition review mockingly put it, people would take better care of the area, and parents would not allow their children to vandalize its equipment.[3] The drawing, which was inspired by suprematist aesthetics and based on a view from a window in Lapin's own home, included several direct and indirect allusions to representatives of the architectural elite: the central obelisk commemorated the longstanding head of the Architect's Union, who had been in charge of all three mass housing projects in Tallinn; there was a common grave for the Union of Architects, and a constructivist gravestone marking the resting place of Lapin himself.

These references to modernist expansion and the exhibition's use of the avant-garde aesthetic pose a question regarding the relationship the Tallinn architects had with technological rationality and progress. Throughout the 1970s, Lapin demonstrated in his writings a somewhat ambivalent attitude towards modernization and the machine, not contradicting dominant Soviet technocracy, yet keeping a distance from it. Instead of architecture that was produced by a machine, he looked for architecture that could perform as a machine in the service of the user.[4] It is, then, not surprising that in his design for the cemeteries in the courtyards among the panel houses, Lapin did not demolish the new towns (which had occurred in Shein's work) but preferred to deterritorialize them through the insertion of what had so far been excluded from modernist urbanity.

Four years later, in 1982, an exhibition of ten architects from the same group took place at the Tallinn Art Salon. Initiated by Lapin and designed by Jüri Okas, it documented discussions held at the turn of the decade and new works by the architects.[5] It also reflected the new attitude of the Tallinn School, influenced, among other things, by their breakthrough into the Architects' Union board. There was an aspiration to establish a band of designers as a group (who now preferred to present themselves as the "Tallinn Ten"[6]), and with this a return to traditional ways of practicing and repre-senting architecture, a "striving for a certain classical order and clarity," as Vilen Künnapu explained in the exhibition catalog. Much attention was given to the exhibition design itself, which formed an independent installation inside the gallery that was reinforced by several "architektons"—or tempo-rary sculptures—referencing temples or classical columns.

In both exhibitions, the architects' aims may have been to increase the formal vocabulary of architec-ture and to "humanize" the environment. However, the means for achieving this were entirely differ-ent: in the first case, in 1978, architecture was opened up to neighboring disciplines, while the 1982 exhibition withdrew inside the fixed borders.

Moscow

Similarly, at the end of the 1970s, a group of young architects emerged in Moscow positing a critique of the architectural establishment and displaying a shift in approach to design practice in their works. Trained in the Moscow Architecture Institute, these practitioners already became known during their studies for their successful entries in international architecture competitions, initially those organized by UNESCO and the International Association for Scenographers, but later also in conceptual competitions sponsored by journals like *Japan Architect (JA)* or *Architectural Design (AD)*, where no restrictions in terms of budget, site, or building systems could rein in their fantasy. In 1981, the Architects' Union started to approve participation in these competitions for its members, making the sending of works abroad easier (previously, this was done illegally); in the same year, Mikhail Belov and Max Kharitonov won first prize in the *JA* residential design competition, giving rise to a sudden increase in entries from the Soviet Union and teams who concentrated solely on "paper" projects.

The paper projects attracted attention for their detailed and time-consuming graphic style and for unexpected and irrational scenarios on future use of the buildings, occasionally presented in comic strips or storyboards. Although the conceptual and often abstract competition briefs played their role in this, it was specifically the narrative approach and use of fiction that brought success to the young Moscow architects. As Belov explained, the key to their approach came from professor Ilya Lezhava, a legendary reformer of architecture from the 1960s, who taught them to think in paradoxes and do the opposite of what was expected: "everyone drafts, we draw, everyone draws perspectives, we build an enormous model."[7]

On August 1, 1984, the exhibition *Paper Architecture* was opened in the premises of the editorial office of the youth magazine *Yunost,* where a selection of competition entries from more than thirty architects were put on display. The space for the show was organized by Belov, who had previously collaborated with the magazine; the exhibition was put together by Yuri Avvakumov, who asked his colleagues and friends to contribute their recent works or proposals for the urban context, in

[Figure 3]

addition to competition designs. In contrast to Tallinn, the Moscow show did not include any built works. Therefore, the name of the exhibition, devised by Avvakumov a few nights before the opening, was simultaneously an ironic reference to the same phrase used pejoratively in the 1920s by critics of the avant-garde, as well as a criticism directed at an architecture profession subject to the planned economy that measured success solely on the basis of built output. As Mikhail Belov later wrote in *Yunost* magazine:

> [T]his incompatibility of the term harbors both a challenge and an irony. All these works were related in that they drew up architecture as seen by their authors in their dreams.[8]

The challenge to the existing architecture profession was underlined by the location of the exhibition venue: the editorial office was located across the street from one of the country's largest state design offices, Mosprojekt, whose numerous architects visited the show over the coming weeks and became the prime interlocutors in discussions over the function of these works. Some were shocked, saying at the discussion evening following the opening that the young architects should "stop fooling around and get to work"; other more favorable critics preferred to interpret the paper production as a laboratory of ideas and referred to the genre of architectural fantasies that existed in the past.[9]

The exhibition was displayed along the corridor and in the two smaller halls of the editorial office, with works and photographs hung along the walls between two plates of glass. With the varying size and media used in the works (it combined both originals and copies), witty models and randomly placed red name tags, the show gave a spontaneous and even rebellious impression. This was further emphasized by the mix of diverse styles and approaches adopted by the different participants. Mikhail Belov, Igor Pichoukevich, and Dmitri Velichkin's colored cardboard model for a UNESCO competition for architecture students—*The Architect as Enabler of User House Planning and Design*— was a proposal for rebuilding a typical multistory Soviet panel house set in a fictional people's republic in Africa [Figure 4]. Called *Village House in a Metropolis,* it presented the story of peasants who had recently moved to the city and needed to adjust the prefabricated building to their everyday needs: the rigid outer wall panels were replaced by freely positioned panels, the inner walls were not straight, each apartment had a terrace, the staircase was replaced by a ramp on the facade, and the roof became a gathering place where a sanctuary would be placed in the future. Meanwhile, a watercolor by Mikhail Filippov and Nadezhda Bronzova for a sculpture museum (competition entry for *JA*) showed a glass pavilion in an eighteenth-century Baroque park, which would act as a space for growing flowers in the winter and displaying snow sculptures in the summer.

Andrei Savin's entry for the *JA* competition, "Dwelling in Historicism and Localism," placed hanging gardens between Manhattan skyscrapers. In an entry to the same competition, Alexander Brodsky and Ilya Utkin submitted a house for Winnie the Pooh that inserted an octagonal private house between apartment blocks in a large city—for people who enjoy the urban life, but feel a "nostalgia for a house of one's own."[10] The building was, nevertheless, connected to the city's electricity network and operated by a "Very Modern Machine" that supplied it with the necessary comforts.

This ambiguous relationship to modernization could be further followed in Yuri Avvakumov's and Sergey Podemshikov's self-erecting house of cards, a pop-up toylike building, constructed for the *AD* Dolls' House competition in 1983, out of "playing cards, scotch tape, and rubber bands."[11] This project was, in fact, a paraphrase of a self-building house by Vyacheslav Koleichuk (who was Avvakumov's colleague in VNIITE, a research institute of technical aesthetics), representing the 1960s utopian discourse that coupled panel building with cybernetic technologies: leaving the factory in a flat form and equipped with autonomous control systems, the structure would have been capable of being assembled on site without human participation.[12] Avvakumov and Podemshikov's design did not so much satirize panel buildings as unstable houses of cards as present an attempt to alienate the denounced anonymous panel construction and abstract technocratic language by introducing an uncanny mass-cultural element.

This relationship to experimental modernist projects of the past becomes more clearly articulated in Avvakumov's and MArchI students' project, a prize-winning entry in the "Style for the Year 2001" competition organized by the magazine *A+U* [Figure 5].[13] The proposal reclaimed the Russian avant-garde aesthetic by redefining a 1960s prefabricated panel house area in Moscow. Focusing on similar wastelands between houses, as in Lapin's design for the cemetery, the constructivist elements were used to build open-ended and transformable structures where the users themselves could come up with possible functions: amateur clubs, dovecotes, minitheaters, and pavilions. The authors explain this paradoxical reinterpretation of the 1920s avant-garde, which for them is "an agitational architecture from its origin and way of life," as "a circus rather than a theatre, axonometric drawing rather than perspective, a barricade rather than a colonnade."[14] Therefore, it is not revived only as a past aesthetic language, but still considered a valid form for experimentation in the name of engaging local inhabitants in the rebuilding process.

Following the exhibition, paper architecture quickly made its way towards broader recognition and was used in several exhibitions representing new Soviet architecture: in 1985 at the international festival of youth and students in Moscow, in 1986 in Ljubljana, in 1987 in Helsinki, Stockholm, and Amsterdam. Since 1988, major exhibitions of the paper projects toured in Paris, Milan, London, and Frankfurt. In the above-mentioned discussion evening following the exhibition opening in Moscow in 1984, a prominent poet and former architecture graduate, Andrei Voznesensky, called the approach of the paper architects a "sublimation of despair"—it was an escape from architectural reality for architects feeling excommunicated from real architecture and remaining 'alongside' architecture."[15] Already two years later, in 1986, architecture critic Alexei Tarkhanov wrote, however, that paper architecture as a phenomenon had become so known and familiar that it was already difficult to question it critically. "There is no one to convince, fame has been achieved, its recent enemies have calmed down and even the masters of the older generation . . . start step by step to understand and use their subtext, irony, grotesque, multiplicity of meanings."[16]

Late-Socialist Public

How then, in the case of the architects in Tallinn and Moscow, should we understand this position, which, on the one hand, allowed a distancing from the dominant architectural elite and room to criticize the reduction of architecture as an appendage of the construction industry, but, on the other hand, allowed an intervention in the institution of architecture in order to alter this very system?

In a recent book, *Everything Was Forever, Until it Was No More: The Last Soviet Generation* (2005), anthropologist Alexei Yurchak has addressed the specific life practices of the late-Soviet period—the fascination for rock music, telling jokes and anecdotes, or sitting in the café societies with their specific atmosphere—criticizing their widespread representation through binaries like dissident versus activist, official versus unofficial, or a homogeneous "us" versus the oppressive power structures of "them." Instead, he proposes that these practices belong to a sociality of *svoi* ("us" or "ours" in Russian) that did not run in opposition to the state but was produced out of mutually embedded notions—of "us," "not us," "the state," "the state representatives," and "the people."[17]

It was also this sociality of *svoi* that offered the most productive relationship in terms of culture and knowledge in society. In Yurchak's words, this was done through a performative shift in relation to authoritative discourse in the late-Soviet period: this language was followed and repeated as a ritualized act, without its meaning being taken as true or false; rather, it functioned as a dynamic way of bringing forth new meanings and practices. As a result, the dominant discourse shifted, and the system itself deterritorialized in a peculiar way, with several of the values of socialism retained.

Thus, even if the rhetoric was followed ironically, the ethics upheld by the socialist (and modernist) system were taken seriously:

> Unlike the dissident strategies of opposing the system's dominant mode of signification, deterritorialization reproduced this mode at the same time as it shifted, built upon, and added new meanings to it.[18]

This new deterritorialized way of life existed neither "inside" nor "outside" the system: reinterpreting and appropriating the means and knowledge available, these milieus of *svoi* were greatly dependent on both the system's financial and institutional support, and the hierarchies and cultural ideals the system set.

In many ways, the activities of both groups—the architects working in Tallinn and Moscow—fit well with the description of the production of the deterritorialized public of *svoi.* Countering the authoritative discourse of the governing architectural elite, they produced their alternative discourse—partly appropriating the authoritative terms and formats, but extending them and using them for new meanings. This included not only verbal language, but also exhibitions and various forms of representation. In some cases, positioning oneself outside society was clearly marked (e.g., in Tõnis Vint's projects for the *Mandala house* or Brodsky and Utkin's imaginative drawings). In other instances (e.g., Lapin's design for the cemetery or Avvakumov's house of cards and courtyards), avant-garde aesthetics blurred the boundaries between withdrawing to an "outside" and engagement: their emphasis on suprematism and constructivism embodied the values of experimentation and utopianism in agreement with the socialist country, but they also believed that radical aesthetics could counter the dullness of official building production by ironically adapting, while still maintaining, socialist values. Concentrating its critique around issues of housing, living environment, and everyday urban spaces, the exhibitions played a role in the production of this new public, which was further reinforced by similar discussions among writers, actors, and other intellectuals. Rather than being openly antagonistic, this new discourse was constructed within, and in contiguity with the official one.

[Figure 4]

[Figure 5]

[1] For different accounts of the Moscow paper architects see: Helene Larroche, ed., *Architecture de Papier d'URSS* (Paris: Editions du Regard, 1988); *Nostalgia of Culture. Contemporary Soviet Visionary Architecture* (London: The Architectural Association, 1988); Heinrich Klotz, ed., *Paper Architecture. New Projects from the Soviet Union* (New York: Rizzoli, 1990).

[2] Leonhard Lapin, *Pimeydestä valoon. Viron taiteen avantgarde neuvostomiehityksen aikana* (Helsinki: Otava, 1996), 122.

[3] Mati Unt, "Arhitektuurinäitus," *Sirp ja Vasar,* June 9, 1978, 8.

[4] See: Leonhard Lapin, "Masinaajastu ja kunst," *Kultuur ja Elu,* no. 9 (1973): 55–56.

[5] See: *Tallinna Seminar* (Tallinn: Union of Estonian Architects, 1980), unpublished manuscript, Museum of Estonian Architecture.

[6] See: Karin Winter, ed., *Tio arkitekter fran Tallinn* (Stockholm: Museum of Swedish Architecture, 1990).

[7] Mikhail Belov, "Rassuzhdenija molodogo cheloveka po povodu arhitektury," *Yunost,* no. 8 (1981): 82.

[8] Mikhail Belov, "Zametki "bumazhnogo" arhitektora," *Yunost,* no. 2 (1986): 107.

[9] See: Aleksei Tarkhanov, "Bumazhnaja arhitektura po ee sostojaniju na 1986 g.," in *God arhitektury,* (Moskva: Strojizdat, 1987), 77.

[10] "Winners in the Shinkenchiku Residential Design Competition 1983," *Japan Architect* 322 (February, 1984): 30.

[11] "Dolls' Houses," *Architectural Design* 53, no. 3–4 (1983): 57.

[12] Vyacheslav Koleichuk, *Mobil'naja arhitektura* (Moskva: CNTI, 1973).

[13] Fumihiko Maki, ed., *A Style for the Year 2001. JA* and *A+U* joint extra edition (Tokyo: Shinkenchiku, 1985).

[14] "Panorama molodyh. 12 novyh imen," *Dekorativnoe iskusstvo* 361, no. 12 (1987): 11.

[15] Mikhail Tumarkin, "Bumazhnaja arhitektura: piknik na obochine ili zadel na budushhee," *Arhitektura,* no. 1 (January, 1985): 4–5.

[16] Aleksei Tarkhanov, "Bumazhnaja arhitektura po ee sostojaniju na 1986 g.," 77.

[17] Alexei Yurchak, *Everything Was Forever, Until It Was No More: The Last Soviet Generation* (Princeton: Princeton University Press, 2005), 103.

[18] Ibid., 116.

Curatorial
Acts

Demonstrations as a Curatorial Practice: The Exhibition Scene at Moderna Museet from *She* to *ARARAT*, 1966–1976

Helena Mattson

Is it a paradox to exhibit architecture? Here, this question will be approached from the position of fine arts, with a focus on how the art world has used architecture to formulate a critical position towards both fields. Importantly, rather than reducing architecture to conventional modes of representation, such as models, drawings, or photos, this essay investigates a series of exhibitions, which capitalized on architecture's ability to construct real-life experiences and to create a participatory situation within the space of the art museum. The exhibitions investigated in this essay all took place at the Moderna Museet in Stockholm under the legendary director Pontus Hultén between 1966 and 1976. It will be argued that this "architectural turn" constituted a curatorial endgame of sorts where the celebration of the immediacy of sensory bodily experience meets the anesthetization and commodification of the architectural experience itself, which was not problematized by the artists and architects during the period.

[Figure 1]

Demonstrations at the Museum

The turmoil in the years around 1968 was clearly visible in Stockholm—public streets and squares became scenes for the voicing of political opinion, protests, and large demonstrations, which ultimately changed the meaning and use of urban public space. During this time, the idea of constructing "demonstrations" migrated to the art world and various European artists and curators began to describe their shows as "demonstrations" rather than exhibitions. For example, in the foreword to the catalog for the exhibition, *Superlund,* which was shown in the southern Swedish city of Lund in 1976, the philosopher and curator Pierre Restany asks: "Is it a real exhibition? I see it more as a demonstration, as an overture to the future."[1] And he goes on: "The viewer/participant whose active participation is more and more needed, becomes a key in the synthesis."[2] When artist Björn Lövin held a show at the museum in 1971, he called it a "demonstration" of a consumer's life rather than an exhibition.[3] The research collective ARARAT followed suit in declaring that they wanted to "demonstrate things" rather than exhibit in 1976.[4] Other examples include Palle Nielsen's exhibition, *Modellen: En modell för ett kvalitativt samhälle* (The Model: A Model for a Qualitative Society), which took place at the Moderna Museet in 1968 and *HON – En katedral* (She – A Cathedral) from 1966.

First, we should be reminded that all these demonstrations could be traced back to exhibitions such as El Lissitzky's *Demonstrationsräume* (1923–1927), and the Independent Group's *Parallel of Life and Art* (1953). As Maria Gough points out in her essay, "Constructivism disorientated: El Lissitzky's Dresden and Hannover *Demonstrationsräume,*" the concept of demonstration in the early twentieth century "was at once broader and more specific" than the idea of an exhibition.[5] It implied a political protest; it unfolded an argument in space and time; and it produced an art of extreme sensuality by immersing the visitor within an environment. The postwar demonstrations follow a similar format, with the difference being that the objects in the space are not presented as "art," but rather as full-scale environments or spatial constructs filled up with everyday things that build up a full-scale world—a "showroom"—inside the actual exhibition space through assembling things from everyday life. The visitor is being considered an active participant who is constructing meaning when moving through/in the installation. Many of these postwar demonstrations aimed at reconfiguring the relationship between the man-of-the-street to the everyday life world and, in so doing, were conceived as political acts.

Three of the exhibitions already mentioned, shown at Moderna Museet in Stockholm, will be addressed here. The first example is *HON – En katedral* from 1966; the second is *Modellen: En modell för ett kvalitativt samhälle* from 1968; and the last is *ARARAT* from 1976 [Figure 1]. I will highlight three techniques of what I call an architectural turn in these "demonstrations": the use of the architectural promenade; the idea of the collaborative and open-ended working processes; and the institutional reframing. By covering the full life of the exhibition, from its conceptual development to its construction and ultimately to the visitor experience, allows the questioning of the art institution, which, I will argue, was their raison d'être.

From *HON* to *ARARAT*

In 1955, when shooting the short film *En dag i solen* (A Day in the Sun), Hans Nordenström, Jean Tinguely, P-O Ultvedt, and Pontus Hultén discussed how to make "a theatre-art-exhibition."[6] They decided that such an event should be a combination of a happening, mechanical theater, and a labyrinth space. In 1958, they built a test structure at Liljevalchs Konsthall in Stockholm, but it would take a further eight years—not until 1966—before the ideas were realized. Pontus Hultén was the Moderna Museet's director at that time and was responsible for mounting the exhibition *HON – en katedral.* The working group had changed slightly and then consisted of Jean Tinguely, P-O Ultvedt, Niki de Saint-Phalle, and Pontus Hultén.[7]

HON was a huge object—28 meters long and 8 meters high—in the shape of a woman lying on her back with legs spread apart. The body nearly touched the roof and seemed to expand the museum space. The fact that it was designed as an architectural structure was emphasized by the exhibition title: "She – A Cathedral." The visitor's path through the installation began between the half-bent legs, passing through the body's sex and into the dark interior. This inner space was filled with moving, rotating machines, meant to resemble the working organs of a body, but it also contained functional stations such as a bar, a cinema, and a gallery. The installation presented a corporeal experience that influenced all the senses but had an architectural sensibility in that it operated like a city, with its own sounds, light, and myriad functionality.

The original idea was to include American artist Robert Rauschenberg in the collaboration, but the team ultimately questioned his Pop Art approach. As Tinguely put it in a letter to the other artists involved: "Don't you feel the four of us would be enough, since the castle would become a unity? Why have an enormous hamburger next to it?"[8] Reasons to exclude the American artist could be also interpreted as a result of the critique of the Vietnam War, which had led to a strong anti-American sentiment in Europe.

The idea for *HON* originated in Niki de Saint Phalle's "Nana-figures," first debuted in a 1965 exhibition held at the Alexander Iolas Gallery in Paris. The figure of a reclining female was scaled up to become an architectural structure with an interior space that could be accessed through her vulva. The exhibition thus marked a break in curatorial practices at Moderna Museet by aligning itself both to women's liberation as well as sexual liberation, but was ultimately criticized for conserving traditional women's social roles. However, the critical dimension was its use of architectural space and corporeal sensibilities, which made it typical of the European full-scale demonstrations.

During his years as the museum's director, Pontus Hultén put Moderna Museet on the international art map. The museum solidified its role as a site for critical experiments outside the traditional role of fine arts in 1968 when the museum was used as a platform for the activist group, *Aktion Samtal* (Action Dialogue), working together with Nielsen. In October of that year, *Modellen* opened at Moderna Museet, following a number of actions that had taken place in Stockholm.[9] The exhibition title had a political connotation to the so-called Swedish [welfare] Model and implied a critique of a system regulated by bureaucracy and norms. As Gunilla Lundahl from *Aktion Samtal* formulated it: "We must build our own models for a new reality, where we have taken the responsibility ourselves."[10]

The layout of the show was reminiscent of a kindergarten. In the middle of the room there was a huge playground, with a wooden structure to climb into and a large "sea" of foam rubber pieces to play in. One of the most often-published images shows the Minister of Education, Olof Palme, jumping into the foam [Figure 2]. Kids as well as the adults could build things, paint, or just jump into the "foam-rubber-sea." Nielsen worked with play as a transformative power in a manner reminiscent of the ideas put forth by Herbert Marcuse in *Eros and Civilization* (1955). The unpredictable play, driven by lust and desire, was intended to activate the visitors, and, subsequently, the society at large.

The last example is the exhibition, *ARARAT,* or *Alternative Research in Architecture Resources Art and Technology,* that opened in 1976.[11] Though Philip von Schantz had been the museum director since 1973, the exhibition can be seen as a continuation of Hultén's idea of the museum as an open critical space.[12] The show was formulated in relation to what were seen as urgent environmental issues: new energy sources, sustainability, alternative building materials, and new lifestyles. The first UN Conference on the Human Environment held in Stockholm in 1972 was disrupted with protests and demonstrations and the group ARARAT was formed to deepen this critique. It was decided that the group could present their research outcome at Moderna Museet. The show involved an extensive network of people, from experts to amateurs, and consisted of full-scale objects like buildings, tools, and practical workshops for the visitor to take part in. As in both *HON* and *Modellen,* the bodily experiences and the element of participation were crucial to the critical dimension of the show.

In opposition to the former exhibitions, where the objects in the exhibition were placed inside the museum, the exhibition space in *ARARAT* was extended to the yard in front of the museum building. Full-scale building structures—real houses, in fact—were erected outside the museum without any attempt at mediation. They were, simply buildings [Figure 5]. It is significant that part of *ARARAT* was presented in the Nordic Pavilion at the Venice Art Biennale in 1976, and became a precursor of sorts for the first full-fledged architectural Biennale that took place in 1980.

An Architectural Turn and a New Form of Criticality

As pointed out earlier, the postwar demonstrations under consideration here could be understood both in political terms and as spatial presentations. Furthermore, three themes that characterize the investigations into new forms of criticality could be traced in all of these exhibitions: walks through programmed stations; collaborative and open-ended working processes; elaboration of the museum as a framework. There was a tension between architecture and art, or applied art and fine art, which meant that the frame constituted by the art institution was under continuous elaboration.

These shows were often organized like architectural structures with predefined circulation routes and programmatic areas, and conceived through conventional architectural plans and sections. In *HON,* the visitor could stroll around as in a city—take a drink in the bar; go to the cinema and watch Greta Garbo's first movie from 1922; and/or climb up to the "space-café" and gain perspective over the whole body. In one of her legs there was a switchback to ride and in the other an exhibition with imitations of well known paintings. After the tour, the visitor emerged, "newborn." *Modellen* was also organized as stations with different functions. In the middle of the room a large area was filled with foam rubber, and the other functions were spread out in the room: a climbing net; a typewriting studio; and a carpentry workshop [Figure 3]. In *ARARAT,* the predefined circulation route started in the court-yard outside the museum, moving through buildings and structures that were standing in front of the museum. The route continued inside the museum where one would be exposed to information regard-ing sustainability. Finally, the walk ended outside the museum in the outdoor workshops where the visitor could experiment with practical construction [Figure 4]. If the walk started as a *tour* of architec-tural environments, it ended in *participatory work* where everyone was part of forming the future.

All of these "demonstrations" followed the same strategy: Through participation and bodily experi-ences the visitors were prompted to think critically and to "act." This was seen as an alternative to the norm of intellectual and aesthetic reflection, as well as of traditional art object that governed a traditional art exhibitions. A similar critical technique was already articulated by filmmaker Sergei Eisenstein: "The new art must set a limit to the dualism of the spheres of emotion and reason . . . It must plunge the abstract process of thought into the cauldron of practical activity."[13]

It was not only the unique art object that was questioned but also the traditional way of making art. The process was organized as an architectural project—as a collaborative work with an open-ended result. *HON* was the result of a limited work period at the museum: six weeks. When the group started work, there was no predefined idea—the end result would be the outcome of their collective work on-site. *HON* existed as art only during the exhibition; after the show, the body was destroyed. *Modellen* was also a result of a collaborative process. *Aktion Samtal* arranged several months of activities in the city, protesting against the building of motorways, backyard slums, the lack of public space, and so forth. They invited Nielsen, who had been working with building spontaneous playgrounds for children in Copenhagen, to take part. He introduced his method, not only based on "direct action," but also on reaching people and decision-makers through new media, which resulted in the show at Moderna Museet. The starting point for *ARARAT* was similar. It had a political starting point discuss-ing environmental questions in relation to the UN conference on Human Environment. Personnel included engineers, architects, urban planners, ecologists, and artists, among others. This collec-tive of people worked together for several years, and the process took the form of a research or an architectural project.

[Figure 2]

[Figure 3]

[Figure 4]

The relations between the institutional framework and the architectural and spatial configurations were quite different in these three examples, but in all cases important to the result. In *HON,* the institutional framework was never questioned, but was rather a precondition. All the creators came from the art world and *HON* was primarily perceived as an event inside the realm of fine arts. In *Modellen,* the institutional framework was not questioned, but was used to gain media attention and to create a debate. In *ARARAT,* the museum as a privileged site was as sharply questioned. In this case, the boundaries of its walls were transgressed as well as the idea of a unique art object along with it. In the catalog to the 1976 Venice Biennale, Lennart Mörk writes: "The important thing is that we as artists have given up our ambition to produce a unique work of art."[14] This notion was supported by the theme, "environmental art," put forward by the scientific committee led by Hultén. Yet, even if the research collective ARARAT used the Biennale as a platform for communication and activism, they never questioned the effects of being part of an art scene and exhibiting "the demonstrations" as objects.

Conclusion

The late 1960s and early 1970s were marked by crises in established ideologies. Conflicts and misgivings within Marxism and other left wing movements resulted in new ideological formations. In the aftermath of what was often understood as the failure of 1968, significant changes in radical philosophy were formulated, especially in France. Universal claims of Marxism were questioned and, instead, concepts such as the local, the ephemeral, and the multiple gained currency among intellectual and artistic circles. The rethinking of the foundations of critique and critical theory led to various intellectual and aesthetic experiments. In this context, the demonstrations I have looked into could be seen as investigations into new formats of criticality expressed through corporeal experiences rather than intellectual and rational explanations. They also mark a paradoxical moment when what was aimed at social and institutional critique paved the way for the commodification and fetishization of architectural experience that plagues much of architecture culture still today.

[Figure 5]

[1] Paul Restany, "Ett Nupanorama," in *Superlund,* exh. cat. (Lund: Lunds konsthall, 1967), 5.

[2] Paul Restany, "En Framtidsfilosofi," in *Superlund,* 18.

[3] See Björn Lövin, *Konsument i oändligheten,* exh. cat. (Stockholm: Moderna Museet, 1971). Translated in *Från P till C— kampen om verkligheten | From P to C—The Struggle for Reality* (Stockholm: Kulturhuset, 1988).

[4] *ARARAT,* exhibition catalog for the Venice Biennale, (Stockholm: Moderna Museet, 1976), 10.

[5] Maria Gough, "Constructivism disoriented: El Lissitzky's Dresden and Hannover *Demonstrationsräume"* in eds. Nancy Perloff and Brian Reed, *Situating El Lissitzky: Vitebsk, Berlin, Moscow* (Los Angeles: Getty Publications, 2003), 89.

[6] See *HON: en katedral byggd av: Niki de Saint Phalle, Jean Tinguely, Per Olof Ultvedt,* exhibition catalog (Stockholm: Moderna Museet, 1966), 6.

[7] The exhibition *Dylaby* (1962) at the Stedejlik Museum in Amsterdam was an earlier example of a full-scale architectural exhibition, in which P-O Ultvetd and Jean Tinguely took part. Even *La Menesunda* (1965) in Buenos Aires was a similar manifestation which Pontus Hultén and Jean Tinguely visited.

[8] Hiroko Ikegami, *The Great Migrator: Robert Rauschenberg and the Global Rise of American Art* (Cambridge: MIT Press, 2010), 139.

[9] For an in-depth analysis of *Modellen* see Lars Bang Larsen, *The Model: A model for a qualitative society* (Barcelona: Museu d'Art Contemporani Barcelona, 2010).

[10] Gunilla Lundahl in exhibition catalog *Modellen: En modell för ett kvalitativt samhälle* (Stockholm: Moderna Museet, 1968), 6.

[11] For a discussion on *ARARAT* see Christina Pech, *Arkitektur och motstånd* (Stockholm: Makadam förlag, 2011), 98–131; Hans Hayden, "Double Bind," and Anette Göthlund, "Activites in the Workshop and Zon" in eds. Anna Tellgren, Martin Sundberg, Johan Rosell, *The History Book* (Stockholm: Moderna Museet, 2008), 177–200; 257–280.

[12] The Swedish artist Philip von Schantz was the director of Moderna Museet 1973–1977.

[13] Maria Gough, "Constructivism disoriented: El Lissitzky's Dresden and Hannover *Demonstrationsräume,"* 89.

[14] *ARARAT,* exhibition catalog for the Venice Biennale, Moderna Museet, Stockholm, 1976, 5.

Hans Hollein as "Everythingizer," Hans Hollein as Curator

Liane Lefaivre

Though he curated many architecture exhibitions throughout his long and extraordinary career, Hans Hollein is perhaps most well known for his contribution to *Strada Novissima* at the Venice Biennale of 1980, which was one of the architectural events that launched postmodernism. The present essay covers the first phase of that career—from his *Plastic Space* shown at Berkeley in 1960, to *MANtransFORMS,* presented at the Cooper Hewitt Museum in Manhattan in 1976. This period of Hollein's was anything but postmodern in its conservative, "citationist" and "façadist" sense. His purpose, like so many cultural figures of this time, was to flaunt conventions and received truths, to liberate the architectural imagination and allow it to roam unexplored territories and associations. This is when he was one of what may be termed the architectural "everythingizers" typical of the era.[1]

It is difficult to draw the line between Hans Hollein's work as a curator of architecture from his work as a curator of art, and also, for that matter, from his work as an architect, artist, sculptor, designer, writer, and magazine editor— especially during this period. This line is difficult to draw because of Hollein's inherent *forma mentis* or mindset. He was exceptionally multifaceted. His collage approach to architecture reflects this as does his collage art, collage sculptures, collage writings, and collage editing. Just one measure of how agile he was in "crossing over"—straddling media and disciplines—is that, between 1960–1976, besides being the future Pritzker Prize-winning architect we all know, he was an artist who was exhibited by some of the greatest gallery owners and curators of the time, among them Sidney Janis (1963), Richard Feigen (1964), and Johannes Cladders (1972). In the early 1970s he was selected by curators Harald Szeemann and Rudi Fuchs to be part of an exhibition representing Austrian art with five other Austrian artists in the early 1970s (not materialized).[2]

This *forma mentis,* in turn, was invigorated and strengthened by the *Zeitgeist* of the late 1950s when Hans Hollein, the artist—as opposed to Hans Hollein, the architect—was exposed to the idea of crossing over and "everythingizing." At the time, it was a novelty to blur the line between art, film, video, sculpture and, of course, curating, but it was also a period when happenings, performance art, conceptual art, and installation art started to dissolve the boundaries between the curator and the artist. Artists first took charge, and they did so outside the confines of the gallery and the museum, breaking down the barriers separating art from the world at large. Harald Szeeman's show, *Live In Your Head: When Attitudes Become Form* at the Kunsthalle Bern of 1969—which was reconstructed at the Prada

Foundation by Thomas Demand and Rem Koolhaas for the 2013 Venice Biennale—was a landmark show, one of the first exhibitions to dissolve the boundaries between diverse art forms and curating. In the same spirit, Richard Feigen had already curated, in 1964, a show that brought together Claes Oldenburg, Frei Otto, Christo, Buckminster Fuller, and Hollein.

Between 1960 and 1976, Hollein exported the concept of crossing-over from art to architecture. His ultimate statement in this respect was his April 1968 article, "Alles ist Architektur (Everything is Architecture)," in *Bau* magazine. This publication consisted of a one-thousand-word manifesto that gave the issue its title. Following this introduction was a succession of ninety images whose logic was not verbal, but visual. Hollein's curating in this case consisted of adding the same "caption" to each diverse image: *Alles ist Architektur* (Everything is Architecture). In this publication, structured like an exhibition, Hollein was one of the avant-garde architects who opened up the closed world of architecture to the realities of the time. Things not usually associated with either "architecture," or affiliated with architects, were suddenly and startlingly equated with them: a pill, a lipstick, a photograph of Sergei Eisenstein, an image of Che Guevara. Niki de Saint Phalle and Jean Tinguely are seen emerging from the vulva of de Saint Phalle's giant Pop sculpture of a supine woman in one photograph. Hollein's ninety-plus images reflected the most pressing issues of contemporary culture: the Vietnam War, war criminals, sexual liberation, sexual exploitation, the third world, oil cartels, political revolution, pop culture, transience, social unrest, violence, consumer society, space technology, computer technology, thermonuclear technology, the loss of tradition, labor unrest, Dadaism, public space, disastrous urban renewal, and ecological disaster.[4]

Hollein's development as a curator did not occur in a vacuum. Le Corbusier actually coined the phrase "tout est architecture." In addition, being from Vienna was a distinct advantage for someone who was going to go into a creative rethinking of how to expand the concept of curating. There was one inventive artist-architect-curator, in particular, to whom Hollein could look as a precedent: the "correalist" cross-over architect-set designer-furniture designer, Frederick Kiesler. In fact, Hollein met Kiesler in New York though the architect-philanthropist Armand Bartos, who was an architectural collaborator of Kiesler's.[5] In 1925, when Josef Hoffmann invited Kiesler to design the theater section of the Austrian pavilion at the *Exposition Internationale des Arts Décoratifs et Industriels Modernes* in Paris, he built *Raumstadt* (City in Space). Kiesler's monumental structure offered a vision of a colossal Proun-cum-De Stijl-inspired floating city of the future. Van Doesburg praised the work, saying it was something that he himself could not have envisioned. After moving to New York the same year, 1925, Kiesler continued to expand the multidimensional scope of his curating. Between 1937 and 1942, Kiesler developed a Vision Machine for exploring visual perception and for viewing images of the work of Marcel Duchamp. It was installed in his 1942 design of Peggy Guggenheim's gallery, Art of this Century, an architectural environment that offered new methods of exhibiting the surrealist art that she was collecting at the time.[6] Even his two pieces of furniture designed for the gallery, the Correalist Rocker and the Instrument, were enlisted to serve not only as chairs, but as exhibition supports as well. The Instrument, in particular, was conceived to fill eighteen different functions, as Kiesler purported. Another precedent for Hollein may have been the postwar Viennese art scene, which was remarkably avant-garde— particularly the activities of the Wiener Gruppe, a loose collaboration of poets and writers established in 1952 that included Friedrich Achleitner, Oswald Wiener, Konrad Bayer, Hans Carl Artmann, and Gerhard Rühm. By the early 1950s, they were combining *avant la lettre* performance art with jazz, concrete poetry, and collage.[7] To put their progressive approach in perspective, it was not until six years later, in 1955, that Allan Ginsberg performed *Howl* for the first time at the Six Gallery in San Francisco. The Wiener Aktionisten would grow out of the Wiener Gruppe, with performances like Gunter Brus's *Wiener Spaziergang* (Vienna Walks) and Valie Export and Peter Weibel's gender-inverting walks, which featured the woman walking the man on all fours through the streets of Vienna, like a dog.

Hollein, as opposed to other Austrian architects and artists, was as exposed to the American art scene as the Austrian one. Thanks to a Harkness Commonwealth travel grant, he spent two years in the U.S. between fall 1958 and fall 1960. The grant allowed recipients to attend the university of his or her choice. Hollein, accordingly, enrolled first at Illinois Institute of Technology (IIT), because he thought he would be studying with Mies van der Rohe. After one year, he transferred to the avant-garde, multi-disciplinary, regionalist School of Environmental Design at the University of California/Berkeley at the invitation of architects Joseph Esherick and its founder, William Wurster, where in 1960 he completed a Masters of Architecture with Esherick and the sculptor James Prestini, also a professor at the school, both of whom he greatly admired.[8] During his stay in the U.S., Hollein gravitated towards American poets and artists, largely staying clear of the world of architects, except for the Bay Area school of Esherick and Wurster, which he believed was the most modern of all. In fact, he expressed disappoint-ment with American architecture's "East Coast establishment." The 26-year-old's final report to the Harkness Foundation was categorical: "People like Eero Saarinen, Philip Johnson, Marcel Breuer, Yamasaki, Rudolph," he wrote, "are altogether overestimated in their importance and competence. Recent efforts of some of them to get off the beaten track and break away are more an intellectual real-ization that something other has to be done than a genuine new way and attitude, which comes from the heart. Of course . . . one man whose work has great potential is Louis Kahn. Certainly no potential has Edward Stone and his school." As for the latter statement, Hollein compared Stone's buildings to Hitler's *Reichskanzlei* (Reich Chancellery) and to the *Foro Mussolini* (Mussolini's Forum).[9]

Among the people he met in the U.S., Allan Kaprow, the inventor of the Happening, was arguably the most significant to Hollein's future career as a curator. Before returning to Vienna in 1960, he befriended Hollein and took him to visit his famous collection of Mondrian paintings. Hollein attended some of Kaprow's earliest happenings, including the very first, *Eighteenth Happenings in Six Parts,* which was presented in 1959 at the opening of the Reuben Gallery in New York.[10] One has to read the accounts of the time to get an inkling of the shock that these happenings created.

In 1962, Susan Sontag, one of the most alert minds of the time, wrote about these early happenings in her article titled, "Happenings: the Art of Radical Juxtaposition." What struck her was the way they were structured. She wrote: "There has appeared in New York recently a new and still esoteric genre of spectacle. At first sight apparently a cross between art exhibit and theatrical performance, these events have been given the modest, somewhat teasing name of 'happenings.'" She goes on to mention that the work resembles, "assemblages, a hybrid of painting, collage, and sculpture, using a sardonic variety of materials, mainly in a state of debris, including license plates, pieces of glass, machine parts, newspaper clippings, and the artist's socks. From the assemblage to the whole room or 'environment' is only one step further. The final step, the Happening, simply puts people into the environment and sets it into motion." The purpose of this astonishing hybrid art form, Sontag surmised, was to "destroy conventional meanings, and create through radical juxtapositions (the 'collage principle.')".[11]

Kaprow's "everythingizing" tendency came to a great degree from his mentor John Cage, who formu-lated the famous dictum that "everything we do is music." Whether or not it was the result of a con-scious borrowing on Hollein's part, his own dictum, "everything is architecture," goes back not only to Le Corbusier but also to Cage, with Kaprow acting as a conduit. This is the context in which Hollein's *forma mentis* matured. Let us look at how these ideas translated into his architectural curating between 1960 and 1976.

Hollein's first exhibition, held in 1960 when he was twenty-six years old, was his Master's thesis presen-tation at Berkeley, called *Plastic Space; Space in Space in Space.* This event is the first in which he trans-ferred concepts from the field of art curating to the field of architecture curating. Although Hollein tends to leave this very early work out of his list of exhibitions, it is the matrix from which all of his other works of art, architecture, and curating sprang between 1960 and 1976. It announced his intention to bend the definition of what architecture was, and to break down the boundaries separating it from art, sculpture, urban design, regional planning, and concrete poetry. *Plastic Space* included an example of installation art—or rather installation architecture—which he called "City," which was made up of large clay structures in which Hollein crawled. Like many of the happenings in the art world at the time, it was presented in a public space outside the confines of the gallery [Figure 1]. Added to this action

[Figure 1]

Akten

Bevölkerungszunahme

Frustration

Gedränge

[Figure 2]

[Figure 3]

[Figure 4]

was a series of clay sculptures, collages, drawings in India ink, and concrete poetry.[12] He presented much the same material in 1963 at the Galerie nächst St. Stephan in Vienna, run by Otto Maurer, in the exhibition in which he participated jointly with Walter Pichler.[13]

The exhibition *Selection 66* was curated by Hollein at the request of the Museum für Angewandte Kunst's (MAK) director Peter Noever in 1966. Although the exhibition was relatively small, it was conceptually groundbreaking. While there is nothing new about an exhibition devoted to design today, Hollein could be considered a pioneer in the field. Instead of just hauling objects from storage and placing them on pedestals, Hollein organized selections from the collection. In this case, he applied the art of curating to an exhibition of chairs from the MAK collection. His innovation was to display design objects within specially made architectural environments in the manner in which art would be presented [Figure 3]. Noever ran with this idea in the 1990s and commissioned other artists to install MAK exhibitions. Among them were Barbara Bloom, who created an installation of Thonet chairs; Donald Judd, who assembled a Baroque room; and Jenny Holzer, who organized a Biedermeier room.

The year 1968 was an *annus mirabilis* for Hollein. That year, he produced the "Alles ist Architektur" issue of *Bau* magazine and organized the madcap, exuberant *Austriennale*—the Austrian contribution to the Milan Architecture Triennale of 1968, called *The Greater Number,* which was curated by Giancarlo de Carlo.[14] What singled it out from all the other architectural exhibitions of the Triennale was, again, its introduction of concepts of curating from the art world. For this exhibition, Hollein devised a zany, Dadaist romp—a happening of sorts. A specially constructed machine churned out Österreichbrillen (Austria glasses), with lenses fabricated in the red-and-white pattern of the Austrian national flag, which allowed visitors "to see things through Austrian eyes." Visitors to the exhibition could not remain mere spectators but were forced to negotiate a labyrinthine installation involving innumerable doors. Doors leading to dead ends, doors to false leads, closed doors, doors to illusionistic halls of mirrors—all meant to represent the absurd claustrophobia of Austria. A series of photographs depict Peter Noever's first wife, the famous Viennese model, Katarina Noever, who was squeezed tightly into spaces crammed with filing cabinets and in rooms with locked doors, or spaces with doors without handles or with multiple handles, none of which worked [Figures 2, 4-5].

Hollein's next two architectural curating projects are polar opposites in content, although formally both were exercises in crossing over. The first was his *Dada Mobile Office* of 1969—part pneumatic architecture, part performance, part video art—it involved him landing a small Cessna airplane on a runway, then deploying an inflatable, transparent plastic office in which he could be seen talking on the telephone and typing. The second was a shocking exhibition devoted to the subject of *memento mori.* Commissioned in 1969 by Johannes Cladders, the director of the avant-garde Abteiberg Museum in Mönchengladbach, Germany, it was titled *Alles ist Architektur: TOT (Everything is Architecture: DEATH).* In Hollein's words, it addressed "death, archaeological excavation sites, archaeological burial grounds, mortuary shrouds, deathbeds, tombs and graves." As Cladders explains in his introduction, *Alles ist Architektur: TOT* was the first of the Mönchengladbach exhibitions to break down the boundary between the museum and the real world.[15] Hollein staged a happening outside the museum's walls, inviting visitors to dig for archaeological remains in the earth around the museum. They were then directed back inside the museum to an artificially created earthen mound which was another "archaeological site." "What will the objects buried in the earth in our time disclose to archaeologists in the future? It contains a hard hat, a golf club, the shards of a Coca Cola bottle, a crayon, and a pair of crampons (traction devices for mountain climbing)." The theme of death was carried throughout the museum: shrouds were hung from the ceiling of some galleries, while another contained a sarcophagus-like box covered with flowers left to wilt. The "archaeological finds" were given deliberately erroneous captions: a fool's cap, for example, was attributed to a king, a spiked helmet to a clown.

With this project, Hollein became, along with Joseph Beuys, among the first artists in the German-speaking world to break the taboo against confronting the sinister reality of Germany's role in World War II. Whereas Beuys's art referred to his own experiences in the German Wehrmacht, Hollein dared to address the Holocaust directly. A metal hose with a sprinkler attached—a reference to the gas jets at Auschwitz—was one such "archaeological find" of the exhibition, labeled "a cleansing instrument for the preservation of racial purity." Two small pamphlets, in a limited edition of fifty copies apiece, accompanied the exhibition. One was the actual catalog, introduced by Cladders and with a running commentary by Hollein. It also contained photographs of the exhibition opening, featuring, among other images, a performance by Joseph Beuys, Hollein and others in the act of excavating the "archeo-logical" site. The other was a catalog of his multifaceted oeuvre up to that time, as a means of stressing that the "everything" of architecture must also comprise a reflection on the dark side of German and Austrian history. Adding to the solemn, funereal aura of the exhibition, the catalogs were placed two-by-two in black, casket-like cardboard cases, each of which also contained two flowering sprigs of the type one might toss into an open grave.[16]

Never one to shy away from controversy or difficulty, with *Work and Behaviour, Life and Death,* his exhibition at the Austrian Pavilion for the 1972 Venice Biennale, Hollein once again returned to the theme of death. The display was divided into two parts. In the first, his transformed the interior of the Josef Hoffmann-designed pavilion into a minimalist and chilling morgue-like installation. He covered the walls, floors, and all objects within the space with sanitary white tiles and placed a grim dissecting table in a hallway next to a pool filled with blood. The installation, painful to behold, was based on a childhood memory of the death of his own father, which occurred when Hollein was six years old. The other half of the exhibition touched the other end of the emotional spectrum, containing an installation based on extreme tenderness and elation. It consisted of a raft fitted with a chair floating on a canal at the back of the pavilion. The image represents a reconstructed memory: he as a small child floating with his father on an Austrian lake. He reenacted the scene on the lagoon behind the Austrian pavilion with his own six-year-old son, Max.

In *MANtransFORMS,* presented at the Cooper-Hewitt Museum of Decorative Arts and Design (now the Cooper-Hewitt, Smithsonian Design Museum) in New York in 1976, the "everythingizing" intent was emphasized, both by Hollein and by the director of the design museum, Lisa Taylor. For one thing, although it was an architecture show, it contained no architecture proper. Hollein instead presented a series of rooms: one filled with dozens of different kinds of breads; another with various definitions of stars; another with dozens of door handles; a room containing brassieres; and a room constructed of paper. He invited a number of collaborators to create works for the exhibition. They included the architect Arata Isozaki, who created an installation in the form of a giant bird cage with an angel inside, Buckminster Fuller, who contributed a geodesic structure, and a divergent array of other designers, including George Nelson, Richard Meier, Murray Grigor, Ettore Sottsass, and Oswald Mathias Ungers. Lisa Taylor noted that, "The exhibition is different from a traditional object-show simply because it is 'experiential' in nature." She wrote, "each visitor's reactions will be affected by his or her unique back-ground and experience. It is participatory in the sense that it is demanding: there is nothing to tell the viewer whether this or that is to be looked at in a certain approved way."[17]

The exhibition was Hollein's ultimate exercise in curatorial "everythingizing." As Hollein put it: "Design is here understood as an approach to a problem, as an attitude toward action, shaping life and environment . . . . Design as process, and design as product, encompasses practically any aspect of life. Design can be urban design or architectural design or product design or dressmaking, but it can also be cooking or singing or making war or making love."[18] Taylor summed it up by stating that everyone is an artist.[19] In a 1974 interview conducted by Barbara Lee Diamonstein, Taylor says that Hollein was chosen to curate the first show of the new design museum because of his "everything is architecture," approach. "Design is everywhere," Taylor says, echoing Hollein. "We see it on the streets, in stores, in our own homes. The role of the Cooper-Hewitt Museum is to help people see design, to show how things are designed, and how they affect our lives. Not like streamlined design. No designer names on items, no famous manufacturers, no labels of 'good' or 'bad.'"[20] *MANtransFORMS* signaled the end of the first phase of Hollein's curatorial work and it was also the end of an era. It was 1976, the year—to recall the opening paragraph—that Charles Jencks introduced the concept of

Postmodernism to architecture in a lecture of the same title in the Netherlands, at the University of Technology of Eindhoven. It was also the year that MoMA organized the exhibition on the Beaux-Arts curated by Arthur Drexler.

From then on, a postmodernist retrenchment replaced a rebellious modernizing spirit of experimentation that had fired the cultural world of the late 1950s and 1960s in general, and Hans Hollein's work in particular. A generalized exuberant tendency toward "everythingizing" that had infused architecture would soon come to a halt. With postmodernism, architecture withdrew from the horror of war, ecological disaster, the alienating effects of new information technologies, and oppressive sexual politics.[21] Although Hollein's multifaceted work entered a new postmodern phase, in his curatorial activities, in spite of the *Strada Novissima,* he never completely abandoned the ambitions he had nurtured in the previous phase that we have just looked over. His installation for the Munich Olympic Games (1976) and his *Traum und Wirklichkeit* in Vienna (1984) are cases in point. But these are the subject of another essay.[22]

[Figure 5]

[1] For a further discussion of "everythingizing,"see Liane Lefaivre, "Everything is Architecture. Multiple Hans Hollein and the Art of Crossing Over," *Harvard Design Review* no. 18 (Spring/Summer 2003).

[2] For more information about the Richard Feigen Gallery, see Liane Lefaivre, "Hans Hollein's Richard Feigen Gallery," *DOCO-MOMO Journal,* 2003. For more about the exhibition to be curated by Rudi Fuchs and Harald Szeemann, see John Sailer interview with *Der Standard* (January 21, 2010).

[3] Hans Hollein, "Alles ist Architectur," *Bau* magazine (April 1968).

[4] This article is based on Liane Lefaivre, "Everything is Architecture. Multiple Hans Hollein and the Art of Crossing Over," and on my forthcoming *Modern Architectures, Austria* (London: Reaktion and Chicago: University of Chicago Press, 2015).

[5] Hans Hollein interview with Liane Lefaivre, August 7, 2000.

[6] For further discussion about the gallery see Susan Davidson and Philip Ryland, *Peggy Guggenheim. The Story of Art of the Century* (Venice: Peggy Guggenheim Collection, 2004).

[7] Peter Weibel, *Die Wiener Gruppe. Ein Moment der Moderne, 1954–1960* (Vienna: Springer Verlag, 1998).

[8] Hans Hollein interview with Liane Lefaivre, August 7, 2000.

[9] Hans Hollein, *Report to the Harkness Commonwealth Foundation,* 1960. Cited with a kind permission from Hans Hollein.

[10] Hans Hollein interview with Liane Lefaivre, August 7. 2000.

[11] Susan Sontag, "Happenings: The Art of Radical Juxtapositions," 1962, reprinted in her *Against Interpretation and Other Essays* (New York: Penguin, 2009), 263–273.

[12] Hans Hollein, *Plastic Space,* thesis submitted in partial satisfaction of the requirements for the degree of Master of Architecture, College of Environmental Design in the Graduate Division of the University of California, approved by James Prestini and Joseph Esherick, July 19, 1969.

[13] See forthcoming Liane Lefaivre, *Modern Architectures in Austria,* Ch. 7 and 8 for a fuller exposition of this exhibition.

[14] *Austriennale,* ed. Hans Hollein, *Austriennale - Österreich auf der 14. Triennale di Milano 1968: die grosse Zahl : vierzehnte Triennale di Milano, Internationale Ausstellung fr⬚ moderne dekorative und angewandte Kunst und moderne Architektur = L'Austria alla 14. Triennale di Milano 1968 : il grande numero : quattordicesima Triennale di Milano,* *Esposizione internazionale delle arti decorative e industriali moderne e dell' architettura moderna = Austria at the 14th Triennale di Milano 1968 : the great number : fourteenth Triennale di Milano, International Exhibition of Modern Decorative and Industrial Arts and of Modern Architecture* (Vienna: Regierungskommissar für die 14. Triennale, 1968).

[15] Johannes Cladders, "Eröffnung," 1970, reprinted in *The Austrian Phenomenon* (Vienna: Architekturzentrum, 2009) 872–874.

[16] *Alles ist Architektur: TOT,* exhibition catalog, ed. Hans Hollein (Mönchengladbach, Germany: Abteiberg Museum, 1970).

[17] Lisa Taylor, "Einleitung," Introduction in *Hans Hollein, MAN-transFORMS, Concepts of an Exhibition* (Vienna: Loecker Verlag, 1989), 9-12. Taylor writes: "It was my hope that the inaugural exhibition would present a new and holistic view of design."

[18] Lisa Taylor, "Press Release," 6. Unpublished manuscript. Cited with a permission of the Cooper Hewitt Museum Archive. Special thanks to archivist Elizabeth Broman.

[19] Ibid., 6.

[20] Lisa Taylor interviewed by Barbaralee Diamonstein-Spielvogel in "Inside New York's Art World: Lisa Taylor, Coorper Hewitt Museum" on October 6, 1976. Part of the Diamonstein Spielvogel Video Archive at the Duke University. Accessed online: htts://www.youtube.com/watch?v=5DVITZudHg.

[21] Alexander Tzonis and Liane Lefaivre, "The Narcissist Phase in Architecture," in *Harvard Architecture Magazine,* No. 1 (1980).

[22] The author would like to acknowledge her gratitude to the late Hans Hollein for agreeing to be interviewed in the summer and fall of 2000 and for kindly providing archival material related to his time in the U.S. as a Harkness Commonwealth fellow and to his curatorial work. The help of the late Madeleine Jenewein, his assistant, was invaluable. The Cooper-Hewitt Museum kindly provided electronic versions of texts of Hans Hollein and Lisa Taylor from the Cooper-Hewitt archive. The Beinecke Library at Yale and the librarians of the MAK Library in Vienna provided important assistance as well.

Exhibiting Ideologies: Architecture at the Venice Biennale, 1968–1980

Léa-Catherine Szacka

> Following the painters and film-makers, the architects have now been admitted to
> the Venice Biennale as well. The response to this, the first Architecture Biennale
> was one of disappointment. The participants who exhibited in Venice formed
> an avant-garde with the fronts reversed. Under the slogan 'the presence of the
> past' they sacrificed the tradition of modernity in the name of a new species of
> historicism.[1]

So complained, in September 1980, the German philosopher Jürgen Habermas, when awarded the
Adorno prize by the city of Frankfurt. This public pronouncement ignited a virulent polemic within the
press as well as connected architectural discourse, via exhibition, to the nascent philosophical debate
opposing modernism to postmodernism.

The 1980, or arguably the first[2] Venice Architecture Biennale, remains one of the strongest curatorial
acts in the history of contemporary architecture: Paolo Portoghesi, with the assistance of an international advisory board,[3] created an exhibition named *La Presenza del Passato (The Presence of the Past)* in
which form, discourse, content, venue, catalog, press coverage, and circulation constituted a highly
coherent apparatus delivering a message that, despite its plurality, remained in tune with postmodernism's main ideas. The 1980 Venice Architecture Biennale, and, more particularly, *The Strada Novissima,*
created a space in which architecture functioned as postmodernism's avatar [Figure 1].

Yet, as I would like to suggest here,[4] this exhibition and its effects on the architectural scene and far
beyond, cannot and should not be read as an isolated event, but rather as the end of the beginning and
the beginning of the end of a fertile period of exchanges between ideologies, disciplines, and cultural
institutions.

In the summer of 1968, the Venice Biennale, like the Milan Triennale a few weeks earlier, was assaulted by demonstrators. The rebels, led by painter Emilio Vedova, were suggesting a boycott of the Biennale, an exhibition that was still operating according to models put in place by the Fascist regime and was seen as the receptacle for the commodification of art mainly intended to please the dominating class.[5] The Biennale, like many other cultural institutions, was criticized for being too elitist and far from people's daily concerns [Figure 2].

In Venice, the Biennale's organizers had anticipated troubles that they hoped to prevent by reinforcing police presence. In the opening of the exhibition catalog, Giovanni Favaretto Fisca, president of the institution, and mayor of Venice, declared:

> The organization of such important exhibitions always raises some problems, but this time the problems are extraordinary. You could say that every Biennale is like a large eye, open to the evolution of artistic problematics within the world; but I think that never before has it been opened in a climate of such profound transformation like the current [one], where aesthetic needs are ever more united and even become an expressive means of that anxiety for renewal, which tends to radically mute the existing relationships between individuals and social groups.[6]

The state of affairs, as described by Fisca, would result in a transformation of the Venice Biennale and of a broader landscape of worldwide cultural institutions.

After the summer disruptions, the Comune di Venezia held, in November 1968, a congress on the Biennale's reform, opening an intense debate regarding the dilemma between reforming or closing the Biennale. The option of reforming the institution was finally adopted, and concluded in July 1973 in the Biennale's new status. This new *modus operandi* tried to respond to the agency of the time by fulfilling many of the protestors' demands, including the abolition of the Biennale's sales office and awards. A "new" and more "social" Biennale, renovated both conceptually and in its core organization, would come to life, and, among other things, would open its doors to architecture.

. . . "Long Live the Biennale!"

After minor local events organized by the Biennale in 1974 and 1975, a first major exhibition, nicknamed *Biennale Anno Zero,* was put together in the summer of 1976 under the directorship of the Italian archi- tect Vittorio Gregotti.[7] Renamed *International Visual Arts & Architecture Exhibition,* it attempted to investi- gate the visual arts as it opens up to new disciplinary identities. In inviting an architect to direct a visual arts event, the Biennale's president Carlo Ripa di Meana was facing two conditions: first, Gregotti sug- gested that the grand exhibition would, from now on, be organized around a unitary theme, which, in 1976, was the relationship between art and the anthropogeographic environment; second, for Gregotti it was essential that the Biennale extended its scope to the discipline of architecture.

In 1976, three small architectural displays were part of the general exhibition. All three were concerned with the heritage of the Modern movement. While two were historical, questioning the origins of the movement—one on rationalism under the Fascist era in the Chiesa di San Lorenzo,[8] and one on the history and legacy of the Werkbund at Ca' Pesaro[9]—the third display focused on contemporary pro- duction. The exhibition, *Europa/America: Architetture Urbane – Alternative Suburbane,* if not memorable as a curatorial act, laid the ground for many of the ideas that would later resurface in the 1980 exhibition, *The Presence of the Past,* by bringing together a group of twenty-five of the most preeminent figures of European and American architecture to share and discuss their recent work and ideas —fostering the discursive turn in architecture. At least partially, it provided architects with a platform for creation and research, promoting the exhibition as a site of production. It reused and most probably helped

[Figure 1]

[Figure 2]

[Figure 3]

[Figure 4]

salvage the Magazzini del Sale, an old salt warehouse on the Guidecca Canal which was threatened by imminent destruction by the municipality of Venice. In short, as Joseph Rykwert phrased it: *Europa/America* was nothing more than a public display of faith in contemporary architecture, a discipline that had suddenly been propelled into the position of mediator for the visual world [Figure 5].

"Enough Demonstrations. Let's go to the Discothèque!"

The 1970s represented a major turning point in the history of modern Italy: the political and social changes in Italy in the years immediately preceding the 1980 Venice Architecture Biennale might have been instrumental in making such an event possible. It took place at the watershed moment between the *anni di piombo* (years of lead)—a period characterized, in Italy, by a strong political dialectic that translated in sociopolitical turmoil, violence, and terrorism—and the 1980s, witnessing depoliticization and the need for lighter matters, as well as more playfulness. In 1978, a major breakthrough occurred: on March 6, Democrazia Cristiana (Christian Democrats) leader Aldo Moro was kidnapped by the Brigade Rosse, and on May 9 he was killed after the government refused to negotiate with the terrorists. After 1978, Italians found themselves ideologically orphaned and did not want to be involved in any political or social cause other than a return to private life. Paired with this turn of events, a loss of faith in any collective form of liberation or realization took place. This phenomenon represented a sort of 180-degree turn that has been termed a *riflusso verso il privato* (return to the private life). This turn signified, among other things, a sexual revolution and an upsurge in hedonism and individualism, accompanied by an increasing Americanization of society. In Venice, the Carnival, a cultural tradition long gone, was reactivated as yet another way of making life more light-spirited, by bringing joy and color into people's lives. And if the organizers of the 1979 Carnival were afraid of failure, to their great surprise, the lagoon was invaded with people dancing in the piazzas, something that had not happened for at least two centuries.

Also important in the late 1970s was the transformation of the Italian Socialist party (PSI) towards a more center-left position. With their move to the center of the political spectrum, the Socialists, led by Bettino Craxi, adopted a more progressive position, away from traditional values linked to Catholicism and a rural mode of living promoted by the ruling Christian Democrats; they also dissociated themselves from the massive Marxist culture aligned with the working class endorsed by the Italian Communist Party (PCI). Since the PCI had historically been linked to a socially engaged architecture and to the Modern movement in general, a new Postmodern style that was neither modern nor conservative seemed perfectly adaptable to the image the Socialists wanted to project. The 1980 Venice Architecture Biennale, with its lack of social claims or ideological debate, its spatial and discursive individualism, consumerism, and competition between architects, and its promotion of Postmodernism might have been facilitated or patronized by the PSI.

The Exhibition as Media Event

The curatorial act in favor of contemporary architecture that took place at the Biennale in 1980 was largely authored by the architect and historian Paolo Portoghesi. Named director of the Architecture Biennale in 1979, Portoghesi strongly believed in the necessity of making—of creating, with the exhibition—a performative space and an occasion for a real physical encounter between architecture and the public. The *Strada Novissima,* an enchanting full-scale scenographic street of facades built inside the Corderie dell'Arsenale di Venezia, gave young and inexperienced architects a hands-on opportunity to develop their own architectural language, contributing to the blossoming of Postmodern architecture, while changing the minds of those like Leon Krier, who famously declared, "I do not build, therefore I am an architect."

Portoghesi, in an attempt to generate an authoritative event for postmodernism, decided—perhaps in a political and strategic gesture—to seek the assistance of an international committee of influential personalities who he thought shared his ideological view on architecture: Charles Jencks, the

Anglo-American guru who had officially coined the term *Postmodernism* in 1977; Vincent Scully, the American defender of the Venturis; the British historian Kenneth Frampton; the American architect Robert A.M. Stern; and, of course his long-time friend, the Norwegian phenomenologist Christian Norberg-Schulz. Together they formed an advisory board, meeting on several occasions to determine the form and content of the exhibition [Figure 4].

In the winter of 1979, while the show was slowly taking shape, Portoghesi commissioned his friend Aldo Rossi to design a small floating construction for a theater-architecture joint event.[10] More than mere construction, the Teatro del Mondo was a poetic event, a living version of Rossi's theory of the analogous city. It served as a testing ground for the curatorial strategy later adopted in building the *Strada Novissima.* In late 1979, perhaps prompted by the successful experience of the Teatro del Mondo, the organization committee intended to ask each architect to design and build a new public transport terminal (or *vaporetto*) stop for the Laguna. Though, as is often the case with the Biennale, time and budget restrictions made this idea impossible to implement. This impossibility coincided with the discovery of the magnificent abandoned space of the Corderie dell'Arsenale, which for Portoghesi was reminiscent of a visit to a German Christmas market and the historical image of the Genovese Strada Nuova. Thus, the *Strada Novissima* was envisioned as a sort of Venetian masquerade version of the 1927

[Figure 5]

Weissenhof Siedlung completed in (and for) a media-dominated society. As Charles Jencks recalls it, "Instead of building the buildings—we didn't have the time nor the money—we built the facades and we took the message through because it was amplified by the media, just in the same way as Johnson's AT&T building became a media event."[11]

Conclusion

The 1980 Venice Architecture Biennale changed the significance of architectural exhibitions. Simulacra have long been used for architectural exhibitions. In the modern tradition of exhibitions, three-dimensional, full-scale models have often served as prototypes or experimental devices, integral to the production of architecture, and representing something that either did, might, or could have existed. The houses built in the garden of New York's Museum of Modern Art in the 1940s and 1950s, for example, served as projections into the future, both for the creators and for the public. Yet, in the 1980 Biennale exhibition, simulacra were employed purely to generate images. *The Presence of the Past,* with its *Strada Novissima,* was not raw documentation of architectural projects and it was not a prototype. Neither was it a formal abstraction, suggesting what the future might look like.

In the postmodern era, characterized by an ever-increasing flow of information, the usefulness of exhibitions was put into question. In an exhibition, models are more powerful than drawings, allowing the visitors to project themselves into space. By creating a giant reproduction of a street, the organizers of the 1980 Biennale allowed the visitors not only to look inside the model but to physically experience it and to become part of the street. The political and social space of the street, as simulated in the Arsenale, thus becomes fully performative: a place to see and be seen, between consumption and exhibitionism.

Unlike other architectural exhibitions whose displayed individual objects—drawings and models—may survive the ephemerality of the ensemble and event, not much remained of the 1980 Venice Architecture Biennale. The *Strada Novissima* existed for a very short time—between 1980 and 1982—and the full-scale parts of the exhibition were mainly temporary and dismantled or lost after the show's presentation. Thus, once the show was over, nothing was left but a scattered collection of photographs, some video footage, the exhibition catalogs, and individual recollections [Figure 3]. In a way, the 1980 Venice Architecture Biennale not only preceded the buildings, but surpassed them. The temporariness of the facades and their explicitly theoretical quality drew attention to the ephemerality of the object, and pointed to an underlying duplicity about the nature of representation itself. Flipping the relationship between reality and representation, the facades of the *Strada Novissima* were a hybrid between full-scale images and models, yet one with no reference attached to them. It was truly its ephemerality that contributed to its appeal.

As with the case of the overly circulated black-and-white shot of the Villa Savoy model surrounded by six photographs of Le Corbusier's built work in the 1932 MoMA exhibition, it might be difficult, when seeing a single view of the *Strada Novissima,* to grasp what exactly happened in Venice in the summer of 1980. Nobody, not even Vittorio Gregotti or other anti-postmodern purists of the time, would today deny the paramount importance of the curatorial act that *The Presence of the Past* represented. Operating a particularly successful connection between form and content, many features of postmodernism converged in *The Presence of the Past* exhibition: from consumerism, pluralism, and communication to the performative space, the supremacy of images, and the cult of personality with its ensuing paradigm of self-representation.

In the wake of the 1980s, through debate and publications, architects and critics expressed their views with a marked tendency towards more publicly oriented exhibitions. The Biennale was at the forefront of this shift. No longer exhibiting ideologies it became an important part of the architectural media apparatus with its mechanism of control and validation. It adopted a new formula, as much as a means to save the Biennale as well as a means to reinvent the way to exhibit architecture.

[1] Jürgen Habermas "Modernity – An Unfinished Project," in *Critical Essays on The Philosophical Discourse of Modernity,* eds. Maurizio Passerin d'Entrèves and Seyla Benhabib, (Cambridge: MIT Press, 1997), 38.

[2] It is sometimes said that the 1976 Venice Biennale, including three smaller architectural exhibitions, was the first architecture Biennale. I considered that the period spanning from 1975—date of the exhibition on the Mulino Stuky—to 1979, year of the creation of the architecture sector of the Biennale, can be seen as the "pre-history" of the architecture Biennale. The real independent exhibition dedicated solely to architecture, and called First International Exhibitions of the Venice Biennale, opened on 27, July 1980.

[3] The advisory board was composed of Robert A.M. Stern, Costantino Dardi, Rosario Giuffré, Udo Kultermann, and Giuseppe Mazzariol. This board was joined by the group of critics: Charles Jencks, Vincent Scully, and Christian Norberg-Schulz.

[4] This essay is extracted from my PhD dissertation, "Exhibiting Architecture: Three Narratives for the History of the 1980 Venice Architecture Biennale" (Bartlett School of Architecture, University College London, 2015).

[5] See Pascale Budillon Puma, *La Biennale di Venezia dalla guerra alla crisi 1948–1968* (Bari: Palomar, 1995).

[6] Giovanni Favaretto Fisca in *Catalogo della XXXIVth Esposizione Biennale Internazionale d'Arte di Venezia,* (Venezia Alfieri Edizioni d'Arte, 1968), XVII. See appendix 61.

[7] See my article "Debates on Display at the 1976 Venice Biennale" in *Place and Displacement: Exhibiting Architecture,* ed. Thordis Arrhenius, Wallis Miller, and Jéremie McGowan (Zurich: Lars Müller Publishers, 2014).

[8] A 2,000-square-meter display presented in the disused sixteenth-century church of San Lorenzo situated in the Sestiere of Castello from July 14 to October 10, 1976.

[9] A 1,500-square-meter display at Ca' Pesaro from July 18 to October 10, 1976.

[10] The Teatro del Mondo was commissioned for the exhibition *Venezia e lo Spazio Scenico,* an event organised by the architecture sector of the Biennale, together with the theater sector.

[11] Charles Jencks, interview with author and Eva Branscome (February 16, 2009).

"We fight the battle with the drawings on the walls": Exhibiting Architecture at the Architectural Association

Irene Sunwoo

In April 1973, the Institute of Contemporary Arts in London hosted an exhibition commemorating the 125th anniversary of the Architectural Association (AA).[1] Founded in 1847 by two students as an educational alternative to the apprenticeship system, the AA—as the exhibition's survey of student work sought to illustrate—had maintained its progressive ethos for well over a century.[2] Providing a portal into the history of this independent institution was a reconstruction of an interior from 36 Bedford Square, the Georgian townhouses in central London that the school has occupied since 1918 [Figure 1]. Winding through an adjacent sequence of rooms that displayed student projects from the late nineteenth and early twentieth centuries, the visitor would have witnessed the school's "Beaux-Arts" phase and its subsequent "Disintegration" before entering a large room bounded by an expansive undulating wall. Fittingly, this modernist display device (evocative of Aalto's interior at the 1939 Finnish Pavilion) chronicled the school's participation in the "Modern Movement," as town planning projects from the late 1930s gave way to postwar institutional, housing, and urban schemes in a subsection on "Architecture and Social Objective." With a sharp turn at the end of this wall, however, the Modern Movement's own disintegration unfolded in subsections on "Technocracy," "Formality,"

[Figure 1]

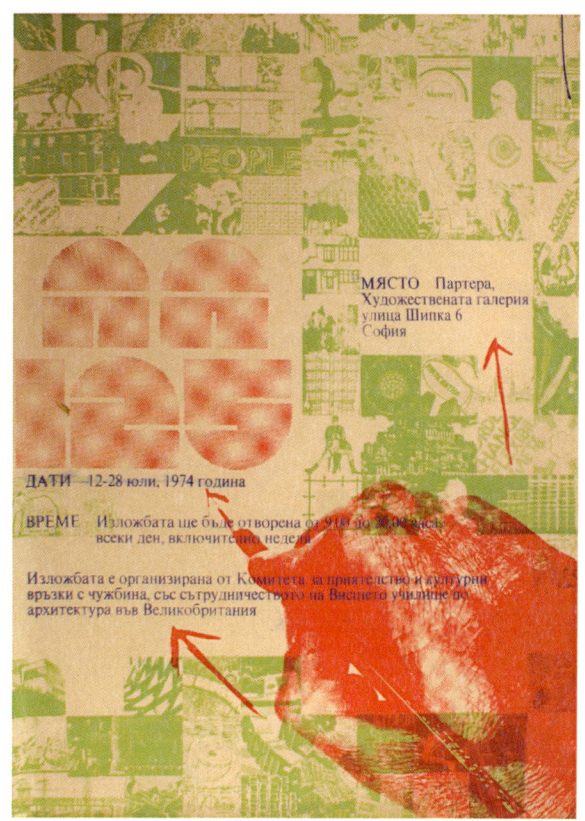

[Figure 2]

and finally "Style." From this point in the exhibition, visitors would have been drawn to what was the concluding and ultimate focal point in this historical itinerary.[3] Nestled into the opposite side of the undulating wall, and therefore located on the other side of the "Modern Movement," a suspended drum delineated a historical episode identified as *The AA Now.* Its interior surface functioned as a screen for projecting student work of the late 1960s and early 1970s, illustrating the tail end of an "electric decade" when tutors, including members of Archigram and Cedric Price, had ruled the school.[4]

But beyond the AA's most recent student output, what this display mechanism also illuminated was an overt consciousness—an anxiety, even—concerning its institutional present and immediate future, and with good reason. Just two years before the AA's anniversary exhibition opened at the ICA, financial woes and an institutional revolution nearly led to the school's closure, a fate thwarted by the instatement of the Canadian-born architectural educator Alvin Boyarsky as the school chairman in 1971.[5] On the one hand, then, the exhibition positioned *The AA Now* as the next chapter in a long and complex institutional history of pedagogical shifts—a history that, in the exhibition, doubled as a narrative framework for Modern architecture's rise and fall. On the other hand, *The AA Now* also presented an open-ended, seemingly *unfinishable* chapter, as its simultaneous and flickering projections rendered the school's postmodern coordinates elusive and resistant to linear narrative. Totalizing an inconstant sphere of production, this display mechanism spectacularized a dialectic that would inform Boyarsky's institutional transformation of the AA in the coming years.

Indeed, a significant component of this institutional transformation was Boyarsky's development of a rigorous exhibitions program at the school. Over the course of his two decades as chairman (1971–1990), the AA staged an extraordinary range of architectural exhibitions which featured student projects, historical research, as well as the work of contemporary architects and artists. Accounts of Boyarsky's career often gloss over this aspect of his chairmanship, and instead privilege his groundbreaking innovations in AA studio pedagogy.[6] Through a reconsideration of the AA's increasing commitment to exhibiting architecture during the 1970s and 1980s, however, I want to insist that exhibitions did not play an auxiliary role in its educational program. Rather, as chairman, Boyarsky engineered and institutionalized a reciprocity between exhibitionary and pedagogical practices that would fuel and complicate the school's engagement in architecture's emerging postmodern trajectories. But if the following discussion deepens an understanding of his pioneering stewardship of the AA, it might also give us pause to reflect on the role of exhibitions in early-twenty-first-century schools of architecture, where curatorial activities have seemingly become requisite modes of production.

The AA's 125th anniversary exhibition was not only one of the first major projects that Boyarsky tackled as school chairman; it was also his first time wearing a curatorial hat.[7] During the 1960s, previous academic posts at the University of Illinois in Chicago, the University of Oregon, and even at the AA had not presented him such opportunities. Nor were exhibitions a feature of the International Institute of Design Summer Sessions, the London-based summer school that Boyarsky directed in the early 1970s.[8] Though he was lacking firsthand curatorial experience, a likely source of inspiration for a public exhibition of student projects was the 1971 show *Education of an Architect.* Hosted by the Museum of Modern Art in New York, this showcase of recent work by Cooper Union architecture students was the public debut of John Hejduk's groundbreaking new curriculum, launched at the school in 1967 and developed with the painter Robert Slutzky. Compounded by its handsome accompanying catalog and enthusiastic reviews, Boyarsky's visit to the exhibition surely ignited a competitive streak in the AA's new chairman, who throughout his career maintained a friendly rivalry with Hejduk.[9]

As he began to cultivate the AA's international profile during the 1970s, the agency of exhibitions was certainly not lost on Boyarsky. Following its first appearance at the ICA in 1973, the anniversary exhibition traveled for five years. With stops including New York, Berlin, Paris, Zürich, Warsaw, and Adelaide, each iteration was chaperoned by an AA staff member and, at times, the school chairman himself [Figure 2]. Commenting on Boyarsky's inaugural curatorial project, long-time AA tutor Peter Cook shrewdly observed that the anniversary exhibition had had a dual function: first, to cull an increasingly multinational student body at a time when cuts in government grants to the AA—and the resulting increase in fees—saw a dramatic decrease in the enrollment of British students. The second function of the exhibition was to impress upon staff and students that they were the "continuing part of an extraordinary and unique institution." In this way, the intention, Cook implied, was to "spur the [AA's] inmates to push and produce and clarify their thrust so that they, too, might be included in the ongoing tourist show."[10] To turn out pedagogical end products that could define "The AA Now," and in turn enter into the space of institutional history directed at design tutors and students, this provocation explicitly imposed stakes on pedagogy—a tactic characteristic of Boyarsky's approach to architectural education, broadly speaking, and certainly pervasive in his AA chairmanship.

Under his direction, the AA abandoned its postwar professionalized curriculum and instead began to operate as a laboratory for an international network of avant-garde architects, historians, and theorists during the 1970s and 1980s. Among many others, tutors who contributed to this vibrant episode included Nigel Coates, Peter Cook, Robin Evans, Zaha Hadid, Charles Jencks, Daniel Libeskind, Rem Koolhaas, Léon Krier, Robin Middleton, Bernard Tschumi, Dalibor Vesely, and Elia Zenghelis. In conjunction with his role as impresario of this rather remarkable cast of teachers, Boyarsky's most well known pedagogical innovation at the AA is its unit system. Established as the basis of the school's five-year undergraduate design program in 1973, this competitive framework of vertical studios (or units) marked an abrupt departure from the horizontal modernist curriculum that had dominated its postwar educational program. Alternatively, the unit system provided tutors autonomous pedagogical territory in which to develop highly individualized, year-long teaching agendas—whether engaging with Russian Constructivism or the pre-industrial city, whether exploring sustainable technologies or conceptual art practices. Structured to support a plurality of investigations and teaching methods, the unit system thus signaled a broader shift in the education of architects: from a modern system of professional training that codified the architect's responsibility to design and build for the needs of society to a postmodern educational model premised on the continuous production of theoretical and critical inquiry.[11]

Exhibitions played a strategic role in the AA's new model of studio pedagogy. Pressuring tutors to develop and pitch their unit agendas at the start of each year, and in turn pressuring students to perform as discerning consumers, the so-called "marketplace" of the unit system concluded each of its academic cycles with an end-of-year exhibition. While this was a common practice that preceded Boyarsky (at the AA and indeed elsewhere), at Bedford Square the display of student work was now choreographed to amplify and concretize the competitive sphere of its "marketplace." As the school declared in the mid-1970s, the end-of-year exhibition was more like a "bazaar" where "[c]onsumer durables co-exist with the bring-and-buy stalls, hand crafts, cottage industries and obscure purveyors of precious goods."[12] Accordingly, each unit was allotted a space within the school not simply to illustrate, but to further pitch its now highly crafted theoretical stance [Figure 3]. Projected across every available interior surface of the school was the continual reinvention of "The AA Now": an institutional topology fraught with ideological clashes that were to stimulate the next season of the "marketplace." And as if to prolong this inherent friction and publicize its fruits, each year this collection of fleeting architectural projections was strategically arrested in the form of a supporting display mechanism that was introduced in 1975: the *AA Projects Review,* a catalog of student work that, in effect, functioned as an exportable encapsulation of the school's yearly exploits. A series of well orchestrated adjustments to the AA's operations thus saw the display of student work begin to function as but one element within an increasingly complex matrix of pedagogical, publishing, and curatorial practices.

Likely prompted by his experience with the anniversary exhibition's world tour, early on in his chairmanship Boyarsky pushed the school to regularly play host to traveling exhibitions; these were usually mounted in the Front Members Room, a public space located on the second floor of the AA's Georgian interior. Several of these early shows, interestingly, focused on French and Belgian modernist avant-gardes, and were sent to Bedford Square courtesy of Maurice Culot, who was then in the midst of building an Archive of Modern Architecture in Brussels and found in the AA a willing host for his research discoveries.

[Figure 3]

[Figure 4]

Reevaluating its in-house curatorial potential, the AA soon sought to expand its enterprise through the production of its own exhibitions based on original research. The first of these was organized and designed by unit tutor Robin Evans in 1976. Based on his doctoral thesis at the University of Essex, the exhibition, *The Fabrication of Virtue,* examined the design of penal institutions during the eighteenth and nineteenth centuries; in 1982 Evans expanded and refined this study in a book of the same title. Installed in the Front Members Room, this rigorous scholarly investigation was, however, largely overshadowed that year by the AA's second original exhibition. *Islamic Art and Architecture in Libya* was curated by George Michell, an Islamicist who was then offering a lecture course on this subject at the AA. Funded by the Libyan government, the exhibition was part of the "World of Islam Festival" in London. A massively scaled cultural event, the festival spanned across multiple institutions in the city.[13] The AA's own contribution was truly spectacular. On display at Bedford Square were "maps, photographs, wooden doors, carved stone inscriptions, coloured tile panels, costumes and archaeological finds," all of which filled the school to the brim—from its public meeting rooms to its reception area, from the lecture hall to the main stair.[14] A blockbuster show, *Islamic Art and Architecture in Libya* revealed how the AA could further strategize its curatorial projects: funding could be acquired through foreign agencies and, importantly, the whole of its premises could be exploited all year round.

The creation of additional exhibition space therefore became a key concern as the school embarked on the renovation of its premises in the summer of 1978. Supervised by AA tutor Rick Mather, the building renovation entailed new lavatories and a bookshop; the refurbishment of the lecture hall, restaurant, and bar (unquestionably the true heart of the school, to this day); and a new exhibition gallery. This reorganization of institutional space not only enabled the rapid infiltration of exhibitions throughout the school, but its newly reconfigured interior also made it possible to stage multiple exhibitions simultaneously: in the new gallery (ground floor); in the Front Members Room and in the bar (second floor); and now even in the new restaurant (basement level). Architecturally, pedagogically, and institutionally, Bedford Square was fully programmed for the production of architectural exhibitions. As testimony, in the 1979/1980 academic year—a particularly fruitful period of curatorial activity—the school put on a staggering total of seventeen exhibitions.[15]

One can discern even deeper layers of complexity within this "exhibitionary complex," to borrow Tony Bennett's notion of those sites where discipline, education, and spectacle converge.[16] Building upon its earliest curatorial forays, the AA continued to stage monographic historical shows. Topics spanned from the illustrations of Joseph Gandy to the paintings of Alvar Aalto, from Czech Functionalism to the career of Dimitris Pikionis. Often enabling the school to lay claim to being the "first" UK venue to show certain historical material, such exhibitions testified to "the AA's continuing interest in nineteenth- and earlier twentieth-century work," and, in turn, Boyarsky's ongoing support of architectural research.[17] Moreover, such curatorial projects should also be understood as part of an educational strategy to expose students to historical topics and issues not addressed elsewhere in the AA's academic program.

Indeed, as Cook remarked in 1981, the "style and range of AA exhibitions during the developed Boyarsky regime can now be seen and discussed as an instrument."[18] Flourishing during the 1980s, this "developed regime" aggressively yielded a constant stream of lectures, publications, and exhibitions that worked in concert with the unit system to realize and institutionalize an intensive and international culture of exchange. Accordingly, exhibitions also became an "instrument" for monitoring the AA's own unique breed of design pedagogy, the unit system. In 1981, the school launched a joint exhibitions and publications series titled *Themes,* which traced the evolution of selected units—including those taught by Dalibor Vesely and Mohsen Mostafavi; Bernard Tschumi and Nigel Coates; Peter Cook, Christine Hawley, and Ron Herron; and Michael Gold. The *Themes* series, then, functioned as self-administered, critical close-ups of the unit system that supplemented the expansive institutional portraits the annual publication of the *AA Projects Review* was relentlessly documenting.

It's just a chandelier—which is an eighteenth century chandelier—[and] an eighteenth century marble fireplace, with nice windows overlooking a green London square, and a bar which sells whiskey and wine, [with] lots of comfortable chairs. Students get their crits in the bar or under the chandelier. It's like downtown. You come to meet people to talk.[22]

Enamored by this vignette, Boyarsky summed up the "relative informality" of the AA by declaring "there's no place, there's no money, and nobody's there for very long periods of time. It's very interesting." The chandelier, the fireplace, and even the fine views of Bedford Square were vestiges of an old-world conviviality that had withstood the winds of change. And, at the same time, these were highly performative anachronisms, ossified symbols of tradition that clung to the skeleton of an institution now eviscerated to maximize the circulation, pursuit, and consumption of ideas, and to provoke the continual reinvention of "The AA Now."

[Figure 5]

The dynamics of the AA's "exhibitionary complex" were further complicated as historical episodes from architecture's past and the ongoing evolution of units were juxtaposed with the work of contemporary artists and architects (including AA tutors), whose projects regularly graced the school's interiors in the form of exhibitions. Shows spotlighted the work of Peter Eisenman, Zaha Hadid, Daniel Libeskind, Future Systems, James Wines, Lebbeus Woods, Eduardo Paolozzi, Mario Botta, and Daniel Weil, for example. With its decorative moldings, fireplaces, and scenic views, the Georgian interiors of the school paradoxically created a level playing field across generations and ideologies. And yet, even the architecture of the school premises could not always support this influx of theories and projects. As an extension of the drawings and models displayed within the townhouses—and as if the AA had burst at the seams—full-scale outdoor installations by John Hejduk, Mary Miss, and Coop Himme(l)blau began to occupy the square in the late 1980s [Figures 4-5].

In the AA's prolific publication of accompanying catalogs for nearly all its exhibitions, a similar logic is discernible, stemming from an acute awareness of the programmatic limitations of the very space of the school. Nowhere was the intertwined relationship between exhibitions and publications more deftly handled than in Boyarsky's lavish *Folios* series, introduced in 1983. Packaging essays and reproductions of drawings in twelve-by-twelve-inch boxes, the *Folios* were not just exhibition catalogs; they were portable exhibitions in and of themselves. For, as Boyarsky encouraged readers, the enclosed drawings could be hung on the walls of one's own home.[19]

Certainly, drawing gained new currency at the AA during Boyarsky's "developed regime," so much so that, for the chairman, drawing had become inextricable from the very identity of the school. In an interview conducted in 1983, Boyarsky offered the following remarks, which amount to an institutional mission statement.

> If you have a curriculum then you are absolved of any other responsibility. It is as if you can wage the battle of architectural education with a typewriter, and having the best curriculum makes you the best school. We're into something quite different. We create a very rich compost for students to develop and grow from and we fight the battle with the drawings on the wall. We're in pursuit of architecture, we discuss it boldly, we draw it as well as we can and we exhibit it. We are one of the few institutions left in the world that keeps its spirit alive.[20]

The "battle of architectural education": a battle over what, precisely? To my mind, it is not simply a matter of "curriculum" versus "no curriculum." Rather, the "battle" that architectural education "fights" is for the disciplinary preservation of architecture; but, more specifically, it is the "pursuit" of an architecture that exceeds the "autonomy of form" as much as it does what Boyarsky called postmodernism's "dead hand of historicism"—the latter a tendency, as the chairman and his tutors asserted, to which the AA had remained immune, despite the teachings of Léon Krier and Charles Jencks during the 1970s. Instead, in its "battle," the AA sought to sustain an expansive culture of architecture, one harvested from an arable terrain of polemic. As the genesis of discourse, production, and events, drawings fueled this "pursuit" that was, according to Boyarsky, the onus of architectural education. Like trophies, they were valiantly—though only fleetingly—hung on the walls of the AA to document an unending succession of victories.

To conclude, another veritable mission statement, offered by Boyarsky at the very start of his chairmanship, casts this "battlefield" in different light. In place of a traditional curriculum, the AA offered an "interactive kaleidoscopic situation," he explained in a 1972 lecture.[21] Saturated by a cacophony of positions and with no tenured tutors, it was a highly mutable atmosphere. Indeed, with students and staff primarily working at home and in nearby offices, respectively, Boyarsky announced (with a touch of pride) that the AA "doesn't have any facilities."

[1] The exhibition took place at the ICA from April 5–April 29, 1973.

[2] For a brief yet informative overview of the AA's nineteenth-century origins and its early twentieth-century development, see John Summerson, *The Architectural Association, 1847–1947* (London: Architectural Association, 1947).

[3] Separate from this chronological exhibition scheme was a gallery corridor in which a display of student projects was organized around the theme "The AA's Contribution to Housing."

[4] Peter Cook, "The Electric Decade: An Atmosphere at the AA School 1963–1973," in James Gowan, ed., *The Architectural Association: A Continuing Experiment* (London: The Architectural Press, 1975), 137–147.

[5] On the institutional context and circumstances leading to Boyarsky's chairmanship, see Irene Sunwoo, "From the 'Well-Laid Table' to the 'Marketplace': The Architectural Association Unit System," *Journal of Architectural Education* 65, no. 2 (March 2012): 24–41.

[6] An exception is to be found in Igor Marjanovic, "Lines and Words on Display: Alvin Boyarsky as a Collector, Curator and Publisher," *Architectural Research Quarterly* 14, no. 2 (June 2010): 165–174.

[7] Assisting the AA chairman were various AA staff members, including James Gowan, Charles Jencks, Peter Cook, and Dennis Crompton. Through Archigram's newly established professional office, Cook and Crompton were also responsible for the exhibition's design.

[8] See Irene Sunwoo, "Pedagogy's Progress: Alvin Boyarsky's International Institute of Design," *Grey Room* 34 (Winter 2009), 28–57; and the forthcoming volume, *In Progress: The International Institute of Design Summer Sessions,* ed. Sunwoo (London: Architectural Association, 2014).

[9] See *Education of an Architect: A Point of View,* ed. John Hejduk (New York: Cooper Union, 1971). Along with the museum's controversial 1977 exhibition of nineteenth-century drawings by students from the École des Beaux-Arts, *Education of an Architect* today remains a rare example of MoMA's curatorial attentiveness to architectural education.

[10] Peter Cook, "Cook's Grand Tour: Highlights of Recent History," *Architectural Review* (October 1983), 39.

[11] On the history of the AA unit system, see Sunwoo, "From the 'Well-Laid Table' to the 'Marketplace.' "

[12] "End of Year Exhibition," *AA Events List,* June 24–28, 1974, Week 31, 1974, unpaginated.

[13] For a critical reading of the festival, see Anneka Lennsen, " 'Muslims to Take Over Institute for Contemporary Art': The 1976 World of Islam Festival," *Middle East Studies Association Bulletin* 42, no. 1/2 (Summer/Winter 2008), 40–47.

[14] See an exhibition plan in *AA Events List,* March 22–26, 1976, Week 11, Spring 1976, unpaginated.

[15] The exhibitions during this year were diverse in focus and content. They featured, for example, original drawings by nineteenth-century architect Hector Horeau; drawings by Giuseppe Terragni from the personal collection of Peter Eisenman; prints by the nineteenth-century Italian architect Luigi Rossini; and drawings and collages by Daniel Libeskind.

[16] Tony Bennett, "The Exhibitionary Complex," in *Thinking About Exhibitions,* ed. Reesa Greenberg, Sandy Nairne, and Bruce W. Ferguson (New York: Routledge, 1996), 81–112.

[17] *AA Projects Review* (1979/80), unpaginated.

[18] Peter Cook, "Larger than Life," *AA Files,* no. 3 (1981), 78.

[19] Alvin Boyarsky, "Foreword," in Daniel Libeskind, *Chamberworks: Architectural Meditations on Themes from Heraclitus,* AA Folio 1 (London: Architectural Association, 1983), unpaginated.

[20] "Alvin Boyarsky interviewed: Ambience and Alchemy," *Architectural Review* (October 1983), 28.

[21] Alvin Boyarsky, "Participants Forum" at the International Institute of Design Summer Session, London (1972), audio recording, Alvin Boyarsky Archive, London.

[22] Ibid., audio recording.

Dialogues

Contemporary Exhibitions in Dialogue

At a panel discussion and presentation at the Yale School of Architecture organized by David Andrew Tasman, panelists Brennan Buck, Carson Chan, Ariane Lourie Harrison, Nina Rappaport, and Joel Sanders share their perspectives with additional comments from Barry Bergdoll, Pedro Gadanho, and Philippe Rahm.

David Andrew Tasman In addition to your professional activities as teachers, writers, critics, and practitioners, you all participate in exhibition making. What role do exhibitions play in your practice?

Joel Sanders During my architectural career I have executed a series of speculative commissions for museums and galleries. At the beginning, the gallery represented not only a venue in which to present my work, but also a subject of inquiry that led me to consider the way building types shape spectatorship and sensory perception. I first addressed this theme in 1992 when I designed an installation titled, *Sighting the Gallery,* at New York's Artists Space that considered how track lights regulate the eye and body of the spectator, transforming him or her into a kind of idealized, disembodied observer who encounters works of art through unmediated visual perception. These insights, which are derived from thinking about art galleries and about visuality and space, subsequently informed three speculative projects, all commissioned for museum exhibitions: *Kyle Residence, Site-specific,* and *Bachelor House.* While the focus of my practice has shifted to built work, these early projects formed the conceptual foundation of my teaching and architectural practice.

Ariane Lourie Harrison My firm, Harrison Atelier, creates gallery-based installations integrating performance. In these works, the audience is invited to resist conventional interpretations of complex phenomena resulting from the intertwining of humans and technology. For example, our performance-installations address the aging body in an era of technologically enabled longevity (*Anchises,* 2010), the placebo effect (*Pharmacophore,* 2011), and the life cycle of the industrial food animal (*Veal,* 2013), and in each case, we try to reveal the complexities of these issues. In *Veal,* rather than simply condemning industrial meat production in a tableau of gore, we sought to present a future scenario in which the ties between human labor and population growth, ecological exploitation, and new technologies involving genetic manipulation of animal life could be visualized [Figures 1-2]. As designers, we propose that the phenomena addressed in these installations, which are all too rarely represented in cultural production, can be physicalized as a performance and installation in which the audience participates physically, interacting with performers, designed objects, and seating/stage sets. For Harrison Atelier, the invention of possible relations—through designed objects, installations, and spaces—and the performance of these relationships in a manner that draws the audience into the work, represents a means of explication through design, to use Peter Sloterdijk's term to describe a process by which something becomes the subject of intention and operation: a process of making certain hidden relationships explicit.

Brennan Buck For FreelandBuck, my joint practice with David Freeland, exhibitions have served as a forum or an excuse for us to design and make a number of small but full-scale structures. The gallery context for us brings an interdisciplinary influence more in terms of form than content, so we are not addressing issues of exhibition, the art world, or art institutions; instead, we are looking at these projects as experiments for how we might build buildings in the world. That said, exhibition spaces both eliminate common architectural requirements (keeping the rain out) and bring uncommon modes of reception into play (such as the close visual attention of gallery visitors, a kind of scrutiny that a building rarely receives). Designing gallery-based installations has pushed our work in specific directions that building projects may not have afforded—for instance, toward the study of visual effects or toward the relationship of drawing and structure, as we addressed in our *Slipstream* [Figure 3] and *Technicolor Bloom* projects.

Nina Rappaport As an architectural critic and curator, I look in a proactive way for meaningful relationships between architecture, urbanism, and culture. Curating for me has become a mode of communication unto itself, the connective tissue through which I am able to reach beyond the architectural audience to the public and to transform research into a call to action.

Carson Chan I see myself equally as a writer and a curator; the two activities offer different ways to express the same concerns. Where writing allows me to expand the topic through a set of controlled ideas, exhibitions enable those ideas to be perpetuated non-linearly as an experience. While both mediums allow us to speculate about architecture in ways that building design doesn't, exhibitions—especially of full-scale representations—enable an immediate spatial and physical engagement that approximates the way we experience buildings. This spatial and experiential aspect of exhibition is becoming ever more important to consider in curating architecture. What we present in an exhibition should be unique and offer something that is not available through other mediums. In today's world, with images and drawings so widely available through digital communication, I see little value in presenting reproductions of photographs and drawings. I see exhibitions as an irreducible form, not simply a book or blog translated spatially.

DAT Has your involvement in exhibition making changed the way you structure the relationship between architecture and its users?

BB I think one of our anxieties (something, Carson, that your work often transcends) is the specificity and limited nature of the audience that we feel will encounter the work in the gallery setting. As architects, our ultimate goal is to create buildings in the city, where—compared to one of our temporary deployments in a gallery—a large number of people intentionally or unintentionally will feel the effect of the project. We aren't entirely comfortable operating within the frame of the gallery, given its limitations, or with the expectation to produce something didactic—that is, something that communicates in the mode of art, rather than architecture.

JS I wonder if the exclusive frame of the traditional gallery has virtues today in our age of distraction, as museums and galleries invite viewers to pay attention, rather than sleepwalking through buildings, which they take for granted. The gallery can be a dangerously elitist space, but also one in which people think.

CC If ever there was *not* a built-in audience, it was during the 2012 Marrakech Biennial that I curated with Nadim Samman, which occurred during the so-called Arab Spring [Figure 4]. It took place in a location where there was no contemporary art museum and limited access to art. In addition, as many of the languages in Morocco are solely oral, all of the commissions had to communicate one-to-one between body and exhibition. For example, artist Elín Hansdóttir decided to work with the villagers of Tassoultante to make something using mud bricks. What surprised everyone was that the project began to take on almost urban qualities and issues that transcended traditional exhibition formats. Elín was staying in an artist residency next to the village. The Western-style residence and the village were separated by a wall. Because Elín had to walk around it every day to work on the piece, the owner of the residency created a door for her. Subsequently, this doorway provided access to the residency

[Figure 1]

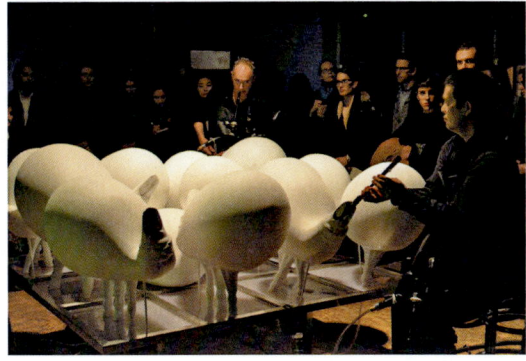

[Figure 2]

[Figure 3]

[Figure 4]

[Figure 5]

to the town's children, who began using its library. In addition, the social structure of the town itself changed as the residents began using Elín's mud-brick installation, which constituted a kind of spiral amphitheater. The space was adopted by the community for town meetings in which residents spoke openly through a microphone in front of an audience—something that they had never done before. In using a form of communication that was completely foreign to the people of Tassoultante to validate yet another foreign form of communication—the town meeting—Elín's project exemplifies the power an architecture exhibition can have.

ALH Carson, that project really sets up the condition for a range of different behaviors to take place, specifically within an installation where there wasn't necessarily a predetermined outcome. It was especially fascinating to see that potential materialize as it did. Similarly, when our studio is working with a topic innately steeped in pathos, like the life cycle of an industrial animal, we try to allow the outcome to gain an undetermined dimension by attempting to pull the audience into playful relationships with designed objects. For example, in our 2013 piece *Veal,* the heads of our milled foam bagpipe creatures, which were attached on springs, bobbled if an audience member chose to pet them. The idea here was to contribute a designed element that prompted unpredictable, if not playful, behaviors and potentially new ways of thinking about a charged subject, such as industrially produced meat.

NR What's interesting about your observation, Ariane, is that it identifies this unpredictability; we don't know, really, who's going to be seeing the show or the installation. By allowing the audience to participate, layers of actual agency are produced. It has been my experience that viewers have the power to impact the work itself, or to potentially shift you from your original intentions to something that evolves with their perspectives.

DAT While agency in the educational environment is encouraged, to the degree that projects take on a criticality that mirrors conceptual art or institutional critique, in practice only the most exceptional architectural oeuvres communicate the principal concerns of the studio that made them. How have your experiences shaped your view of this paradox? Put another way, what is the relationship between exhibition-making and professional practice?

JS During the emergence of my professional practice, curators were important role models. My early work was driven by the influence of cultural studies, performance studies, and, particularly, feminist and queer theory. These speculative issues and ideas were first showcased by museums or institutes such as Artists Space, the Wexner Center for the Arts, MoMA, and the Cooper-Hewitt, Smithsonian Design Museum, and supported by curators such as Mark Robbins, Terence Riley, and Donald Albrecht. All of this led me to ruminate about issues that are still embedded in my work today.

ALH Performance has been a medium of exhibition making that has allowed us to implement a type of speculative architecture often impossible in the traditional sphere of practice. In the 2011 performance work, *Pharmacophore,* which took place in the Storefront for Art and Architecture's wedge-shaped street-side gallery, we were interested in opening the installation to urban feedback—traffic, passersby—by integrating the Storefront's dynamic facade, designed by Steven Holl and Vito Acconci, into our performance. Rather than envisioning the performance as a work contained within the gallery, performers manipulated the facade's rotating doors and windows: this created a performance that played out across the facade and onto the sidewalk, in addition to revealing the audience inside, on display to the street's informal viewers. Our agency, you could say, could be found in our ability to activate the observation by the literary theorist Ihab Habib Hassan, who said (to paraphrase) that we perform and are performed every moment. This concept is something the studio really draws into our practice.

NR As the curator of the *Vertical Urban Factory* [Figure 5], which goes beyond the idea of exhibition, I am able to use historical evidence as a didactic material and as a way to speculate on an imaginary near future. The project was motivated by urban, economic, and social issues and by the philosophies of Vilém Flusser, which focus on the human species for its distinct characteristic of making: *Homo faber.*

My curatorial position allowed me to identify an issue of concern, in this instance the loss of manufacturing within the urban sphere, and to explore the proposition of a typology of the vertical that became a provocation, or a call to action, as to how we can reinsert manufacturing back into cities.

CC After working at the Neue Nationalgalerie with Andres Lepik, together with Fotini Lazaridou-Hatzigoga, I established Program, an initiative for art and architecture in Berlin. One of the first things we did was to return to an idea that K. Michael Hays had raised during a seminar we both had with him at Harvard, from which we were able to develop our own redefinition of architecture: the spatial practice of a body of knowledge that incorporates its historical, political, social, and economic contexts. For us, thinking of architecture and exhibition making in this way allowed us to emancipate the former from its more functional requirements of building design.

DAT Toward the close of the '70s, Douglas Crimp's exhibition, *Pictures,* at Artists Space featured appropriation-based practices that he described as "representation freed from the tyranny of the represented." Around the same time, Rem Koolhaas demonstrated in his book, *Delirious New York,* a similar acceptance, analysis, and recombination of the banal to achieve a similar level of speculation. Can we expect today's architectural representation techniques and exhibition-making practices to have a similar social impact expected by the vanguard?

Mark Wigley Exposing systems, revealing invisible but influential forces—or hiding them—is something we think a lot about as architects. Brennan started out by setting up this distinction between the gallery and the world outside, which makes me question where you see the most interesting explorations in turning the world into a kind of ready-made gallery—not in designing specific installations as a way of talking about architecture, but using existing architecture as the exhibition. Are there particular examples that come to mind?

NR There has been an interesting shift in how walking tours have been organized lately, where they are being used as a polemic, as a way to see architecture and urban issues in the city in a unique way. These tours have become a form of curating or activation of the city that do not necessarily have anything to do with an art installation, or with the act of exhibition, but the architecture is seen as it is.

CC The idea of making the whole city into a giant ready-made exhibition has precedents in projects like the Hansaviertel in Berlin made for *Interbau '57,* and the Weissenhofseidlung houses of Stuttgart (1927). We can also think of all the open-air museums, like the Norsk Folkemuseum in Oslo, which is essentially a little town in which every house is from a different era of Norway's history. For the Biennial of the Americas in Denver (2013), we invited architects to design and build full-scale temporary architecture throughout downtown Denver. Each pavilion was site-specific in the sense that each responded to the particular problems and challenges of their respective sites through built form.

ALH To Mark's question about existing architecture used as the exhibition, the early work of Diller and Scofidio comes to mind . . . for example, their 1986 piece, *The Memory Theatre of Giulio Camillo,* which animated the hidden architecture of the Brooklyn Bridge Anchorage by introducing a set of performances into it. I had not seen this piece, but Seth, my partner at Harrison Atelier, had seen it, and it prompted us to think about ways to draw on the industrial remnants of the former leash factory where our installation, *Veal,* was staged.

BB There is a seduction for architects in working on exhibitions because many of the issues that we normally consider are intensified: visuality, attention, tactility. All those things are dulled in someone's experience of a building they are moving through repeatedly, day after day. That background quality is potentially powerful though, which makes me worry that the world as gallery is not only impossible, but a distraction from how buildings actually operate.

[Figure 6]

[Figure 7]

189

[Figure 8]

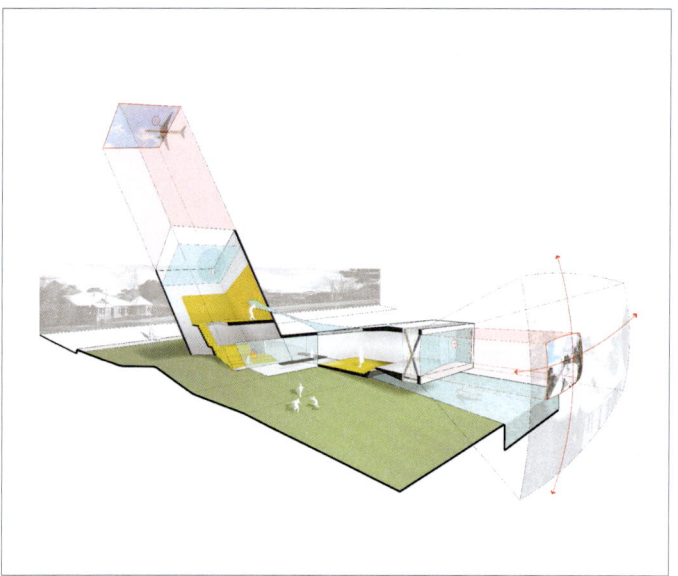

[Figure 9]

Barry Bergdoll The past six years of the Young Architects Program at MoMA PS1 is interesting in terms of the variety of approaches being discussed—between understanding the exhibition as a feedback mechanism relating directly to practice, or the insistence on operating on a kind of parallel economy that almost shouldn't affect a practice. When Terence Riley started the Young Architects Program, it was very much about the exercise of curatorial power—granting young designers the opportunity to build something in the great space that is the PS1 courtyard, which is not the same thing as the PS1 gallery, but has a similar relationship to the city. Over the years I've been organizing the juries, a role now taken on by Pedro Gadanho, there has emerged a very interesting phenomenon, and that is that so many of the nominees have already done a great many installations. This circumstance makes me question the role that "the institution" plays in the feedback loop: is it actually still open, or is it closed, and is it still desirable or not? Some of you talked about the exhibition space as a laboratory and incubator from which a practice can emerge. Other practices—like yours, Ariane—are not actually architecture at all, but more in the tradition of performance art and multimedia installation.

ALH Yet, to me, it seems clear, if we consider the trajectory of a firm like Coop Himmelb(l)au, that certain types of performance work offer a doorway into architectural practice and new perspectives on architecture. Some of the people with whom Carson has worked, such as Alex Schweder, use performance to raise new and destabilizing sets of questions about architecture itself.

JS Looking at this issue from a historical perspective, I think in many ways that architects are ten years behind artists. The long history of institutional critique, particularly in the 1960s and 1970s, was about breaking down the boundaries between art and life, criticizing the museum as a privileged container promoting an elitist formalism. The Museum of Modern Art has been a famous whipping post, but I think we are beyond that critique. The boundary between the museum, the gallery, and everyday life is something that I don't think we want to blur entirely. Each is a different space, but, like Foucault's concept of heterotopia, I think that they reflect one another and that is important. When I was a young architect, we were incredibly suspicious of practice. We were not using the museum as a venue to get our work known, or as a vehicle to get "real" commissions, which is how it functions for some people today. We were interested in exploring our agency as architects, as cultural producers, making work visible within the social and public sphere—work that was as independent (as possible) from the hegemony of outside forces that dictate what will be built and how it will function.

BB There is a commonly understood hierarchy that Joel refers to, which is that exhibition work is a stepchild of designing a building—it's a step below that other, better level. I don't want to reinforce that hierarchy. The installation work provides a different set of constraints that can be productive. At the same time, there is a justifiable backlash, or new doubts being raised, about what this parallel economy of pavilion-making is doing for architecture. How does a sea of digitally fabricated pavilions advance the broader discipline?

Phillip Rahm For us, installations—or, rather, art spaces—are laboratories for form in which to explore new design principles and test compositional tools. The goal is to apply later in the real world what we research in art spaces. As Brennan said, for architects, working in the gallery is only a transitional—but necessary—moment for experimentation. However, there is maybe a paradox about the role of the architecture curator: Why stay in the "art" world? Why not imagine that the ideas developed and tested in the art world could be later applied in the real world? The architectural curator is, like a politician, capable of defining the future of architecture and the city.

CC The Biennial of the Americas was initiated by the City of Denver. As executive curator of the 2013 edition, I worked closely with the city [Figure 6]. The experience illustrated for me the very different methods that politicians and policy makers employ, compared to those used by artists and architects. Where politicians are strategically geared to effect policy, architects and artists are able to involve citizens in alternate visions of the world. Where politicians impose change, architects can sow the seeds of change in organizing the way we all engage in public space . . . this is not to say that politicians and the creative fields can't learn from one another. The mayor of Bogota, Antanas Mockus, in office until 2003, was very influenced by theater and performance art. He donned costumes to perform other forms of citizenry and played the part of a "supercitizen." In this way he brought to life new ideas of civic engagement that policy making could not.

NR As a curator-turned-activist, or advocate, I give tours of factories and actually work with manufacturers to see how they can maintain production spaces, especially in New York City. And, in every city to which the *Vertical Urban Factory* exhibition travels, we do a specific installation on the manufacturing spaces in that city as well as ask the local politicians and economic development offices to participate in panel discussions. These are both ways in which I work to make curating an active position.

Pedro Gadanho The paradox in the center of this conversation lies in the fact that architects are typically expecting exhibition devices to be at the "service" of their practice. So, for the architects the exhibition of architecture becomes a question of considering different ways by which to represent one's production. Then there is the position of curators, who arise from a different tradition and a specific practice, who intend to go beyond only exhibition making—and may want to develop more of a critical project. I think this is a very interesting dialogue or contrast, especially when these curators bear a very strong connection to specific traditions of art curating—and this connection suddenly influences the ways in which we are thinking about architectural exhibitions and their potential roles. Certainly, it suggests that emerging forms of curating are productive—rather than just reactive—and can challenge traditional views and presentation formats for the architectural profession. They can also appear as an embodiment or continuation of the role of criticism, and they present a form of research or enquiry that has an immediate output before a broader audience. In a way, this is a moment in which, more than ever, curating itself arises as an autonomous, not necessarily subservient, practice.

Exhibitions Matter

At a panel discussion and presentation at the Yale School of Architecture, organized by Carson Chan, panelists Eva Franch i Gilabert, Pedro Gadanho, Andrea Phillips, and Henry Urbach share their perspectives.

Carson Chan How did your interest in architecture exhibitions begin?

Eva Franch Although I've been the Executive Director and Chief Curator at the Storefront for Art and Architecture since 2010, I am not interested in architecture exhibitions per se. I am interested in architectural projects that are able to articulate, construct and test the different forces that constitute and reconstitute a context for architecture—from beauty to politics.

Pedro Gadanho As for me, I first became interested in art and design shows as an exhibition designer. Through my connections with the art and design worlds I designed exhibitions on several different subjects. Only then came an interest in using that medium to also produce critical reflections on architecture. When I finally pursued curating architecture exhibitions, the impulse came out of a need to explore and represent certain themes for which exhibitions—rather than books, for instance—were a better vehicle. The first curatorial projects were ambitious exhibitions that took advantage of contextual circumstances, such as the joint Cultural Capitals of Europe 2001, in Porto and Rotterdam, or the fact that I was involved in organizing an independent biennale on design culture, *ExperimentaDesign,* in Lisbon, in the same year. In one case, that led to an exhibition in Porto that explored the diversity of Rotterdam-based practices, including architects such as Rem Koolhaas, MVRDV, and others. In the other, it led to a collaboration with the British Council for a show on young British architects, *Space Invaders.* From the very beginning, these endeavors felt as if they were a means to analyze a certain condition, and to offer a point of view through both the visual apparatus of the exhibition and its curatorial text. In a way, the exhibition was the necessary means to the end of writing about something.

Henry Urbach I became interested in architecture exhibitions in the early 1990s, and was part of the curatorial team for the *Queer Space* exhibition at the Storefront for Art and Architecture in 1994. In 1997, I opened Henry Urbach Architecture, a gallery in New York that presented exhibitions of contemporary art and experimental architecture, with a strong focus on installations.

Andrea Phillips I come from a Marxian tradition of cultural investigation and have spent much time discussing and writing about the assumptions made by producers, commissioners, and critics regarding art and its urban environment. Questions of what is made public and for what reasons concern me. In this context I have always attempted to find links between architectural and artistic production. In 2007, I set up a research project and think tank at Goldsmiths College, London, called Curating Architecture in order to investigate these ideas further with colleagues who were artists, architects, curators, philosophers, and urbanists. We had many heated debates about the social-shaping mechanisms of urbanism debates that we recognized had a long historical tail. The discussions were very informed by what at the time we perceived as a transcendent practice of hagiographic exhibitions on architectural production—in a European context, this included the curatorial work of AMO, for example, touring exhibitions of Herzog & De Meuron, Zaha Hadid, and David Adjaye, etc., as well as the Serpentine Gallery pavilion series. What excited some people and grated others was the flirtatious relationship between art and architecture. We attempted to analyze these spectacular events in relation to movements of transnational capital, and growing inequality, both local and global. Looking back, it is interesting that this stream of exhibition making has largely dried up, which for me can only be read as a response to the financial crash of 2008 and the rhetoric of austerity that has followed in its stead.

CC Architecture, articulated in one form or another, surrounds us all the time. What are the challenges of bringing something ubiquitous into an exhibition?

EF There is an assumption in the formulation of the question that implies exhibition as representation or exhibition as display of something outside of itself. I think of exhibitions as generative devices through which one can take higher architectural risks. Therefore, the only challenge in relationship to "exhibition making" is to understand the rituals and limits embedded within the specific protocols of "exhibition making," while identifying and delineating new constraints and forms of engagement.

HU I'd add that an important challenge is to present architecture as a form of knowledge and a medium of cultural representation. Exhibitions offer the chance to explore the values and beliefs that are inscribed in buildings and architectural space. They reframe architecture according to the questions they ask.

AP I have learned that it is both almost impossible and useless to try to bring architecture into exhibitions. Together with the participants of Curating Architecture, I made a research-based exhibition in collaboration with The Showroom, a project space that was in London's East End. We worked with four groups of practitioners: the architecture practices AMO and Hirsch & Misselwitz, and the artists Walid Raad and Angela Ferreira. All participants contributed with interesting and provocative work, but the exhibition itself was not able to produce a collective imaginary space that enabled its viewers to think through the complex questions of urban space, our projected goal. Instead, it produced individual and highly specific works. Of course, this is not an issue with the works themselves but with the phenomenological category of the exhibition itself and its restrictions as a culturally capitalized form. It is also to do with the process of making exhibitions in such a traditional format where practitioners are individualized and to a certain extent seek individualization. Architecture has the capacity to break with this; it is a collective enterprise. At one point in the Curating Architecture discussions, Eyal Weizman said that the only really logical place for architecture to be exhibited is when plans for new buildings need to be posted in public spaces for community consultation for legal reasons. This has stuck with me: the link between display, publication, and making public. At this point, the architect's plans—to use Bruno Latour's term—become "matters of concern." This is what I think architectural exhibitions should be, but rarely are.

CC Architecture is a form of spatial communication, and for ideas to be imparted, everyone needs to be speaking the same language. What techniques have you seen or developed in order to express spatial ideas in exhibition displays? Henry, I'm curious about your reflections on communicating spatial ideas to the very mixed publics at the SFMOMA.

HU I was curator of architecture and design there from 2006 to 2011, and I organized a show called *Cut: Revealing the Section.* The exhibition combined various media to explain what a section is. I showed Mario Botta's section drawings of the museum itself (which he designed), section models including Joel Sanders's *Bachelor House* (1999), photographs of Gordon Matta-Clark's *Splitting* (1974), in which the artist split a house down the middle, and a work by the artist Peter Wegner that cleaved the gallery in two with a double-sided, chromatic wall made of one and a half million sheets of paper. In addition, there was interpretive text that presented the idea of the vertical section and its relative opacity compared to the horizontal section or plan view that is commonly understood.

EF Well, I disagree in essence with the assumptions the question puts forth. I do not think architecture is only a form of spatial communication. That would imply architecture as the medium of something preexisting and of the past, and not the future. Secondly, I reject the categories of "exhibition" and "display." I'd rather use "project" and "project." While I do think architecture articulates and carries within itself spatial practices with economic, political, and historical baggage, the ultimate aim of architecture is to reconstitute them anew in the generation of something else, something other. This otherness is a thing in and of itself. Regarding techniques of "exhibition making" that I've employed, I would list questions and ideas such as "curatorial objects" and the "art of no communication" in relation to the 2013 exhibition, *Past Futures, Present, Futures,* or the Hitchcock "McGuffin" in relation to the annual drawing exhibition at the Storefront, or the idea of Trojan horses in relation to *OfficeUS* at the 2014 Venice Architecture Biennale, or the "art of hyper communication" with the ongoing Storefront TV Studio. However, none of these techniques have any meaning without the understanding of what is at stake in each one of them, what context they try to transform, and on what grounds of doubt they are being developed.

PG I try to use narrative devices that are somehow able to convey the conception or experience of space to a wider audience. I've found that when architects speak, they are often clearer in expressing their thoughts about space than when they write. I've made video interviews to try and capture these ideas and then insert them into the general exhibition narrative. And while I believe the ability of models to convey spatial ideas is a popular misconception, and neither am I an advocate of architectural installations, I seek to collaborate with professionals, namely graphic designers, to produce strong visual narratives that are able to capture the audience's attention. The aim is that the narratives in each show will eventually convey spatial concepts in clear, accessible language, be it in a verbal or nonverbal way. In this sense, in its diverse formats and possibilities, video has proven to be an instrument that is more informative and more able to capture and transmit the spatial experience. Two recent examples in MoMA's *Conceptions of Space* show offer good proof of its versatility: in one case, the experience of photographer Cristóbal Palma—himself educated as an architect—translates into a narrative sequence that offers a complex, poetic portrait of Pezo von Ellrichshausen's Casa Cién (2011). In the other case, the architects themselves are able to transform a typical project presentation into a more explanatory video. As such, SO-IL's video for the Kukje Gallery in Seoul describes the whole process of conception behind the architect's project, making the ideas accessible to a general audience. In any case, I'm trying to address the audience with language that has more chance of reaching out to them on their own terms, and this without necessarily concealing the specific complexity of architecture.

AP Architecture is a matter of civic concern. Any display device that allows people to access plans and discuss them is a good display device.

CC Architecture exhibitions started as the display of drawings, models, and building fragments, but today they occupy a significant and separate body of work for many architects. What potentials do you see in architecture exhibitions as a separate discipline from architecture proper?

AP The separation of exhibition from architecture proper is for me part of a historically attenuated publishing device that in itself could be a useful medium of communication. The problem is that most architectural exhibitions are celebratory rather than socially and politically quizzical. There are of course really impressive exceptions to this. The question of architectural exhibition also cannot be divorced from a more general discussion about the role of galleries and museums in contemporary culture per se—the ways in which they are funded, or the increased need to exhibit the types of exhibitions that will enable patronage.

EF Exhibitions about architecture are not necessarily architecture exhibitions. I strongly believe there should be a clear distinction between those two. They actually have very little to do with each other.

PG I think architecture exhibitions pertain to something that we can call the culture of architecture. I don't see them as separate from any other form of production, like writing or building.

HU But architecture exhibitions offer an opportunity to state an argument about architecture and open new avenues of interpretation in ways that writing or building cannot. Exhibitions can also offer an effective and experiential introduction of ideas to a larger public, especially for younger practitioners. Architectural thought remains a somewhat mysterious domain for the general public, and exhibitions, along with other media, can serve to bridge that gap.

CC Henry makes a good point about how exhibitions, being events that allow information to be spatially experienced, have the potential to give large, diverse audiences access to architectural ideas. Eva, who would you say is your main target audience at Storefront? Why?

EF Individuals with a growing curiosity. The audience is always in construction and changes according to each project. In *Letters to the Mayor (2014),* with a compilation of letters by architects to mayors around the world, there was a very clear target audience that we do hope will continue to follow other projects that do not directly relate to them individually but contribute to their understanding of architecture, cities, and civic life. In other projects, less direct or didactic, we hope to be able to raise the level of curiosity of art and architecture experts as well as of "ignorant" experts or random passersby. Unfortunately, curiosity decreases with age, and the world is aging. There is a lot of work to be done if one believes that one constructs audiences.

CC Pedro, how have you tried to formulate an audience in your work at MoMA?

PG I try to speak to two very different audiences. One is the audience made up of professionals who look at the artifacts produced in their field in order to understand their own position. The other is an audience that knows very little about architecture, even though they might be able to recognize a Picasso, and place it within a history of painting. The general public knows very little about the culture of architecture, its history, its modus operandi, or conceptual tools. There is the need for a permanent pedagogical project, one that does not exclude the complexities of architectural culture. Knowledgeable professionals shouldn't be ignored either. To reconcile the two extremes of familiarity, I use Umberto Eco's idea that a text—both the visual and written components of an exhibition—has the capacity to speak simultaneously to very different cultural recipients. It just depends on the recipients' "cultural baggage"—how much information they retain, how much they can absorb of the same text. Curators must be aware of the disparity in knowledge to be able to produce a viable "text."

CC Henry, how have you been able to address both professional audiences and the many other publics that might visit your exhibition?

HU I've been interested in how the exhibition itself can provide a compelling spatial experience or enact architectural thinking at a 1:1 scale. Installations can do this, as can exhibition design strategies that express spatial concepts beyond the organization of information or artifacts.

EF I simply leave all the doors open.

CC Traditionally, curators have been mediators of cultural artifacts like art, presenting it in ways that would give visitors access to them and their ideas. What would you like to see change in architecture curating in order to give more access to what can be a pretty opaque profession?

EF I don't think there should be curators. At best, it is an alternate title for a historian—of the past or the future—or in the worst case, a disguise for an economist of networks. On the other hand, currently we fetishize transparency—perhaps a residue from the project of modernity—but I don't think architecture needs to be less opaque. As J.V. Foix, a Catalan poet, writes: "It is when I sleep that I see clearly."

CC Architecture curating is a young discipline, but many of its practices have simply happened without too much reflection. Unlike the curating of art, it does not seem like it has reached a self-critical point yet, with perhaps the exception of the 14th Venice Architecture Biennale, directed by Rem Koolhaas. What would you like to see change most in the professional practice of architecture curating?

PG I like it as it is. Architecture curating is evolving in its own way, but if the 14th Venice Architecture Biennale is to be considered a moment of self-criticality, then I think something is terribly wrong. The last editions of the Venice Biennale have been exactly the opposite of what architectural curating should be. They have been the product of brand-name architects who are able to fundraise but who are not particularly concerned with any conception of architectural curating. To give the Biennale back to curators, as it inevitably happens in the art field, would be a good start for a change in the field.

HU I don't agree that the discipline hasn't reached a point of self-reflection; I think the conference at Yale demonstrates otherwise. The historiographical papers suggest one way to build awareness of norms that have guided curatorial practice, as do the range of approaches suggested in this panel. Still, there is plenty of room for expansion, both within more traditional frameworks, such as the museum and biennial, as well as other possibilities, including historic sites and urban space.

EF The best architecture exhibitions are made first by artists and then by architects (and I include historians within the second category). I am concerned with the fact that at some point there might be so-called "architecture curators" who are not architects or artists.

CC The architecture biennial exhibition is something we have seen proliferate for the last two decades. It is a model borrowed from art biennials, and perhaps without too much consideration as to its suitability. Most notably, architecture's relationship to the city is not like that of fine art, and for an iterative exhibition in the same city (e.g. Venice, Rotterdam) one might expect more of a relationship between the exhibition and the city. If not the biennial model, what would you suggest to be a viable model for a large-scale iterative architecture exhibition?

PG Well, there are good historical examples: the *Weissenhof Estates* in Stuttgart (1927), and the *International Building Exhibitions* in Berlin, provide models in which certain typologies and ideas of the city were curated as a full-scale urban experiment. I triggered a curatorial project of that nature, one that was extremely important for my practice. In 2002, I made an exhibition in a public square for the winners of a "curated competition" for a number of new vertical parking lots in Lisbon. Had the project been taken to full expression—which it hadn't—today one would find eight car-parks in the city that constitute an exhibition of experimental buildings, a survey of the best young Lisbon architects, and also the built expression of an urban laboratory proposing mixed uses for an otherwise banal program. At a certain point in the process, though, it became both impossible and undesirable to "curate" the corruption and economic interests that exist in any given city.

EF The WorldWide Storefront (WWFS) is an ongoing project I started as a reaction to the proliferation of architecture biennials, mostly fueled by political and economical desires. WWFS, in that regard, is a mode of action; its aim is to unveil, produce, and discuss experimental cultural works on a global scale, but from local points of view. As a new initiative, the WWSF wants to provide a simultaneous, multi-locus of alternative spaces around the globe and a digital platform for the expression and exchange of latent desires within contemporary art and architecture practices, with new relationships to politics, economy, and, ultimately, power.

AP Actually, I prefer the Venice Architecture Biennale to the Art Biennale. While I recognize that they both develop out of very specific conditions, I think that the architecture edition often achieves a more relaxed, discursive, playful, and experimental arena. Though I am generally critical of exhibitions of architecture, the space of the biennial could be put to much better use in this way. As architecture is inherently a consultative process, which necessarily draws across disciplines, it is often most recognizable within the multivalent format of the biennial. There is an opening there for reinvention, I think. But the biennial would have to be made a free event and dispense with its aura of aesthetic legislation. A tall order, I know.

Contributors

Barry Bergdoll is the Meyer Schapiro Professor of Modern Architectural History at Columbia University and a curator in the Department of Architecture and Design at the Museum of Modern Art, where from 2007–2013 he served as The Philip Johnson Chief Curator of Architecture and Design. At MoMA, he has organized, curated, and consulted on several major exhibitions of nineteenth- and twentieth-century architecture, including *Frank Lloyd Wright and the City: Density vs. Dispersal* (2014), *Le Corbusier: An Atlas of Modern Landscapes* with Jean-Louis Cohen (2013), and *Henri Labrouste: Structure Brought to Light* with Corinne Bélier and Marc Le Coeur (2013). He is author or editor of numerous publications, including *Henri Labrouste: Structure Brought to Light* (with Corinne Bélier and Marc Le Coeur, 2012); *Bauhaus 1919–1933: Workshops for Modernity* (2010); *Home Delivery: Fabricating the Modern Dwelling* (2008); *Mies in Berlin* (2001); *Karl Friedrich Schinkel: An Architecture for Prussia* (1994); *Léon Vaudoyer: Historicism in the Age of Industry* (1994); and *European Architecture 1750–1890,* in the Oxford History of Art series (2001). He served as president of the Society of Architectural Historians from 2006 to 2008, Slade Professor of Fine Art at Cambridge University in winter 2011, and in 2013 delivered the 62nd A.W. Mellon Lectures in the Fine Arts at the National Gallery of Art, Washington, D.C. He is a member of the American Academy of Arts and Sciences and an honorary fellow of the Royal Institute of British Architects.

Brennan Buck is principal of the architectural firm FreelandBuck, based in New York and Los Angeles and a Critic at the Yale School of Architecture. His work and writing, which focuses on technology within the discipline and its associated aesthetic culture, has been published in the journals *Log, Frame, Architectural Record, Detail,* and *Surface,* as well as several recent books on architecture and technology. His exhibition projects include the installations, *Technicolor Bloom* (Vienna), *Slipstream* (New York), and *Stacked* (Los Angeles). Prior to forming FreelandBuck, he worked for Neil M. Denari Architects and Johnston Marklee & Associates in Los Angeles and taught at the University of Applied Arts, Vienna, the Royal Danish Academy in Copenhagen, the University of Kentucky, and Pennsylvania State University. Buck received a BS from Cornell University and a MArch from the University of California at Los Angeles.

Craig Buckley is an assistant professor in the history of art at Yale University. He previously taught at the Graduate School of Architecture, Planning and Preservation at Columbia University. Buckley's research interests center on the history of modern architecture and the experiments of the historical avant-gardes, the publishing and media practices of architects, as well as the relationships between artistic and architectural movements through the course of the twentieth century. He is co-curator of the traveling exhibition and research project, *Clip/Stamp/Fold,* as well as *Collecting Architecture Territories* (with Mark Wasiuta), presented at the DESTE Foundation, Athens, and numerous other exhibitions. He is the editor of *Dan Graham's New Jersey,* (Lars Müller Publishers, 2012), *Utopie: Texts and Projects 1967–1978* (Semiotext(e)/MIT Press, 2011), and *Clip/Stamp/Fold: The Radical Architecture of Little Magazines 196X–197X* (Actar, 2010). His essays have appeared in journals such as *October, Grey Room, Log,* and *Perspecta,* among others. Buckley is currently working on a book project entitled *Graphic Apparatuses: Architecture, Media and the Reinvention of Assembly,* which analyzes the legacy of montage and collage in the redefinition of techniques of assembly across a range of architectural practices in Europe from the 1950s to the 1970s. He completed his MA at the University of Western Ontario, attended the Whitney Independent Study Program in New York, and received his PhD from Princeton University in 2013.

Paula Burleigh is a PhD candidate at the Graduate Center, City University of New York, where she is working on her dissertation, entitled *The Labyrinth, the Cave, and the Monolith: Archaic Utopias, 1947–1968.* She is the recipient of the Capelloni Dissertation Fellowship and she is a Joan Tisch Teaching Fellow at the Whitney Museum of American Art. She is a frequent lecturer at the Museum of Modern Art, New York, and she writes for the *Brooklyn Rail.*

Carson Chan is an architecture writer and curator, and pursuing a PhD in architecture at Princeton University. After working for Barkow Leibinger Architects and the Neue Nationalgalerie's architecture exhibitions department in Berlin, with Fotini Lazaridou-Hatzigoga he co-founded PROGRAM in 2006, a non-commercial initiative for art and architecture collaborations. He has curated and overseen more than fifty exhibitions of contemporary art and architecture. His writing on art, architecture, and contemporary culture appears in books and periodicals, including *Kaleidoscope,* where he is a contributing editor, and *032c* (Berlin), where he is editor-at-large. Chan has interviewed a broad range of contemporary practitioners, including Thomas Demand, Udo Kittelmann, William T. Vollmann, MVRDV, Ute Meta Bauer, Greg Lynn, Rick Owens, Hans Kollhoff, and David Simon. With Nadim Samman, Chan curated the Marrakech Biennale 2012, presenting newly commissioned works by more than forty artists, architects, writers, musicians, and composers at five locations throughout the city. Chan was executive curator of the Biennial of the Americas 2013, in Denver, Colorado.

Eva Franch i Gilabert is an architect and the executive director and chief curator of the Storefront for Art and Architecture in New York. In 2004, she founded the solo practice, Office Of Architectural Affairs (OOAA). Franch's work has been exhibited internationally at FAD Barcelona, the Venice Architecture Biennale, and the Shenzhen Architecture Biennale, among other venues. In addition to chairing multiple national and international juries, she lectures internationally on art, architecture and the importance of alternative practices in the construction and understanding of public life. At Storefront, Franch has curated exhibitions including: *Past Futures, Present Futures; Aesthetics–Anesthetics; No Shame: Storefront for Sale; POP: Protocols, Obsessions, Positions;* and *Letters to the Mayor.* She has also initiated a publication series with Lars Müller, launched the Storefront International Series of forums on architecture and the online platform, WorldWide Storefront, and founded OFFIC*EUS,* a project for global architectural prac- tice that represented the United States at the 2014 Venice Architecture Biennale. Franch has taught at the Graduate School for Architecture, Planning, and Preservation at Columbia University, the Università Iuav di Venezia, the State University of New York/Buffalo, and Rice University School of Architecture. She studied at Delft University of Technology in the Netherlands, and earned a MArch from the Escola Tècnica Superior d'Arquitectura in Barcelona, and a second MArch from Princeton University. She has received a number of fellowships and awards, including a Schloss Solitude Residency Fellowship in 2010.

Pedro Gadanho is the curator of contemporary architecture in the Department of Architecture and Design at the Museum of Modern Art, New York. Since he joined MoMA in 2012, he is responsible for the Young Architects Program, and curated the exhibitions *9+1 Ways of Being Political, Cut'n'Paste, Conceptions of Space,* and *Uneven Growth.* Previously, he divided his activity between architecture, teaching, writing, and curating. Gadanho holds a MA in art and architecture and a PhD in architecture and mass media. He is the author of *Interiores 01–010* and of *Arquituraem Público,* and a recipient of the FAD Prize for Thought and Criticism in 2012. He was the editor of *BEYOND* bookazine, writes the *ShrapnelContemporary* blog, and contributes regularly to international publications. He curated *Metaflux* at the 2004 Venice Architecture Biennale and exhibitions such as *Post.Rotterdam, Space Invaders,* and *Pancho Guedes, An Alternative Modernist.* He was also a chief curator of experimental design between 2001 and 2003. Among exhibition layouts, galleries, and refurbishments, his designs include the Ellipse Foundation in Lisbon, and Orange House in Carreço, Family Home in Oporto, and GMG House in Torres Vedras.

Romy Golan is a professor of twentieth-century European art at the Graduate Center, City University of New York. She is the author of *Modernity and Nostalgia: Art and Politics in France Between the Wars* and *Muralnomad: The Paradox of Wall Painting, Europe 1927–1957* (Yale University Press, 1995 and 2009). Among her recent publications are: "Vitalità del Negativo/Negativo della Vitalità," *October* No. 150 (Winter 2014); "Slow Time: The Futurist Mural" in *Italian Futurism: 1909–1944* (Guggenheim Museum, 2014);"The Scene of a Disappearance" in *Giosetta Fioroni: L'Argento* (The Drawing Center, 2013); "Flashbacks and Eclipses in Italian Art in the 1960s," *Grey Room* no. 49 (Fall 2012); "The World Fair:

A Transmedial Theatre," *Encuentros con los años 30* (Museo Reina Sofia, 2012); and "Equivoci: Le Corbusier al Convegno Volta," *L'Italia di Le Corbusier* (MAXXI, Rome, 2012).

Ariane Lourie Harrison is an architect, educator, and co-founder of Harrison Atelier, with Seth Harrison. Harrison Atelier's installation-performances engage themes such as the aging body in an era of medicalized longevity (*Anchises,* 2010), the pharmaceutical industry and the placebo effect (*Pharmacophore,* 2011), and the industrial logic of food-animal production (*Veal,* 2013). The firm was recognized for its innovative installation design at the 2013 World Stage Design exhibition. Harrison Atelier's ongoing work at the OMI International Art Center in upstate New York includes the construction of a 1,500-square-foot outdoor pavilion and a performance sequence, *Species Niches* (2014–2015). Harrison has taught at the Yale School of Architecture since 2006 and also teaches at the Graduate Architecture and Urban Design Program at Pratt Institute. She is the editor of *Architectural Theories of the Environment: Posthuman Territory* (Routledge, 2013), and has taught studios and seminars that focus on the posthuman interpenetration of technology and human and animal life. Harrison received a PhD in architectural history from the Institute of Fine Arts, New York University, a MArch from the Graduate School of Architecture, Planning, and Preservation at Columbia University, and an AB in architectural history from Princeton University.

Andres Kurg, PhD, is an architectural historian and researcher at the Institute of Art History, Estonian Academy of Arts, in Tallinn. His research explores architectural and art practices in the Soviet Union from the late 1960s to 1980s in relation to technological transformations and changes in everyday life and values. He has published articles in *ArtMargins, Journal of Architecture; Interiors: Design, Architecture, Culture;* and *Home Cultures, A Prior Magazine,* and contributed to exhibition catalogs on postsocialist urban transformations and spatial conflicts. Kurg has co-edited and authored *A User's Guide to Tallinn* (2002) and *Environment, Projects, Concepts: Architects of the Tallinn School 1972–1985* (2008). He recently co-curated the exhibition *Our Metamorphic Futures. Design, Technical Aesthetics and Experimental Architecture in the Soviet Union 1960–1980* in Vilnius National Gallery of Art and Estonian Museum of Applied Art and Design (2011–2012), a project funded by a grant from the European Union's "Culture" program.

Liane Lefaivre is professor and chair of architectural history and theory at the University of Applied Arts in Vienna, Austria. Her writing and research relate to the period between the Renaissance and the Enlightenment, and to the twentieth century. Her publications include: *The Child, the City and the Power of Play, or the PIP Principle* (Tsinghua University, 2010); *Ground Up City* (010 Publishers, 2006); *The Emergence of Modern Architecture* (Routledge, 2003); and *Leon Battista Alberti's Hypnerotomachia Poliphili. Re-Configuring the Architectural Body in the Early Italian Renaissance* (MIT Press, 1997). She co-authored, with architect and writer Alexander Tzonis: *Architecture of Regionalism in the Global Age. Hills and Valleys in the Flat World* (Routledge, 2012); *Classical Architecture. The Poetics of Order* (MIT Press, 1986); *Aldo van Eyck Humanist Rebel* (1999); and *Critical Regionalism* (Prestel, 2003). She and Tzonis were co-editors of *Tropical Architecture; Critical Regionalism in an Age of Globalization* (Wiley, 2001). Lefaivre curated the exhibitions *Aldo Van Eyck, The Playgrounds and the City* (Stedelijk Museum, Amsterdam, 2002) and *Santiago Calatrava, Like a Bird* (Kunsthistorisches Museum, in collaboration with the Naturhistorisches Museum, Vienna, 2003). In 2010, she co-curated, with professor Li Kaisheng of the Shanghai Academy of Social Sciences, an exhibition at the Shanghai Art Biennale of their urban design work based on playgrounds. Her forthcoming book is *Modern Architectures in Austria* (Reaktion Books and the University of Chicago Press).

Mari Lending is a professor of architectural theory and history at the Oslo School of Architecture and Design and a senior researcher in the research projects, *The Printed and the Built: Architecture and Public Debate in Modern Europe* and *Place and Displacement: Exhibiting Architecture,* which are administered by the Oslo Center for Critical Architectural Studies (OCCAS). She was a visiting scholar at the Yale School of Architecture in Spring 2014 and is currently working on a book on nineteenth-century plaster cast collections with the working title, *Monuments in Flux: Plaster Casts as Mass Medium.* She recently published, with Mari Hvattum, the book *Modeling Time: The Permanent Collection, 1925–2014* (Torpedo Press, 2014), drawing on the exhibition, *Model as Ruin,* at the House of Artists in Oslo.

Helena Mattsson is Associate Professor at the KTH School of Architecture, Stockholm. Among other publications, she was editor (with S-O Wallenstein) of *Swedish Modernism: Architecture, Consumption and the Welfare State* (2010) and *Kalmar Stortorg* (2006). Mattsson's current project is *Architecture of Deregulations,* which investigates the neo-liberal turn in Swedish 1990s architecture. Mattsson is an editor for the magazine *SITE.*

Wallis Miller specializes in nineteenth- and twentieth-century German and European architecture. Her writing focuses on architecture exhibitions and museums, including the essays "Popularity Contexts: Architecture Exhibitions in 19th Century Germany," "Fitting In: Architecture in the Art Gallery," "Schinkel's Museums," and "Mies and Exhibitions" (for the exhibition, *Mies in Berlin,* at the Museum of Modern Art, New York). She is the co-editor, with Mari Lending, Thordis Arrhenius, and Jérémie McGowan, of *Place and Displacement: Exhibiting Architecture.* Her current project, *Architecture on Display: Exhibitions and the Emergence of Modernism in Germany,* discusses the formative role of exhibitions for architecture in Germany during the nineteenth and early wtwentieth centuries. She is the Charles P. Graves Associate Professor of Architecture at the University of Kentucky and, most recently, has been a visiting scholar at the Oslo Centre for Critical Architecture Studies.

Eeva-Liisa Pelkonen is Associate Professor at Yale School of Architecture, where she teaches design, history and theory. She author of the books: *Achtung Architektur! Image and Phantasm in Contemporary Austrian Architecture* (MIT Press/Graham Foundation, 1996), *Alvar Aalto: Architecture, Modernity and Geopolitics* (Yale University Press, 2009), and *Kevin Roche: Architecture as Environment* (Yale University Press, 2011), as well as co-editor of *Eero Saarinen: Shaping the Future* (Yale University Press, 2006). Her scholarly work has been supported by the Getty Foundation, the Graham Foundation in the Fine Arts, the Finnish Academy of Arts and Sciences, and the Austrian Ministry of Science and Research. Pelkonen received an M.Arch. from the Tampere University of Technology, Finland, an MED from Yale School of Architecture, and a PhD from Columbia University.

Andrea Phillips is a professor of fine art and director of PhD programs in the art department at Goldsmiths, University of London. She lectures and writes about the economic and social construction of publics within contemporary art. Recent and ongoing research projects include: *Curating Architecture,* a think tank and exhibition examining the role of exhibitions in the making of architecture's social and political forms; *Actors, Agent, and Attendants,* a research project and set of publications that address the role of artistic and curatorial production in contemporary political milieus (in collaboration with SKOR/ Foundation for Art and Public Domain, 2009–2012); co-director with Suhail Malik, Andrew Wheatley, and Sarah Thelwall of the research project, *The Aesthetic and Economic Impact of the Art Market,* an investigation into the ways in which the art market shapes artists' careers and public exhibition (2010–ongoing); *Public Alchemy,* the public program for the 2013 Istanbul Biennial (co-curated with Fulya Erdemci); *Tagore, Pedagogy and Contemporary Visual Cultures* (in collaboration with Grant Watson); *How to Work Together* (in collaboration with Chisenhale Gallery, Studio Voltaire, and The Showroom, 2014–ongoing).

Nina Rappaport is an architectural critic, curator, and educator. She is the publications director at the Yale School of Architecture for which she edits the biannual magazine *Constructs,* as well as exhibition catalogs and books. She is the director of *Vertical Urban Factory,* which includes a traveling exhibition and the eponymous book with Actar (2015). She is the author of the book, *Support and Resist: Structural Engineers and Design Innovation* (The Monacelli Press, 2007), co-editor of *Ezra Stoller: Photographer* (Yale University Press, 2012), and co-author of *Long Island City: Connecting the Arts* (Episode Books, 2006), an outgrowth of a Design Trust fellowship. She has written essays for numerous journals, including *Archithese, Praxis, Perspecta, Scapes, 306090, Clog, Log, Metropolis,* and *Architects Newspaper,* among others. Rappaport is the recipient of grants from the Graham Foundation and the New York State Council on the Arts. She also curated exhibitions on the work of photographer Ezra Stoller, in Washington, D.C.; *The Swiss Section* at the Van Alen Institute, New York (2004); on Aalto's Viipuri Library at Columbia University's Avery Hall (1998); and co-curated *Saving Corporate Modernism* at Yale School of Architecture (2001). Rappaport has taught seminars at the Syracuse School of Architecture program in New York City, Parsons the New School for Design, Barnard College, and the Yale School of Architecture.

Simon Sadler is a professor of architectural and urban history in the department of design at the University of California, Davis. Formerly, he taught at the University of Nottingham in the UK; Trinity College, University of Dublin, Ireland; Birmingham City University, UK; and the Open University, UK. His publications include: *Archigram: Architecture without Architecture* (MIT Press, 2005); *Non-Plan: Essays on Freedom, Participation and Change in Modern Architecture and Urbanism* (Architectural Press, 2000, co-editor, Jonathan Hughes); and *The Situationist City* (MIT Press, 1998). His research is centered on the ideological programs of design since the mid-twentieth century. Current projects include a book for MIT Press on holistic architecture that is supported by the Graham Foundation, which he is compiling with Caroline Maniaque; and a book on the study of design in California, including the convening of the Californian section of the Society of Architectural Historians Archipedia. He serves on the advisory board of the Architectural Humanities Research Association and is past Fellow of the Paul Mellon Center for Studies in British Art.

Joel Sanders is the principal of his New York-based studio, Joel Sanders Architect (JSA), and an adjunct professor of architecture at the Yale School of Architecture. JSA projects have been featured in international exhibitions at the Museum of Modern Art, New York, the San Francisco Museum of Modern Art, the Art Institute of Chicago, and the Cooper-Hewitt National Design Museum. The firm has received numerous awards, including six AIA New York Chapter Awards, two AIA New York State Awards, an *Interior Design* Best of Year Award, and two Design Citations from Progressive Architecture. Sanders is the editor of *Stud: Architectures of Masculinity,* and frequently publishes his work and critical writings in international publications such as *Architectural Record, Architect, Interior Design, Architectural Digest, The New York Times, Wallpaper,* and *A+U.* The Monacelli Press released a monograph of his work, *Joel Sanders: Writings and Projects,* in 2005. His most recent book, *Groundwork: Between Landscape and Architecture,* co-edited with Diana Balmori, was released by The Monacelli Press in 2011.

Léa-Catherine Szacka is an architectural historian based in Paris and Oslo. After studying architecture in Montreal and Venice, she completed a PhD in architectural history and theory at the Bartlett School of Architecture, University of London. Her thesis was entitled "Exhibiting the Postmodern: Three Narratives for a History of the 1980 Venice Architecture Biennale." Szacka has worked for the publisher Actar and the Barbican Art Gallery in London. She is now part of the Exhibition History research group at the Centre Pompidou as well as a postdoctoral research fellow at the Oslo School of Architecture. Szacka has taught at Nottingham Trent University, and the École Nationale Supérieure d'Architecture (Versailles, Paris-Malaquais, and Paris-La Villette). She has presented her work at international conferences and has published in *Log, AD, OASE, AA Files,* and *Domus,* among other professional journals and magazines.

David Andrew Tasman is an artist, writer, and founder of DVLPR. He is a regular contributor to *DIS Magazine* where he writes about contemporary issues in art. He spoke at the Talks Program, Salon 2013, at Art Basel Miami Beach, and at the 2012 Milan Triennial on topics of art, architecture, urbanism, and technology. Tasman has exhibited his work in the New York galleries Room East and Eli Ping Gallery. Prior to establishing his studio he worked for artist Tom Sachs, architects Diller Scofidio + Renfro, and KPF Architects where he was an associate principle. At Yale Tasman studied with David Joselit, Peter Eisenman, and Sir David Chipperfield, who nominated Tasman for the H.I. Feldman Prize for design excellence. In 2010 he was selected by Nancy Spector, Chief Curator at the Solomon R. Guggenheim Museum as one of five winners of the competition, *Re:Contemplating the Void.*

Henry Urbach was the Director of the Philip Johnson Glass House from 2012 to 2015. Prior to that he was the curator of architecture and design at the San Francisco Museum of Modern Art, where he organized the following exhibitions: *Your tempo: Olafur Eliasson; Cut: Revealing the Section; 246 and Counting: Recent Architecture and Design Acquisitions; Double Down: Two Visions of Vegas; Patterns of Speculation: J. MAYER H.; Austere; Otl Aicher; Sensate: Bodies and Design; ParaDesign; Tobias Wong;* and, in collaboration with Diller Scofidio + Renfro, *How Wine Became Modern: Design + Wine 1976 to Now.* Prior to joining SFMOMA, for nearly ten years he directed Henry Urbach Architecture, a gallery of contemporary art and architecture in New York. Urbach completed a MArch degree at Columbia University and a MA in the history and theory of architecture at Princeton University. He has taught in several schools of architecture, including the University of California, Los Angeles and Parsons School of Design, as well as the curatorial practice program at California College of the Arts, and the public art studies program at the University of Southern California. Urbach has written extensively about architecture, art, and culture.

Federica Vannucchi is an architect, historian, and theorist. She is currently a PhD candidate in architecture at Princeton University. She holds an architectural degree from the Università degli Studi di Firenze and earned a Master of Environmental Design (MED) at the Yale School of Architecture. Among other design firms, she has worked for Peter Eisenman Architects in New York. Vannucchi has taught architectural history, theory, and design at Pratt Institute, Parsons the New School for Design, Yale School of Architecture, and Princeton University. Her writing and design projects have been published in professional journals and magazines. Among other honors and awards, she is a member of the Fellowship of Woodrow Wilson Scholars at Princeton University; the recipient of a Collection Research Grant from the Canadian Center for Architecture in Montreal; and has received the Sonia Albert Schimberg Prize, awarded by the Yale School of Architecture. She is currently completing her dissertation on the International Exhibition of Decorative Arts and Modern Architecture Triennale of Milan, 1945–1973.